Problems of Economic
and Political Transformation
in the Balkans

Problems of Economic and Political Transformation in the Balkans

Edited by Ian Jeffries

PINTER
London and New York

Pinter
A Cassell imprint
Wellington House, 125 Strand, London WC2R 0BB
215 Park Avenue South, New York, NY 10003, USA

First published 1996

British Library Cataloguing in Publication Data
A catalogue record for this book is available from the British Library.

ISBN 1-85567-319-3

Library of Congress Cataloging-in-Publication Data
Problems of economic and political transformation in the Balkans /
    edited by Ian Jeffries
         p.   cm.
      Includes bibliographical references (p.).
      ISN 1-85567-319-3
      1. Balkan Peninsula — Economic conditions. 2. Balkan Peninsula —
    Politics and government — 1989– I. Jeffries, Ian.
    HC401.P76 1996
    330.9496—dc20   95-26834
                                                                        CIP

Typeset by Patrick Armstrong, Book Production Services
Printed and bound in Great Britain by Biddles Limited,
Guildford and King's Lynn

Contents

Acknowledgements

I am extremely grateful to Alin Teodorescu (now of IMAS, Bucharest) and Ionel David of the Soros Foundation (Bucharest) for their invaluable assistance in producing this book. The Soros Foundation provided generous funding.

My gratitude also extends to Frances Pinter and Nicola Viinikka for their encouragement and support. Fiona McKenzie (House Editor) and the copy editor, Michael Ayton, undertook their duties to the highest professional standard. Because of pressure of work, Cassell kindly provided an index.

Ian Jeffries

1 Introduction: the Balkan Transformation in a Comparative Perspective

Anders Åslund

In the first half of the 1990s, 27 countries in Eastern Europe and the former Soviet Union (FSU) have attempted a transition from communism to capitalism. The results have varied greatly. The Central East European countries have taken the lead, particularly Poland and the Czech Republic. The Baltic republics went through much greater structural changes, but they seem to have got on to the right track very fast. The four formerly socialist countries in the Balkans, Romania, Bulgaria, Albania and Yugoslavia, have gone through much more arduous systemic changes. Their hardships are more reminiscent of those of former Soviet republics than of East Central Europe.

The first purpose of this book is to assess what has been accomplished in the economic transition in the various formerly socialist countries in the Balkans. The picture that emerges, however, is not all that encouraging. Even if all the economies now seem to have bottomed out and are recovering, the social costs of transition have been great and many political, social, ethnic and structural hazards remain.

The Balkan countries have not been fortunate

There are certainly economic reasons for the Balkan countries not having been more successful to date. For instance, none of the Balkan countries has undertaken a comprehensive economic reform, with a combined far-reaching liberalization and strict macroeconomic stabilization, as Poland or Czechoslovakia have done. Nor has any Balkan country pegged its currency on the basis of an internationally-financed stabilization fund, which has proven so successful in Poland, Czechoslovakia and Estonia.[1] In general, the limited international interest and financing for the Balkan states in comparison with East Central Europe were striking from the outset of these states' democratic transitions.

However, none of these economic explanations is particularly surprising.

In a similar collaborative effort in 1990, the ten authors largely agreed that the same economic strategies that had been pursued in East Central Europe should preferably be adopted also in the formerly socialist countries in the Balkans. However, at the same time, there was a strong conviction that the Balkan countries were not very likely to do the right thing for historical, political, social, ethnic and structural reasons (Sjöberg and Wyzan 1991). The developments in Albania, Bulgaria and Romania were relatively predictable to judge from our earlier book, while we turned our attention to Yugoslavia at the very moment when the Markovic stabilization in the summer of 1990 looked like a success, and the political and economic development of Yugoslavia has turned out worse than most observers had anticipated.

It is obvious that liberalization has been insufficient in the Balkans, but it is more interesting to find out why liberalization has not gone further. Concomitantly, the insufficient stabilization was easily predicted from an analysis of budgetary and monetary policies, but the real query is why good sense was not heeded. Privatization has also been comparatively limited, but why has it not been promoted more?

In order to investigate the causes of the not very favourable developments in the Balkans, we found a need to go further and look into more facets of society. This volume was commissioned in the summer of 1994 on the initiative of Ionel David and Alin Teodorescu of the Soros Foundation in Romania, and the Soros Foundation has generously funded the project. They managed to lure most of the original contributors into the project, but they also chose to include a few political scientists and sociologists to delve deeper into the causes of the economic misfortunes in the Balkans.

The explanations are to be sought in different spheres of society. Ethnic conflicts are of significance all over and they are awarded a great deal of attention in this volume. While there are similarities, the peculiarities are more striking, rendering it more natural to discuss each country separately. Religion is usually closely connected with ethnicity. Similarly, historical animosity tends to be connected with religion and ethnicity.

Many features, however, are reminiscent in the various countries. Albania, Bulgaria and Romania were all very severe communist dictatorships, which left them with several similarities. First, the old elite or *nomenklatura* was very strong, while, second, civil society was weak. Third, as a consequence of the underdeveloped civil society, the intellectual elite was rudimentary and a great deal of important knowledge about the functioning of a market economy was missing, both in the elite and among the population at large. Under the surface of overt anti-Marxism, covert, frequently subconscious, quasi-Marxism is often to be found. Fourth, the state as a representation of common interests was frail. Fifth, the economic structures were particularly distorted because of the whims of communist dictators, although these eccentricities had

variations. Nicolae Ceauşescu was particularly fond of large-scale heavy industry and industrial concentration. Enver Hoxha relished autarky and monopoly more than anybody else. In general, Albania, Bulgaria and Romania have
a great deal in common, while Yugoslavia both before and after the break-up
is pretty much apart.

The political economy is reminiscent of the former Soviet Union

When looking upon the political and sociological features of Albania, Bulgaria
and Romania, the observer is easily struck by how great the similarities are
with the Slavic republics of the former Soviet Union, that is, Russia, Ukraine
and Belarus (Åslund and Layard 1993; Åslund 1994). Looking back at their
experiences during the last few years, it is not surprising that they have made
similar economic mistakes. They have all maintained more regulations and
had more inflation than the Central East European states and, as a result,
their national income, standard of living and investments have declined more.
Now when the mistakes have already been made, and the costs paid, we can
assess the causes and offer advice as to how the problems could have
been avoided, or rather mitigated, because the negative forces at play were
strong.

What all these countries offer is a framework for a theory of the political
economy of the transition from communism to capitalism of a broader valid-
ity than that which the comparatively favoured East Central European countries can provide. We can say that Poland, the Czech Republic and Estonia
tell us what should be done in an ideal transition from communism to capitalism, while the Balkans and the Slavic republics of the former Soviet Union
tell us more about what is likely to happen in the ordinary case.

A radical transition is needed, but not likely to occur

The general preconditions, primarily a strong, old elite, but a weak state and
civil society, are common to all these states. In such a situation, the main
political threat to sound economic policies comes from the old elite, and its
prime representatives after the democratic breakthrough are the state enterprises managers and the managers of state and collective farms. They can benefit greatly from inflation through subsidized state loans and from trade
restrictions through monopoly rents and price discrimination both in foreign
and domestic trade. In the absence of overt privatization, the old elite can
embezzle state property to their own benefit. The workers and the popula-

tion at large, however, pose no serious threat to sound economic policies. If anything, the problem is that they are not strong enough to balance the old elite in such elementary matters of justice as receiving agreed pay for undertaken work.

Since these problems are political, they should be encountered with political means. The trick is to reach out to the exceedingly passive people and activate them in the construction of political institutions that can rein in the flamboyance of the old elite. While round-table agreements might have been necessary for persuading the old elite to accept democratization, they should be abandoned in favour of democratic parliamentary elections at the earliest convenience, because a democratically elected parliament is the best popular bulwark against the old elite. However, if the deputies are individually elected without party allegiance, they are all too easily bought by rich interest groups. Therefore, it is important that nascent democratic parliaments are structured and disciplined by political parties. Another fundamental political institution is a constitution. The earlier it is adopted, the better it is likely to be. In the literature on democratization, there is a broad consensus on the importance of holding early parliamentary elections with political parties and adopting a constitution ('Economic Reform' 1994; Linz 1978; Przeworski 1991).

If the old elite is too strong to allow a systemic change that is beneficial for the population at large, it is of course not possible. A basic precondition for a sound transition is that the anti-establishment democrats have come to power. Romania under President Ion Iliescu and Ukraine under President Leonid Kuchma are illustrative examples of members of the old *nomenklatura* who managed to hang on to power after the collapse of communism, and both proved true to their constituencies, doing everything to enrich them. If that is the case, the prime task of reformers seems to be to build a political base so that they can capture power democratically, because the old *nomenklatura* remains the prime adversary of liberal economic reform. However, if liberal reformers have been brought to power in connection with the democratic break-through, they had better act quickly, because the old elite is only down for a short while. It will come back sooner than anybody really believes, and it will come back with a vengeance. The democratic and liberal reformers at the summit of power must swiftly build the pillars both of a democratic society and of a market economy.

The first and simplest economic task is to liberalize the economy as far as possible – prices, domestic trade, foreign trade and entrepreneurship. Frequent arguments about how far the liberalization should go with reference to alternative Western models are not really relevant, for a number of reasons. Any regulation in a state with an endemically corrupt bureaucracy is a boon to corrupt officials and that cannot be defended under any ideology. The number of regulations is immense and the only way of easing up the economy to a reasonable extent is to try to liberalize as far as possible. Nor can anything really be regulated before the market has been re-established and it takes time before all the millions of markets of an ordinary market economy have come alive. On the one hand, a less developed socialist economy requires a more far-reaching liberalization than a more developed one to achieve a satisfactory functioning. On the other hand, less developed socialist economies are likely to liberalize less, because of the greater strength of the old *nomenklatura*. Therefore, at least initially, the laggards in the transition will probably do worse economically during the first few years and they will have more corruption and economic distortions. The only way to solve these problems within a reasonable period of time will be to liberalize further. Then, they might be able to catch up with the pioneers in East Central Europe, which have forged ahead, but they have maintained too large public expenditures, which require extraordinary tax burdens for countries at that level of economic development. The Baltic states might show a more appropriate example to the Balkan states, as they have encountered their greater structural problems with a more radical reduction of public expenditures.

Similarly, a strict macroeconomic stabilization is all the more important for less orderly formerly socialist countries for both internal and external reasons. Internally, these countries have poor control over their finances, with a number of semi-fiscal holes. Subsidized credits, particularly for agriculture, that are not controlled though the budget process are standard; import subsidies through differentiated exchange rates are all too common; certain expenditures are decided above the head of the Minister of Finance who lacked political weight in the command economy. Externally, the international community is simply less interested in these poorer, more distant and more complicated countries than in East Central Europe. For these reasons, the Balkan states need to try to obtain smaller budget deficits than the countries in East Central Europe, but they are less likely to accomplish it. Again, the Baltic countries, which have settled for balanced budgets, have shown a good example. It is noteworthy that even so, they have not escaped relatively high inflation rates of about 35 per cent in both Latvia and Estonia in 1993 (Hansson 1994).

Less obvious are the lessons that are coming out about large-scale privatization from Eastern Europe and the former Soviet Union (Frydman and Rapaczynski 1994). It now appears that either a large-scale mass privatization will be undertaken early on, or there will be so much political dispute that it will not be undertaken. Only Czechoslovakia and Russia have so far managed to transfer large enterprises to a broad range of new owners on a mass scale. Poland, on the contrary, has had the best discussion on privatization, but the result has been that all problems have been raised and all interests alerted so that it has proved impossible to undertake much privatization of large enterprises. Although privatization is legally and technically far more complicated than a constitution, the political problem is of a similar nature: the longer the discussion lasts, the clearer certain influential groups realize that an early solution is not to their advantage, so they choose to block it. The liberal reformers can only win if they move ahead with great speed.

On the basis of these observations, it is possible to suggest a general preferable sequencing of the transition from communism to capitalism. The very start consists of a democratic break-through. Its very nature is of vital importance for subsequent choices, but the reformers cannot do much about it. It is determined by events and the old elite. A clear, unconditional, but unbloody, break is best for the reformers. The Czechoslovak velvet revolution stands out as an ideal and the subsequent evolution has also been ideal. Secondly, when reformers have assumed power, they should swiftly introduce a comprehensive programme of economic reform in one package, including far-reaching liberalization, strict macroeconomic stabilization, and the initiation of privatization. Politically, it is easier to do it early in one package. Economically, one comprehensive reform is much more effective. In a third step, it is time to build political institutions. The optimal time for new parliamentary elections appears to be in the second quarter after a comprehensive reform has been introduced. Then, economic stabilization has bitten, commodities have returned to the shops and people realize that they will survive in a market economy. Their standard of living has initially been depressed, but they are still prepared to make sacrifices for what most are likely to consider a good course. Later on, their standard of living will slowly recover, but too slowly for most, and the costs of readjustments will make people weary. That is another reason why elections should not be held too late. As early as is practically possible a mass privatization should be launched with a distribution of privatization vouchers to the whole population and soon afterwards privatization auctions should be held. They should be national as in Czechoslovakia rather than local as in Russia, and it is important both to allow financial intermediaries (investment funds) to get some strong outside owners and to limit insider ownership (which has become excessive in Russia).

Quasi-Marxism prevails after Marxism

A peculiar feature of post-communist mentality is that overt Marxism is rejected, but often quasi-Marxism prevails, because of popular ignorance or because people do not realize that their concepts pertain to Marxist ideology. Since quasi-Marxist prejudices sound plausible to a wide public, they are particular dangerous. The wrong understanding leads to the wrong decision, which harms the economic welfare of the many, while a few smart members of the old elite are all too often able to make a fortune in the process. While these are likely to be more pronounced in the former Soviet Union than in the Balkan states, many of these impediments also appear to be in evidence in the Balkans. The following are observations from Russia.

One of the most obvious quasi-Marxist sentiments is production fetishism, the eulogizing of both industrial and agricultural production, combined with utter contempt for trade and finance, labelled 'speculation'. As trade, services and finance were utterly neglected in the old economy, they should recover swiftly with the introduction of a market economy and they do. The Marxists, however, do not realize that better allocation raises economic welfare. Instead, they complain that the market under their conditions does not give anything, because it does not stimulate production, only breeds speculation. The danger is that such sentiments lead to the regulation of trade, which slows down the recovery of both production and the economy as a whole.

Less obvious is ownership fetishism, since it is a reflection of reverse Marxism. A standard post-communist view is that no market can exist without predominant private ownership. Therefore, privatization should precede liberalization. However, that has hardly ever happened in practice. Liberalization has typically preceded privatization, because private property is not very private before liberalization, because few private property rights exist, notably the rights to decide over production, sales and prices. On the contrary, market socialism is possible, while private property and a command economy existed only in Nazi Germany, and privatization has never occurred in a command economy with command economy regulations. Moreover, the private enterprises that have existed traditionally have been highly liberalized by Western standards, rarely paying tax, etc. Particularly in Russian agriculture, this undue emphasis on prior privatization has led to so much focus on land reform that little liberalization of agricultural trade has taken place. Hence the old agricultural establishment has preserved its powers and has been perfectly able to block land reform.

Even more curious is the semi-belief in the market typical of the former Soviet Union. Even most reformers did not believe in Adam Smith's invisible hand. They thought of the market as a price-setting mechanism, but they did not believe that it could function as an allocation mechanism. As a result, talk of the catastrophic absence of a market infrastructure is all too common, as if a market could not exist before computers. The very beauty of the market is that it functions in a decentralized and autonomous fashion. Any two persons who happen to meet and discuss a deal amounts to a market and there are millions of markets. The disbelief in the market as an allocator has had very serious effects. It has led to the retention of export regulations, state procurement and a number of monopolistic regulations that hamper the development of the market. It is like children who cannot believe that they can actually swim. Similarly, the Marxist belief in modernity and technical sophistication prevailed. As the market was supposed to be a sophisticated mechanism, people expressed disdain when they saw a 'bazaar', demanding that a market should be computerized, as if the market was a recent innovation.

One of the greatest Soviet myths is that Soviet production was enormously monopolized. The truth is the opposite. In the USSR, there were surprisingly many producers of various goods, and the big enterprises were not dominant and not even particularly big by any international comparison. The problem was instead the regulation of the market that created trade monopolies. In addition, small enterprises were missing, which could be amended by a far-reaching freedom of enterprise, so that new enterprises might be established. However, since the Russian belief was that the economy was dominated by gigantic producer monopolies, the anti-monopoly policy was characterized by price regulation, which further entrenched the trade monopolies. In reality, however, more liberalization and stabilization were needed, so that enterprises both could compete and would feel forced to compete, as they would run out of money otherwise.

The post-Marxist prejudices were all the deeper in the sphere of politics. East Europeans in general appear to find it difficult to think rationally about politics. In general, an extraordinary contempt of political science has taken hold in Eastern Europe and the FSU. As a result, democrats have mostly remained amateurs at forming political strategies. They have not bothered to organize proper parties, as the communists had a party. Nor have they written proper party programmes because the communists made party programmes holy. Similarly, party discipline, political participation and political professionalism have been dismissed as unworthy. Public education and information sound so much like communist agitprop that most democrats discard them. As a result, democrats often insist on making all the political mistakes, and then people are surprised that they lose against communists and others who take party politics seriously. The worst effect is that the democrats tend not to try to reach out to the ordinary people, and then they inevitably feel neglected. Many turn to others that actually pay attention to the ordinary man and woman.

One of the worst post-Marxist confusions is that speed in itself is something bad. It is true that the literature on democracy contains a lot about the virtue of slowness, checks and balances in political decision-making. However, that is not true of the literature on democratization, which on the contrary emphasizes the importance of speed and decisive action. Far too often the democrats accept the communists' arguments about what democracy is and adopt a self-defeating course. Politics is too serious not to be handled in a professional fashion.

The ultimate prejudice, however, is an exaggerated belief in the national uniqueness of each country, taking it so far that no universal laws of social sciences apply to them. Such laws do exist. The question is rather to establish them and their preconditions, because preconditions vary greatly.

The structure of the book

This book consists of nine papers. Most deal with specific countries, but some are of a more general character. It is natural to start with the three countries Romania, Bulgaria and Albania, as their problems are reasonably related. We start with the biggest, Romania, and move to the smallest, Albania. Former Yugoslavia, however, differs more, so that it seems appropriate to put it last. Still, there are sufficient similarities to bring in Yugoslavia in this context.

Per Ronnås summarizes Romania's heritage from the communist regime of Nicolae Ceauşescu and looks at the policies pursued since the revolution in 1989. His conclusion is that Romania inherited an even by communist standards highly distorted economic structure, but after the revolution Romania had a great opportunity to make a clean break. However, no coherent reform strategy came to the fore, and Romania slipped down into what Ronnås calls underdevelopment. Indeed, Romania is one the outstanding example of the social costs of gradualism.

Andrei Musetescu investigates why Romania made such a political choice of 'pathological gradualism' through a study of the evolution of Romania's multi-party system. The political parties have proliferated and fragmented. Legitimacy has been a major factor. However, the historical legitimacy of pre-communist existence has not proved relevant. Instead charisma has been of great significance, which has caused personification. The main source of legitimacy, however, has been participation in the revolution in 1989, which explains much of Iliescu's strength. A variety of politicians have suffered from embarrassing streaks in their past. A Romanian peculiarity is that several major politicians have been returning *émigrés*, but they have not done well. Next, parties are likely to be judged more by what they can do for Romania's future and social bases are likely to become more important.

For Bulgaria, Michael Wyzan provides an economic overview. In terms of reform performance, he puts Bulgaria after East Central Europe, but before the other Balkan countries or the former Soviet republics. Bulgaria faced a particularly severe external shock, which has caused a sharp fall in economic activity. Even so, considerable progress has been made on macroeconomic stabilization, even if inflation remains too high. The weakest link of the transition so far has been privatization.

Gramoz Pashko offers an overview of the economic development during the transition in Albania. Few countries can display more economic oddities than Albania, the poorest country in Europe. The collapse of the communist economic system was certainly dramatic in Albania. Whether it wanted to or not, Albania had little choice but to undertake radical measures, and it had not the practical ability to co-ordinate its reforms. In 1993, Albania had got inflation under some control and could already record a growth of GDP of no less than 10 per cent. Because of its tiny size and poverty, foreign assistance has come to play an extraordinary role in the Albanian economy. In 1992 the total foreign grants and loans disbursed to Albania actually exceeded the Albanian GDP, a record hard to beat.

Örjan Sjöberg has chosen to look into the regional effects of economic transformation in Albania. Although the transition has not lasted for long as yet, he can already detect a tendency towards the kind of migration that is typical of a poor rural society: from poor rural areas in the highlands to richer and more urban areas on the coast.

Alan Smith looks at the aforementioned three countries in one context in an attempt to answer the question why the transition has proved so difficult for these countries. In general, he finds that the fall in national income and industrial output has been greater the more gradual the transition has been, though cause and effect may be questioned. He underlines the problems of introducing 'shock therapy' in the Balkans and factors that complicated the transition there, for instance difficulties in redirecting trade to Western Europe, breaking with the past, and the limitations imposed by poverty.

Although Yugoslavia has fallen apart, we chose to treat it in one context. In two separate but co-ordinated papers, Ivo Bicanic and Will Bartlett provide complementary economic overviews over the five successor states, Slovenia, Croatia, Bosnia-Hercegovina, the Federal Republic Yugoslavia and Macedonia, though Bosnia-Hercegovina is largely neglected because of the war devastation. Not surprisingly, the most common characterization is divergence. In 1993, inflation ranged from a controlled 23 per cent in Slovenia to one of the greatest hyperinflations in history in the Federal Republic Yugoslavia. The analysis is complicated by the large number of possible causes. As would be expected, the cost of the transition has been particularly high in this war-ridden region.

In a final overview paper, Robert Bideleux and Ian Jeffries put nationalism and the transition to democracy and market economies in the Balkans into a historical perspective. They warn against a number of aggressive and exclusive utterances of nationalism, while appealing for a tolerant and inclusive civic conception of the nation.

Note

1. Romania did try to peg its exchange rate early on, but without reserves the pegging was not credible and failed within days. Rump Yugoslavia has pegged its exchange rate, but only after a very severe hyperinflation and without substantial international reserves.

References

Åslund, A. (1992) *The Post-Communist Economic Revolution: How Big a Bang?* Washington, DC: Center for Strategic and International Studies and Westview Press.

Åslund, A. (ed.) (1994) *Economic Transformation in Russia.* London: Pinter.

Åslund, A. and Layard, R. (eds) (1993) *Changing the Economic System in Russia.* London: Pinter.

Blanchard, O., Dornbusch, R., Krugman, P., Layard, R. and Summers, L. (1991) *Reform in Eastern Europe.* Cambridge, MA: MIT Press.

Bruno, B., di Tella, G., Dornbusch, R. and Fischer, S. (eds) (1988) *Inflation Stabilization.* Cambridge, MA: MIT Press.

'Economic reform and democracy' (1994) *Journal of Democracy,* vol. 5, no. 4.

Frydman, R. and Rapaczynski, A. (1994) *Privatization in Eastern Europe: Is the State Withering Away?* Budapest, London and New York: Central European University.

Hansson, A. (1994) 'The Baltic States: poised for growth', *Östekonomisk Rapport,* vol. 6, no. 5.

Linz, J. (1978) *The Breakdown of Democratic Regimes: Crisis, Breakdown, and Reequilibration.* Baltimore: Johns Hopkins University Press.

Lipton, D. and Sachs, J. (1990) 'Creating a market in Eastern Europe: the case of Poland', *Brookings Papers on Economic Activity,* no. 1.

Przeworski, A. (1991) *Democracy and the Market: Political and Economic Reforms in Eastern Europe and Latin America.* Cambridge: Cambridge University Press.

Sachs, J. (1994) *Poland's Jump to a Market Economy.* Cambridge, MA: MIT Press.

Sjöberg, Ö. and Wyzan, M. (eds) (1991) *Economic Change in the Balkan States: Albania, Bulgaria, Romania and Yugoslavia.* London: Pinter.

2 Romania: Transition to Underdevelopment?

Per Ronnås

Introduction

One of the more noble aims of the socialist regime was to deliver Romania from its traditional state of agrarian backwardness through massive industrialization and to reduce the wide development gap *vis-à-vis* the West. This objective bestowed a certain legitimacy on the regime. It was also used to justify the suppression of consumption in favour of very high rates of investment. For decades, the slogan 'we must make sacrifices today for the future of our children' was more or less accepted, because it struck a chord. For a long time the regime was seen to deliver on its promise. Economic development was visible and quite impressive. However, hopes faded quickly in the 1980s as development reversed and the country plunged into a crisis which depressed living standards to levels reminiscent of the first post-war years. The population at large attributed the crisis to gross mismanagement of the economy and the fault was placed squarely at the feet of Ceauşescu. In this way, his highly personalized (mis)rule served to obscure the deficiencies of the economic system as such and of the Stalinist development strategy which had been implemented with such remarkable consistency, not to say intransigence, since the installation of the socialist regime after the war.

The fall of Ceauşescu resulted in a virtual explosion of euphoria. Instantaneous improvements in the form of heating, twenty-four hour electricity and reappearance of meat and other food products on previously bare shelves in the shops reinforced a belief that the removal of Ceauşescu had more or less solved the economic problems. However, the mood of euphoria was short-lived. It gradually turned into bitter disillusion as economic contraction and dislocations combined with acute macroeconomic instability created hardship of a different, but no less painful, kind than in the 1980s. Five years after the revolution, Romanians have to come to grips with the fact that, despite half a century of sacrifices for a better future, their country remains impoverished, and they are seemingly no closer to bridging the economic development gap *vis-à-vis* the West than they were before the Second World War. Indeed, the gap has even widened. While in 1938 the per capita net national income in Romania was a fifth of that of Germany and a seventh of that of the USA, by 1993 the ratios were over one to twenty *vis-à-vis* both countries.

Against this backdrop, the present study takes stock of the situation in terms of social and economic development as it stood on the eve of the revolution and assesses the developments during the first half-decade since the fall of Ceauşescu. The focus of the post-socialist period is on four broad aspects deemed to be of particular importance: (1) macroeconomic stability; (2) price liberalization and creation of efficient markets, with an emphasis on getting the 'big prices' right (for capital, labour, foreign exchange, energy and main raw materials); (3) institutional restructuring and 'depoliticization' of the economy; (4) human resources development. The first two of these aspects are at the very heart of the transition to a market economy and as such require little explanation or justification. The importance of the latter two is distilled from an analysis of the socialist period.

A main characteristic of the socialist period was a profound politicization of the entire economy. This development was a natural and logical consequence of the ruling ideology and the accompanying system of central planning, and, as such, not unique to Romania. However, Romania differed in the sense that, while most of its neighbours tinkered with reform long before 1989, developments in Romania were in the opposite direction, with increasingly desperate attempts to socialize all aspects of the economy. As a consequence, institutional reform in general and a depoliticization of the economy in particular took on a particular urgency as Romania embarked on the road of market-based development.

The importance of human resources development for long-term economic development is indisputable. In post-socialist Romania this aspect adds a particular importance as the previous regime left behind a decidedly mixed legacy, requiring urgent attention and rectification.

The socialist record

The least controversial achievements of the previous regime were probably in the field of education, being particularly impressive during the first half of the period. Seven years of free education was introduced in 1948, of which four years were compulsory. At the same time widespread literacy campaigns, targeting adults, were launched. Compulsory education was increased to eight years in 1961. The amount of resources earmarked for education was increased sharply over the inter-war level. Teaching staff more than doubled between 1948 and 1965 and the number of pupils per teacher declined from 35.4 to

23.7 in the same period (*Anuarul statistic* 1966: 490–1). Scholarships and cheap lodging in student hostels made education beyond compulsory school increasingly accessible to less well-to-do families. The result of these measures was a rapid increase in the educational level of the population. Illiteracy declined rapidly from a level of 23 per cent in 1948 (Golopenția and Georgescu 1948) and all but disappeared over a decade or two. Among the younger age groups seven or eight years of basic education became the norm, while in 1938 only 14 per cent of pupils were beyond the primary level (class V) (*Anuarul statistic* 1966: 490–1, 494–5). Secondary education, too, expanded rapidly. University enrolment increased from 57,000 in 1956–60 to 170,000 in 1976–80, and enrolment in secondary schools increased from 321,000 to 980,300 over the same period (*Anuarul statistic* 1982: 281).

The attempt at demographic engineering introduced in 1966 came to mark a distinct break in the trend of increasing educational standards, as few provisions were made to meet the vast increase in the demand for education resulting from the increased size of the young age cohorts.[1] Deteriorating teacher/pupil ratios in compulsory education and increasingly fierce competition for entry into secondary and tertiary education followed. Tertiary education would seem to have suffered the most as total enrolment actually fell from 192,800 in 1980–81 to 164,500 in 1989–90, while the population in the 18–22 age bracket increased from 1,627,000 to 2,115,000 (*Anuarul statistic* 1981: 579; *Buletin de informare* 1990/3: 9).

Two other aspects of the achievements in education during the socialist regime deserve attention, namely profile and quality. These aspects are not all that relevant for basic education, where the main emphasis is to provide skills in the 'three Rs', but are of crucial importance in higher education. From the very beginning, the socialist regime emphasized technical and professional rather than classical education. This bias assumed absurd proportions during the latter part of Ceaușescu's reign as narrow vocational training squeezed out more broad-based tertiary education. Thus, the educational profile of the graduates from secondary and tertiary education became increasingly narrow and focused on technical professions and blue collar skills. In view of the economic restructuring which was to come this was particularly unfortunate. The educational profile of the young labour force educated during the last decade of Ceaușescu's reign is poorly attuned to the needs of the emerging market economy and civil society, at the same time as the narrow and vocational nature of its education makes retraining more difficult than it needed to have been.

The qualitative deficiencies of the educational system under socialism are somewhat more nebulous, yet often acutely felt. They stem from a number of factors, most notable of which are: the political and ideological straitjacket imposed on all research and teaching; international isolation; a detachment of research from teaching; an emphasis on learning by rote; and a discouragement of the development of analytical skills. All in all, there were very good reasons for the new regime after the revolution to attach very high priority to rectifying and improving the human resource base.

Health care is another field where the socialist regime, at least initially, produced considerable results. The initial achievements are indisputable. Infant mortality, which remained at a level of more than 15 per cent until the late 1940s (with a peak of 19.9 per cent in 1947), was brought down to 4.4 per cent in 1965 and 2.9 per cent in 1980. Inoculation programmes and much improved accessibility to health care, not least in rural areas, accounted for much of the fall in infant mortality. However, as in the case of education, once the easy gains were reaped further improvements proved difficult. Indeed, in line with the general neglect and disregard of the Ceauşescu regime for human resources, the standard of health care fell sharply in the 1980s. Thus, despite the early achievements in basic health care after the war, the lasting impression is that the legacy of Ceauşescu in the field of health care was an unmitigated disaster. The health sector was starved of resources and often decades behind the West in technological development, and the medical staff was to a large extent dispirited and demoralized. While good dispersal of health centres resulted in rather easy access, quality varied widely between the large cities and the smaller localities.

The most controversial aspects of the previous regime were in the field of economic development. To put these in a perspective, one needs to remind oneself of the background. Failure to diversify the economy through industrialization, combined with rather high rates of population growth, forced agriculture to assume the role of an employment buffer in the inter-war period. Primitive production techniques, exceedingly poor capital endowment and a minimum of cash input kept returns to land at a low level, while the deteriorating land–labour ratio led to falling productivity and incomes. In 1930, some 80 per cent of the population was still rural and agriculture was the main source of income for 72 per cent of the population (*Recensămîntul* 1930, vol. 5). By 1941 the share of the non-farm population had increased by a mere 2.6 percentage units (Cresin 1948). The economic depression hit agriculture in Romania particularly severely and was a major factor behind the poor overall economic performance in the inter-war period. However, at the heart of the problem lay the failure to reduce the pervasive role of primitive subsistence farming in the economy. This was a problem which any post-war government would have had to tackle.

The comparative strengths and weaknesses of centrally planned economies are well known. In socialist jargon, they are good at extensive, but not at intensive development, that is, they are good at mobilizing resources, but not at utilizing them efficiently. Romania proved to be no exception in this regard and at the end of the war the preconditions for 'extensive' development were ideal. Yet, despite concerted efforts to develop a strong base of heavy industry during the first post-war decade, there was little apparent change in the occupational structure of the labour force until the late 1950s.[2]

The collectivization of agriculture in the late 1950s and early 1960s, which was combined with forceful efforts to mechanize agriculture and develop industry, marked the end of the economy dominated by subsistence farming. The share of the non-agricultural labour force increased from 30.3 per cent in 1956 to 42.9 per cent in 1966, and to 63.5 per cent in 1977 (Ronnås 1984: 143). In absolute terms the non-agricultural labour force increased from 4,442,000 in 1966 to 6,818,000 in 1977. The shift of labour from agriculture, where labour productivity by any standard was dismally low, to manufacturing and other non-agricultural sectors, where at any rate productivity was a good deal higher than in agriculture, resulted in large gains in productivity. The very high overall economic growth rates in the 1960s and 1970s were a result of these transfer gains.[3]

The shortcomings of the development strategy, while obvious to few at the time, have since become common wisdom. In the Romanian case, they were aggravated by unprecedented mismanagement of the economy in the 1980s (Ronnås 1991; Teodorescu 1991). The legacy resulting from over forty years of increasingly mindless socialist development was a bloated industrial sector, designed according to ideological concepts dating back to the nineteenth century, and to political whims. The industrial sector was dominated by a relatively small number of huge enterprises, yet little benefit was drawn from economies of scale. Chemical and other heavy industry had been assigned a role which was out of all proportion, while other industrial branches, such as food processing, were sorely neglected. One of the most severe handicaps was obsolete technology owing to the tendency towards technological pluralism inherent in the economic system[4] and aggravated by the virtual absence of technological renewal during the 1980s.

Nobody today questions that the physical production capacity left behind by the previous regime requires very comprehensive pruning, restructuring and updating in order to be put on a sound and internationally competitive footing. However, inefficient organizational structures, lack of business and management skills required in a market economy, poor work methods and ethics, and, not least, an absence of incentives to strive for economic efficiency and profitability because of perennially soft budget constraints, were no doubt just as important reasons behind the economic inefficiency and uncompetitiveness of the state industrial sector.

Today's challenges

The persistent curse of inflation

A main task of the government in any market economy is promotion of over-all macroeconomic stability. This task is particularly taxing in transition economies where strong destabilizing forces have to be countered with poorly developed policy instruments. As a synthesis expression of fundamental economic woes and as an economic and social evil of the highest order, inflation deserves priority attention. Indeed, it may be argued that safeguarding the value of the currency is one of the most fundamental obligations of the government. With triple-digit inflation three years in a row, resulting in a more than thirty-fold increase in consumer prices since 1990, the Romanian record of containing inflation is little short of a disaster. The failure to control inflation after the inevitable price increases in the wake of price liberalization and the adjustment of relative prices reflects fundamental weaknesses in the reform policies, which are dealt with below. The cost of this failure in terms of the hardship it has inflicted on the population and as an impediment to restructuring through growth rather than through destruction and contraction has been enormous. At long last, a serious attempt was made in early 1994 to come to grips with the problem through a tightening of the monetary policies. The initial success of this attempt made the need for measures aimed at eliminating the root causes, such as poor financial discipline in the state enterprises, all the more acute.

Replacing the visible hand by the invisible

The issue of 'getting prices right' and creating efficient markets is of fundamental importance to the reform process. Prices reflecting relative scarcities form an indispensable and irreplaceable basis for the entire restructuring of the economy and an absolute prerequisite for economic efficiency, without which no sustainable growth will be possible. The severely distorted relative prices in the past underscore the importance of this issue in the Romanian context. Fundamental steps for reinstating prices as carriers of vital economic information were taken through a series of price liberalizations in 1990 and 1991 and through a liberalization of external trade. In the event, it proved more difficult to make prices matter than to liberalize them. Continued soft budget constraints and monopoly positions on the market made state enterprises largely insensitive to changes in relative prices and resulted in a weak supply response to price changes. More often than not, cost increases were automatically and immediately passed on to the consumers, while their impact on production methods and the restructuring of production lines has been much slower. This would also appear to have been a main cause behind the resilient inflation.

The remedy lies in an increase in the number of actors on the market and in improving the efficiency of markets. Factor markets and markets for inputs, intermediary products and final goods have developed slowly and remain imperfect. The proliferation of new small-scale private enterprises is gradually beginning to make a difference. However, the vast majority of these enterprises are found in the services industries rather than in manufacturing, which in its turn may be explained by the fact that it is difficult to operate manufacturing enterprises in a situation where fundamental markets do not function properly. The development of markets must inevitably take place both from the bottom and from above. In this context, it falls upon the government to create a conducive environment, and to level the playing field through the establishment and enforcement of a legal framework and the removal of administrative and other obstacles. Much of this falls under the heading of institutional restructuring.

However, it may be argued that there are some prices which are of such fundamental importance that active intervention to 'get them right' may be justified and that measures to improve the efficiency of the markets in which they are determined deserve top priority. The foreign exchange rate, the price of capital (i.e. the interest rate), wages, energy prices and perhaps also agricultural prices arguably fall into this category. 'Getting them right', in the sense that they clear markets and that access to these markets is unhindered and non-discriminatory, is very important, not only to promote private enterprise development, but also to promote sound economic growth in general. Indeed, it may be argued that if this issue is not tackled, then most other economic policies will prove rather ineffectual. The Romanian record with regard to getting the 'big prices' right has been rather mixed. Although the difference between the market and the official foreign exchange rate was for a long time quite small, determined steps towards full convertibility were only taken in April 1994. Fear of a rapid depreciation of the leu in the wake of full convertibility and of the inflationary effects of such a depreciation would appear to have softened the political will to introduce full convertibility for a long time. Yet, the leu appreciated considerably in real terms *vis-à-vis* the dollar and other hard currencies in 1993–94. It can easily be argued that the less than full convertibility of the leu has hampered economic restructuring in general and the development of the private enterprise sector in particular.

The lack of a functioning capital market and the practice of rationing credits at often highly negative real rates of interest has probably been one of the most important obstacles to economic restructuring and the growth of private enterprises. The bulk of the credit has continued to be channelled to the ailing state enterprises, while private enterprises have had very little access to credits, at any price. The establishment of special credit facilities earmarked for agriculture and small-scale enterprises did, no doubt, reduce the problem somewhat, but did little to solve it. At the heart of the problem has been the need to let the market, through the price mechanism, determine the allocation of credits. The link between macroeconomic instability and inadequate institutional reforms has nowhere been more obvious than in the field of capital markets. Failure to detach the allocation of credits from political processes has resulted in economically irresponsible credit policies, in terms of both volumes and direction, which has greatly fuelled inflation. On the other hand the high rate of inflation has been a major obstacle to the establishment of a sound capital market.

By comparison, the price of labour has displayed much less distortion. Inflation has severely eroded real wages, which by end-1993 stood at only 63 per cent of the level in January 1990 (*PlanEcon Report* 1993; *Buletin statistic* 1993/12). Thus, real wages have fallen at least as sharply as labour productivity, albeit with a certain time lag. The problem is not inflexible wages, but the reduced geographic and occupational mobility and lack of mechanisms for efficient collection and dissemination of labour market information.

For a long time the shortfalls in energy production resulted in rationing of energy and administrative allocation on the basis of quotas. For obvious reasons, this practice was hardly conducive to either efficient energy use or industrial restructuring.

Institutional restructuring

In terms of economic restructuring, it is useful to distinguish between the restructuring of the institutional framework of the economy and the restructuring of production as such. While responsibility for the restructuring of production must by and large be decentralized to the individual enterprises and left to the market, the responsibility for the institutional restructuring falls squarely on the government. This latter restructuring is just as far-reaching and important as that of the production as such. Successful restructuring of the institutional framework is a precondition for the economic transition and the calibre of the new institutional framework which emerges will have a decisive impact on the long-term development prospects of the country. As a fundamental prerequisite for a transition to a civil society based on the principles of democracy and to a market economy, institutional restructuring had very high priority immediately after the revolution. The comprehensive nature of the changes implied that the restructuring was (and is) in fact a question of destroying much, if not most, of the previous institutions and replacing them with new ones. Not only formal institutions, but behavioural practices and habits need to be replaced.

Driven by the force of circumstances, changes were swift in some areas, notably in those related to the establishment of a civil society. A free press and political pluralism was established virtually overnight and a healthy proliferation of non-governmental organizations began. However, the restructuring and rebuilding of institution with a bearing on the economy has been much slower, partial and incomplete. This vast process may conceptually be divided into two broad areas: (1) a replacement of discretionary decision-making by the rule of law, and the establishment and enforcement of a regulatory framework for the economy; and (2) a general 'depoliticization' of the economy.

The discretionary and arbitrary political interventions in the detailed management of individual enterprises found its most spectacular form in the surprise visits to enterprises regularly undertaken by Ceauşescu. At these visits he would descend upon an enterprise with a helicopter, and spend an hour or two at the work floor in the enterprise, whereupon he would give detailed instructions as to how the enterprise should henceforth be run and, typically, revise the production targets upwards. At a lower level, party cadres would see it both as their right and as their duty to interfere in the management of individual enterprises. As the enterprises were perceived to be mere tools for implementing the economic policy of the party and as the interests of the party had absolute priority over everything else there was not, indeed could not be, any clear-cut separation of power and responsibility between enterprises and the state apparatus, and decision-making was by necessity discretionary.

The first year or two after the revolution saw a very rapid development in the legislative field. A large number of laws which aimed at providing the legal underpinning for the transition to a market economy were put in place. A certain ambivalence towards private entrepreneurship was reflected in the legislation. An initial law, passed as early as February 1990 (but subsequently abrogated), set an upper ceiling on the number of employees in private enterprises (Decret-Lege 1990/53; this ceiling was subsequently removed). The tax burden placed on private enterprises by new fiscal laws was progressive and very heavy. Other laws interfered unduly in the running of the enterprises, such as that establishing maximum trade margins. Yet, a number of fundamental laws are not yet in place. Of these, the absence of a law on bankruptcy has been the most harmful. In its absence, the means of enforcing contracts and financial obligations have remained blunt and very weak. This has been a severe obstacle to the development of an efficient capital market and has resulted in very high transaction costs as creditors are at the mercy of debtors.

Law enforcement remains poorly developed, not least in the economic field. Certain teething problems following the introduction of a large body of new legislation were obviously to be expected. These have been aggravated by the neglect of the legal professions during the past regime and inadequate efforts to enhance the capacity and competence of the judiciary since the revolution. The demoralized and weakened status of the police is particularly noteworthy. Law enforcement is further undermined by corruption. While always an endemic phenomenon in Romanian society, it seems to have taken more visible forms since the revolution. The problem is particularly severe in the economic field as almost half a century of absence of property rights implies that emphatic efforts are required to reinstate them.

Generally speaking, small and medium-sized enterprises are likely to be the most affected by the poor law enforcement. Large state enterprises are usually capable of fending for themselves. At the other end of the scale, poor law enforcement permits micro enterprises to exist without being registered or taxed. However, the medium- and small-scale enterprises in the formal sector, which inevitably must assume a key role in the restructuring of the economy, are highly dependent on well-established and enforceable rules of the game. Their bargaining position is typically weak and they need the backing of an efficient legal system to be able to prosper.

The ambiguous attitude of the government(s) to the transformation of the economy is reflected in a failure to depoliticize the economy: to cut ownership and other links between enterprises and other economic agents on the one hand and the state bureaucracy and the political establishment on the other.

The real estate and the agricultural sectors were privatized within two years. In the case of the real estate sector privatization presented few problems as much of the housing was already in private hands prior to the revolution. The very strong popular pressure for decollectivization effectively precluded any other course of action in the field of agriculture.[5] A first tentative step towards partial decollectivization in the form of a decree issued already in early 1990 (*Adevărul* 1990a, 1990b) was in many parts of the country taken as *carte blanche* for dissolving the collective farms. The full-fledged decollectivization, which was proclaimed in the form of a land law in February 1991 (Legea fondului funciar 1991), amounted to a formal recognition and institutionalization and an attempt to control a process which could no longer be reversed.

By contrast, the privatization of the industrial sector has been painfully slow.[6] After a promising start, which saw the establishment of a law transforming state enterprises into joint stock companies and autonomous state monopolies in 1990 (Legea 15 1990), a law on privatization in 1991 and the creation of an elaborate institutional apparatus for the implementation of the privatization, little has been achieved in terms of actual privatization.[7]Although the technical difficulties of implementing a successful privatization should not be underestimated and the technical solution chosen in Romania was, in retrospect, not ideal, one cannot escape the conclusion that the main reason behind the dismal privatization record has been a lack of will-power to implement it (Ionescu 1994a).

The transfer of the ownership of enterprises from the public to private hands is but one, albeit fundamental, aspect of the depolitization of the economy. It needs to be backed up by an unambiguous transfer of economic and financial responsibility and accountability from the state to the manager and new owners of the enterprise. In other words, the privatization must be accompanied by enforcement of hard budget constraints to be credible and meaningful. The system of central planning forged close ties between enterprises and various levels of the state bureaucracy. These ties were often of a both formal and personal nature. While indispensable under central planning, with the market-based transformation of the economy they lose their meaning and become more often than not counter-productive. Yet, for managers steeped in the old system and ill-equipped to face a new market-oriented environment, they represent a lifeline. At the same time they continue to provide a sense of meaning and importance to government officials and departments whose sense of purpose is eroded as their previous sphere of decision-making is relocated to the market-place. Thus, it is easy to understand why it is proving so difficult to wean enterprises away from state support and guidance. Furthermore, a widespread fear of mass unemployment and social unrest has provided a genuine reason for continued support to state enterprises. However, with the benefit of hindsight it is clear that the failure to depoliticize the huge part of the economy represented by the state enterprises, to decisively cut their links with the government bureaucracy and to enforce hard budget constraints on them has been extremely costly and has yielded little if any real benefit.

The continued support to the state enterprise sector has proved ineffective as a means of maintaining employment (Table 2.1). At best, it has served to delay the retrenchment of the labour force somewhat. Since the revolution, wage employment in the state enterprise sector has fallen by almost 2.4 million, or 30 per cent. Only a very small part of this decline may be attributed to privatization of state enterprises. To the sharp fall in employment may be added continued more or less open unemployment within enterprises. Temporary lay-offs (usually without pay) and involuntary reductions in working hours continue to be widespread in the state enterprises. This phenomenon is not new and there is no evidence that it increased in magnitude in the past year; indeed, the opposite may well have been the case. However,

Table 2.1 Changes in the structure of the labour force 1989–93

	1989	1993	change
Active labour force	10,945.7	10,458,0	− 487.7
Own account workers	2948.6	3983.0	1034.4
Wage workers	7997.1	6475.0	− 1522.1
– state sector	7997.1	5637.0	− 2360.1
– non-state sector	–	838.0	838.0
Registered unemployed	–	1164.7	1164.7

Note: The active labour force does not include unemployed. The figures refer to end-year.
Sources: Anuarul statistic (1992: 124–9); *Buletin statistic* (1993/12).

Table 2.2 Industrial structure of the labour force, end-year 1990–93 (percentages)

	1990	1991	1992	1993
Agriculture	27.9	28.5	28.7	33.0
Industry	38.1	37.0	35.4	31.6
Construction	7.0	6.0	4.2	5.5
Trade	5.9	6.3	8.1	8.9
Other	21.1	22.2	23.6	21.0

Source: Romania Economic·Newsletter (1994).

it does suggest that the contraction of the labour force in state enterprises will continue, unless there is a pronounced revival of production. The reduction of the labour force in the state enterprises has taken place concomitant with a sharp fall in productivity and wages.[8]

Tables 2.1 and 2.2 give an unequivocal picture of considerable restructuring of the labour force, both by forms of employment and across industrial sectors. Private sector employment has accounted for the entire increase in labour absorption since the revolution. The share of the state sector in total employment is down from approximately 73 per cent in 1989 to 54 per cent by the end of 1993. Despite the proliferation of new small-scale enterprises, by mid-1994 there were 352,000 private stock companies and an additional 220,500 'family associations and household enterprises' (*Buletin statistic* 1994, no. 5; the figures refer to the end of May); much of the increase in private sector employment has taken place in agriculture. As the urban labour market has contracted, agriculture has reassumed its perennial role as an employment buffer. Agricultural employment reportedly increased by 354,100 people or 11 per cent in 1993 (*Romania Economic Newsletter* 1994). This increase should be seen in the light of the decollectivization in 1991 which transferred land to some 6.2 million claimants according to a principle of restitution. However, the main factor behind the sharp shift of labour from wage employment in industry to self-employment in agriculture was massive lay-offs of rural– urban commuters working in urban industries. Scattered evidence in early 1993 suggested a 40 per cent reduction of this category of workers, which at the time of the revolution amounted to approximately 900,000 (Ronnås 1993: 226). Their return to agriculture was in most instances involuntary and will have resulted in a sharp fall in their standard of living as incomes from the typically tiny plots of land[9] yield little more than a subsistence income.

The direct and indirect costs of the continued subsidization of state enterprises do not lend themselves to any quantitative estimate, but have by any standard been crippling. The most obvious direct cost has been in the form of lack of control over credit expansion, budget deficits resulting from direct subsidies and government guarantees for financially unsound loans to state enterprises, and ensuing inflation. A lack of financial discipline and the absence of credible sanctions against failure to honour financial obligations have made possible a continuous accumulation of inter-enterprise arrears. This results in so-called economic blockages and when the situation is perceived to have become too critical, the government unfailingly steps in with a large infusion of fresh credits, which invariably are accompanied by solemn statements that they represent a final bail-out and that henceforth the enterprises have to stand on their own feet.[10] A conservative estimate put the inter-enterprise arrears at 3600 billion lei in early 1994,[11] equivalent to 19 per cent of the GDP or 1.6 times total investments, and state subsidies to keep these enterprises afloat cost the equivalent of 10 per cent of GDP.[12] Until the pervasive financial irresponsibility of the state-owned enterprises is brought under control, which will require effective deterrents in the form of credible threats of bankruptcy, it will prove difficult to bring inflation under control.

The opportunity cost of the capital used to keep financially unsound enterprises afloat is very high indeed. The restructuring of the economy is severely impaired by a shortage of capital. At less than 11 per cent of GDP, the level of investment is far too low to ensure a speedy redressing of the economy. The private sector in particular suffers from unequal and limited access to formal credit. There can be no doubt that the continued allocation of the major share of the credits to ailing state enterprises carries a very high cost in terms of forgone economic growth and private sector employment and income generation. As a policy for redressing the economy it is entirely counter-productive. Furthermore, the continued subsidization of state enterprises severely distorts competition and implies that private enterprises cannot compete on the market on equal terms. Not only are private enterprises disadvantaged in terms of access to capital and other factors of production, but as they, in contrast to state enterprises, have to cover their costs to survive, they also have a competitive disadvantage on the markets for their outputs. Besides, the fostering of linkages between small (private) and large (state) enterprises, which has proved crucial to small-scale enterprise development in other transition economies,[13] is impossible as long as contracts with state enterprises cannot be legally enforced. In effect, this situation slows down the restructuring of the economy and the creation of efficient markets for inputs, intermediary products and final goods as new actors on the market do not come forward.

The failure to depoliticize the state enterprises and to put them on a commercial footing also amounts to a major disservice to the state enterprise sector as such. According to senior government officials,[14] the bulk of the losses are concentrated in some 100 to 150 large enterprises, which also are responsible for most of the inter-enterprise arrears, while the majority of the remaining 6000 enterprises are basically sound. According to the same source, an internal spontaneous process of technological upgrading and adjustment to new market conditions is in fact under way in many state enterprises. Seen from this angle, the current policy of relaxed budget constraints is highly detrimental. First, state enterprises, too, suffer from market distortions, the lack of an institutional and legislative framework and the inability to enforce contracts. Secondly, continued subsidies make it impossible to distinguish the potentially healthy enterprises from the hopeless cases. In the absence of hard budget constraints a differentiation of enterprises according to viability and creditworthiness is not possible. They are all tarred with the same brush and there is a risk that the potentially healthy enterprises gradually sink with the hopeless cases. Furthermore, the State Ownership Fund (SOF) uses profits from healthy enterprises to subsidize the sick ones. Thirdly, this risk is heightened by the fact that the policy of continued soft budget constraints does not provide any incentives for internal restructuring of the production and organization of enterprises and replacement/upgrading of enterprise management. On the contrary, good contacts with government authorities rather than marketing, organizational and entrepreneurial skills in general remain the most important characteristics of a successful manager.

It is widely recognized that the poor performance of state enterprises in many instances is due to bad management and organization rather than to inherent weaknesses in the enterprise. The potential for improving efficiency and productivity through improved management and organization is no doubt vast in many enterprises. Based on scattered evidence from cases where professional managers from the West have taken over the management of state enterprises, it would appear that it is often possible to double or even treble production with the existing resources.[15] While the scope for improving the performance of existing enterprises can only be established *ex post* and any *ex ante* estimates are bound to be very approximate, it is nevertheless clear that the continued subsidization of state enterprises carries a very high cost in the form of forgone efficiency gains (which ultimately is borne by the labour force in the form of fewer jobs and lower wages) and that it reduces the likelihood of survival of the very enterprises it is aimed to protect.

Lastly, it should be noted that the failure to depoliticize the economy imposes an opportunity cost on the government and the administration. Preoccupation with the plight of individual enterprises detracts attention from more fundamental and strategic development issues. It also slows down the restructuring of the government apparatus as the old function as a custodian of economic activities and agents is unduly preserved, while other more strategic functions develop but slowly.

Human resources development

Considerable advances have been made in the field of human resources development since the revolution. Major steps have been taken to remedy the dwarfed and distorted system of higher education left behind by the previous regime. University education has expanded by nearly 50 per cent in terms of enrolment and the proportion of the 19–23 age group enrolled in universities as day students has increased from a meagre 4.5 per cent in 1989–90 to 9.8 per cent in 1992–93 (Table 2.3). The structure of the university education has also undergone impressive changes, considering the difficulties involved in rapidly expanding education in individual disciplines. Thus, teaching in economics, law, the humanities and natural sciences has been greatly expanded at the expense of polytechnic education, which in the past accounted for an absurdly high share of the total university enrolment.

Improvements in the quality of education are more difficult to assess. In some disciplines, such as economics and law, it is a question of developing curricula and professional knowledge virtually from scratch. The vastly improved access to information, the large number of Western textbooks being translated into Romanian and the often strong pressure exercised by students on the academic staff to requalify and update their knowledge is clearly bearing fruit in the form of improved quality of teaching, although this is inevitably a slow process. Disdain and an often petty interference on the part of the political leadership combined with virtually complete isolation from the rest of the world created intolerable conditions for research under the previous regime.

Table 2.3   Enrolment in university education 1989–90 and 1992–93

| | 1989/90 | | 1992/93 | | |
	Number	%	Number	%	Index: 1989 = 100
All university	159,465	100.0	235,669	100.0	148
– day students	94,952	59.5	186,419	79.1	196
– technical	113,185	71.0	118,097	50.1	104
– economics	15,493	9.7	35,279	15.0	228
– medicine	16,703	10.5	23,656	10.0	142
– law	2362	1.5	10,865	4.6	460
– natural sciences	9230	5.8	19,426	8.2	210
– humanities	6598	4.1	24,872	10.6	377
– arts	936	0.6	3474	1.5	371

Note: Natural sciences include mathematics, physics, chemistry and biology. Humanities include geography, history, philosophy, philology, sports, sociology, psychology, pedagogics, journalism and theology. The 'university' age group 19–23 numbered 2,089,000 in mid-1989 and 1,895,000 in mid-1992.

Sources: *Anuarul statistic* (1992: 91, 170–1, 208–13); *Informaţii statistice operative* (1993).

Social sciences were particularly severely affected. Against this backdrop, the scholarly advances in the past few years, not least in economics, have been impressive. In many instances young scholars are taking the lead in raising the quality of research and in exploring new fields. While these developments are extremely encouraging, one should not lose sight of the fact that they take place from a disastrous starting point and that determined efforts will be required over a long period of time to bring research, higher education and human resources development in general up to a level where they may become a development force rather than a constraint.

Conclusion

The revolution in December 1989 created a unique momentum for change, and the opportunity for a clean break with the abysmal economic, social and political development and for exploiting the development force embedded in the millions of people whose entrepreneurial drive had been thwarted for over a generation. Half a decade down the road it is clear that, at least in the economic field, the momentum has not been adequately exploited. The existence of a widespread and strong will-power among the population at large to exploit their newly-won freedoms to improve the economic situation for themselves and their children is incontestable and amply reflected in the rapid proliferation of entrepreneurship and small-scale enterprises, and in the resuscitation of agriculture in the wake of the decollectivization despite adverse and seemingly chaotic conditions for production.

Thus, the new government had a singular chance to turn a fresh page and to devote its entire attention to creating an overall economic, social and institutional environment conducive to economic restructuring and rapid growth. The regime(s) in power since the fall of Ceauşescu have largely failed to face up to this challenge. At the heart of the problem is a failure to carry out an adequate institutional restructuring and to 'depoliticize' the economy. The continued macroeconomic instability may largely be seen as an effect of these failures. The most visible costs of the absence of a forceful and coherent reform strategy have been a failure to exploit the potential for increasing the efficiency and viability of state enterprises, forgone consolidation and growth of the nascent private sector and an involuntary retreat of the newly privatized agricultural sector into subsistence farming. At an aggregate level the costs are reflected in an unduly sharp decline of production, wages and living standards in general. A more subtle but equally severe cost has been in the form of an increasing disillusion and despondency among the population at large, who, for good reasons, feel that they are being let down twice. Declining faith in the future invariably results in a reluctance to invest and in a brain drain and may easily become a self-fulfilling prophecy.

The fact that the free-fall of the economy seems to have been halted and reversed into feeble growth offers little consolation. With a per capita GNP of less than $1100,[16] Romania is at the bottom end of the 'middle-income economies', in the same league as Morocco, Jordan and El Salvador. The average wage in 1993 was a mere $80 per month[17] and the number of people living in abject poverty with an income of less than $25 per month had reportedly doubled since 1989 (*Le Monde*, 14 April 1994). The combination of an economic structure of an industrialized country and the economic performance of a preindustrialized one reflects extreme inefficiency in the allocation and utilization of the means of production and other scarce resources. The question is not if Romania is experiencing a transition to underdevelopment, but how to achieve a transition away from underdevelopment.

Notes

1. As a consequence of Decree 1966/779, which banned all forms of contraceptives as well as abortions, the number of births increased from 273,700 in 1966 to 527,800 in 1967.
2. By 1956, 69.7 per cent of the labour force was still in agriculture.
3. According to official statistics, national income grew at an average annual rate of 9.5 per cent between 1966 and 1975 (*Anuarul statistic* 1976: 46).
4. In the absence of any economic efficiency criteria, the introduction of new technology typically did not result in the elimination of previous outmoded technology. Technologies were simply added to each other, even within the same enterprise (Teodorescu 1991).
5. In many places a spontaneous destruction/division of the collective property took place immediately after the revolution.
6. According to the Principal Economic Adviser to the President, Misu Negritoiu, four years after the revolution only 2 per cent of the state patrimony had been privatized (*Le Monde*, 14 April 1994).
7. In all, 6300 enterprises have been earmarked for privatization. By the end of 1993 some 430 'small' enterprises had reportedly been privatized, while very little had been achieved in terms of privatizing the larger enterprises (EFTA 1994). See also Ionescu (1994a).
8. After a fall by nearly 50 per cent since 1989, industrial labour productivity increased by 8.1 per cent in 1993, apparently as a consequence of the sharp retrenchment of the labour force.
9. According to a survey of 25,000 rural households in 1992, the average agricultural holding following the decollectivization was 2.5 ha, of which 2.0 ha was arable land (*Ancheta sociologică* 1992: 16).
10. A 'once-and-for-all' cancellation of enterprise losses accumulated up to 1990 was repeated on an even larger scale in early 1992, when a presidential decree forced the supposedly autonomous banking system to bail out bad inter-enterprise debts to the tune of 400 billion lei through credits.
11. Ionescu (1994). A considerably higher figure, 4200 billion lei, was quoted by *The Financial Times*, 3 May 1994.
12. Ionescu (1994b); *Le Monde*, 14 April 1994. Apparently, this at least in part takes the form of cross-subsidization of enterprises within the framework of the State Ownership Fund. Thus profits from healthy enterprises are channelled into the sick ones.
13. Not least in China and Vietnam: see Ronnås and Sjöberg (1993) and Johansson and Ronnås (1994).
14. Communication at an EFTA High-level Workshop on Economic Policy in Bucharest, 28–29 June 1994. The figure would seem to originate from a study by McKinsey, which identified 130 enterprises as disproportionately responsible for the country's economic woes (*The Financial Times*, 3 May 1994). These enterprises are concentrated in metallurgy, and in machine-building, chemical and electro-technical branches. It would seem that they account for approxi-

mately a third of the labour force in state enterprises.

15. Communication by Percy Barnevik, President ABB, at a conference on 'Russian economic reform in jeopardy', Stockholm, 16–17 June 1994. The remark referred to experiences from East Central Europe and the former Soviet Union in general.
16. According to official statistics, the per capita GNP was 828,000 lei in 1993 and the average exchange rate was 760 lei to the dollar (*Buletin statistic* 12/1993; *The Financial Times*, 3 May 1994).
17. Ibid.

References

Adevărul (1990a) 'Decret-Lege privind unele măsuri pentru stimularea ţărănimii, 1 February.
—— (1990b) 'Decret-Lege privind unele măsuri pentru stimularea ţărănimii şi activităţii economice a unităţilor agricole cooperatiste şi de stat', 2 February.
Ancheta sociologică (1992) *Probleme de bază ale agriculturii României, Rezultatele preliminare ale anchetei sociologice in 500 de comune.* Bucharest: Academia de ştiinţe agricole şi silvice 'Gheorghe Ionescu Siseşti', Institutul de economie şi sociologie rurală.
Anuarul statistic (1966–82) *Anuarul statistic al Republicii Socialiste România.* Bucharest: Direcţia Centrală de Statistică.
—— (1990–92) *Anuarul statistic al României.* Bucharest: Comisia Naţională pentru Statistica.
Buletin de informare (1990) *Buletin de informare publică al Comisiei Naţionale pentru Statistică.* Bucharest.
Buletin statistic (1993) *Buletin statistic de informare publică.* Bucharest: Comisia Naţională pentru Statistică.
Cresin, R. (1948) 'Cîteva aspecte ale rezultatelor recensămîntului agricol din 1948', *Probleme Economice*, no. 4.
Decret-Lege 1990/53 (1990) 'Decret-lege 53 privind organizarea şi desfăşurarea unor activităţi economice pe baza liberei iniţiative', *Monitorul Oficial al României*, Part I, vol. II, no. 20, 6 February.
EFTA (1994) Joint EFTA–Romania Committee. 'Economic developments in Romania'. Note by the Secretariat, Geneva, mimeo.
Golopenţia, A., and Georgescu, D. (1948) 'Populaţia Republicii Populare Române la 25 ianuarie 1948: rezultatele provizorii ale recensămîntului', *Probleme Economice*, no. 2.
Informaţii statistice operative (1993) 'Invăţământul de toate gradele în anul şcolar (universitar) 1992/1993', Seria: Populaţie, no. 1. Bucharest: Comisia Naţională pentru Statistică.
Ionescu, D. (1994a) 'Romania's privatization program: who is in charge?' in *RFE/RL Research Report*, vol. 3, no. 5, 4 February.
—— (1994b) 'Romania's standby agreement with the IMF' in *RFE/RL Research Report*,

vol. 3, no. 18, 6 May.

Johansson, S. and Ronnås, P. (1994) 'Promotion versus protection: a review of Asian experiences of rural industrialization', paper presented at a workshop on 'Rural industrialization in India', New Delhi, August 1994.

Legea 15 (1990) 'Legea privind reorganizarea unităţilor economice de stat ca regii autonome şi societăţi comerciale', *Monitorul Oficial al României*, Part I, anul II, no. 98, 8 August.

Legea 58 (1991) 'Legea privatizării societaţilor comerciale', *Monitorul Oficial al României*, Part I, anul III, no. 169, 16 August.

Legea fondului funciar (1991) 'Legea fondului funciar', *Monitorul Oficial al României*, Part I, anul III, no. 37, 20 February.

PlanEcon Report (1993) 'Romanian monthly economic monitor: soaring budget deficit and inflation delay economic recovery', vol. IX, nos 17–18, 28 May.

Recensămîntul (1930) *Recensămîntul general al României din 29 decembrie 1930*, vols I–X in Manuilă, S. (ed.). Bucharest: Institutul Central de Statistică.

Romania Economic Newsletter (1994) vol. 4, no. 1, April–June.

Ronnås, P. (1984) *Urbanization in Romania: A Geography of Social and Economic Change Since Independence*. Stockholm: EFI.

—— (1991) 'The economic legacy of Ceauşescu' in Sjöberg, Ö. and Wyzan, M. (eds) *Economic Change in the Balkan States: Albania, Bulgaria, Romania and Yugoslavia*. London: Pinter.

—— (1992) 'Romania: ailing state firms may create a roadblock', *RFE/RL Research Report*, vol. 1, no. 17, 24 April.

—— (1993) 'Human resources, employment and incomes' in *Romania: A Strategy for the Transition in Agriculture Working Papers*, vol. 2. Washington, DC: The World Bank.

Ronnås, P. and Sjöberg, Ö. (1993) *Township Enterprises: A Part of the World or a World Apart?* Studies in International Economics and Geography, Research Report 14. Stockholm: EFI.

Teodorescu, A. (1991) 'The future of a failure: the Romanian economy' in Sjöberg, Ö. and Wyzan, M. (eds) *Economic Change in the Balkan States: Albania, Bulgaria, Romania and Yugoslavia*. London: Pinter.

3 Romania: The Emergence of a Pluralist Party System. Challenges and Crises 1989-94

Andrei Musetescu

Central and Eastern Europe: a common pattern of transition

The concomitance and interdependence of the economic, political, social and cultural dimensions of the reform represent the most relevant common feature of the transition in Central and Eastern Europe. The region as a whole has never been homogeneous, as was pointed out by the critics of the Stalinist geopolitical concept of Eastern Europe (Heller and Feher 1994). But the actual and real differences in the premises and in the range and paths of changes in the post-commmunist countries do not decrease the significance of this typical challenge. Similar goals have been successfully achieved in other regions of the world. In Spain and Portugal, for example, the transition from dictatorship to democracy took place under favourable social and economic conditions (private ownership, a developed middle class and the institutions of civil society). In some Far Eastern countries a rapid economic growth was achieved under authoritarian political regimes. This is also the case in China, where what the official language calls 'socialism with Chinese characteristics' means a combination of economic reforms and a non-democratic political system.

For Romania, the main effects of the specific content of transition in the European post-communist countries are as follows:

1. The gap between the strategic and the operational level of the changes to be made. Dahrendorf (1993) has emphasized that the strategic changes, that is, changes which have major long-term consequences, depend on the relationship between these two levels. Several public opinion surveys have shown that the population's support for the concepts of the market economy, privatization and the rule of law is much stronger than for the concrete

consequences. In the political debate the reformist rhetoric is generalized. Even when there is not a nominal but a genuine agreement regarding global objectives, their instrumentalization in sectoral programmes is controversial. This resulted in a 'pathological gradualism' (Munteanu 1993; Serbanescu 1994; Vosganian 1994).

The issue of the strategic changes to be made within the social system was relevant for the process of political party building in Romania. Two periods can be identified in this respect. The first one (December 1989–January 1992) has been dominated by a homogeneous basic message regarding the features of the 'new Romania', considered as corresponding to and compatible with the Western type of social organization. This statement does not imply the absence of political competition; it only emphasizes that all the major political organizations, although critical of the options of their rivals, had a common target. The second period began during the campaign for the local elections (February 1992) and its main new feature is the ascension of alternative political programmes primarily interested in gaining social support by means of an inside-oriented offer, which tried to exploit the increasing social costs of change. It resulted in the emergence of two political messages (nationalistic and reformed-communist), which in the former period were active but included in the heterogeneous, ambiguous and contradictory programmes of the National Salvation Front (FSN) (Tismaneanu 1993).

2. The limited domestic resources for change and the low capacity to meet even legitimate claims. This is an important opportunity and a basis of legitimation for the counter-reformist approaches, which give a degenerative and costly interpretation of the need for social stability. In Romania, at least two political themes were generated by the need for resource mobilization, the national consensus project and the priorities issue. In both cases, positive historical references were given as empirical evidence of rationality. On the other hand, the period when we were 'men in dark times' (Arendt 1974) produced a collective negative experience in Romania related to pseudo-consensus and centralized resource allocation.

More active in addressing proposals for national consensus were Ion Iliescu and the ruling parties (the FSN and the Party for Social Democracy of Romania/PDSR), the main targets being the opposition parties and the trade unions. These attempts have always been backed by intense mass communication, based on the supposed support of the population for an integrative formula. In this respect, although the theme was not absent in its public message, the opposition parties did not manage to gain the initiative. It is a rather stable and costly feature of the post-communist period, that, with the exception of some influential newspapers and private radio stations and TV channels, the institutions outside the 'power structures', including parties and non-governmental organizations, have generally been not successful in imposing the major issues of public interest and debate. The failure of the last significant attempt at building national consensus on the basis of a minimal but commonly accepted policy ('the social and political pact', inspired by the Moncloa agreement) was produced by the lack of commitment on the side of the PDSR relating to the crucial point: the identification and agreement upon a relevant set of genuine reforms to be achieved in a given period. Even so, the project had a direct function in the political competition being presented by its supporters as proof of an 'avoiding responsibility strategy' on the part of the opposition, in order to discredit its claims of operational political alternative.

Romanian political parties: a quantitative approach

One of the main priorities of the post-communist period in all the Central and Eastern European countries was giving legal status to party pluralism. No contradictory debate occurred on this issue. This was perceived as an indicator of political liberalization, a legitimization resource, both domestic and foreign, for the emerging political leadership and a necessary premise for the institutional building of the new political system. It is also a reaction to one general characteristic of the immediate post-totalitarian periods: social activism and political mobilization of the population.

Romania lacked, to a greater extent than some of its allies in the Warsaw Pact, the legal and institutional basis for the rule of law and a democratic political system. As Chirot (1991) noted, 'the tragedy of Stalinism, which Ceauşescu and other East European leaders used as model, was its complete success in some respects'. In Romania Decree Law 8/1989 aimed to compensate for this handicap, at least at the formal level, and provided the legal framework for the organization of political parties. The main feature is its extreme permissiveness (251 signatures are needed for registration), which stimulated the extreme multiplicity of political parties. The negative effects became manifest very soon, a proliferation of satellite parties, 'shadow parties' (the emergence of parties having names quite similar to already influential and attractive ones) and limitations as regards the genuine representation of the real interests of different social classes.

Until May 1990 the lack of electoral legitimization for all the 150-plus political parties provided a rational basis for the existing legal framework. Moreover, the solutions based on a 'non-organic' approach as suggested by some political parties (administrative limitations and interdictions) would imply multiple risks for the development of a democratic political system. But after the 1990 general election, the preservation of the initial legal requirements represents a typical case of abortion of the process of modernization. The analysis of the 1990–94 legislative input (draft laws) and output (laws) proves the low interest in this field.

The multiplication and fragmentation of the political scene is not unique to Romania, but a frequent characteristic of the first stage of post-totalitarianism, based on the high political mobilization of the population (interest in political issues, information and participation). The number of political parties has no real correspondence in the structure of the Romanian electorate. The election certified that party atomization has no equivalent in a comparable atomization of the population's political choices. In the 1992 local elections, only 13 out of 89 participating political parties won more than 1 per cent of votes; together, they won more than 90 per cent of votes. The 1992 legislative elections confirmed the tendency of political concentration and the consolidation of 15 political parties. The core area of the Romanian party system is not homogeneous. The differences in terms of social support, membership and territorial coverage provide the basis for internal mobility and influence reallocation between the competing members. The possibility of ascension of other parties as well as of decline of currently influential ones cannot be excluded; it is another dimension of the mobility of the Romanian party system. In this context, what is relevant is the unconfirmed but persistent information regarding the transformation of a marginal party (the Democratic Centre Party of Romania/PDCR) into the main political organization supporting Ion Iliescu in the presidential campaign of 1996 or the prospects of the dissident group from the Socialist Labour Party (PSM) in their attempt to reproduce the evolution and capitalize on the recent revival of the reformist left in Central and Eastern Europe.

The party atomization phenomenon will remain in the medium term, even though many parties lack a stable and significant social basis. The fusion of different political parties reduced their number. The main intended functions of this process were: (1) increasing public awareness of the parties involved; (2) increasing the credibility of the core member of the alliance (representing a centre of political attraction); (3) increasing the electoral chances of the constituting organizations and of their leaders. It was mainly minor political parties which took part in this process, so that its general influence was low. The potentially effective case could be provided by the present tendency, following successive attempts, towards the unification of several liberal parties having significant networks of local organization and parliamentry and local government representation.

The alliances represent the other pattern of political concentration. It is debatable whether at least some of them end up as an institutional unification/single party. Regardless of their future development, some latent or manifest crises have already been generated by this formula, the most effective being the identity crisis of some component organizations and the hegemonic status crisis. These two sources are now active in the case of the main opposition alliance, the Democratic Convention for Romania (CDR); several projects of reorganization have been proposed and the leadership issue became a central and decisive point of debate.

Another specific crisis, basically linked to and produced by the former two, refers to the mutual harmonization of political programmes and actions of the alliance members. In this context, the comparative advantage of addressing larger and various target groups has some negative side effects: (1) the actions of one alliance member could be costly for the others; (2) a more difficult decision-making process.

An *ad hoc* alliance has been generated by the PDSR, the winner of a relative majority in the 1992 general election, its main objective being to provide parliamentary support for the government. The internal crises have been solved by means of a 'reward distribution policy' which resulted in a continously increasing influence of the allied parties (the Party of National Union of Romanians/PUNR, the Greater Romania Party/PRM and the Socialist Labour Party/PSM) on state institutions, at both national and local level. It is a costly strategy in terms of needed economic, political and social reforms owing to the dominant lack of interest in genuine and modern changes and, if the case, the generally regressive and counter-effective strategic options and practical solutions offered by these parties.

An opposite tendency was the fragmentation of several political parties. If the fusions mainly involved marginal political parties, the fragmentation affected some major ones. Two main causes can be identified, namely an internal doctrinaire debate/clarification and interpersonal polemics and struggles at the top level of the party.

The first relevant case is that of the former National Salvation Front (FSN). The dominance of a movement-type political organization is a regular feature of the first stage of the political process in many post-communist countries. Although the differences cannot be ignored (the most relevant being the legitimacy and the political and ideological background and offer/programme of the leadership), there are also some common characteristics, such as the massive social support and basic heterogeneity in terms of strategic orientation. This internal latent crisis was solved by means of fragmentation into autonomous and often antagonistic parts. It is, also, an important cause for the 'second election crisis' in many of these countries (unlike the case of the first post-communist elections, which resulted in strong majorities, the second ones in many cases generated multiple fragmentation and comparatively low popular support for each significant competitor). In the Romanian case, this evolution generated two parties, one backing and supporting Ion Iliescu (PDSR) and another led by former prime minister Petre Roman (Democrat Party/PD). The liberals provide the second example of major centrifugal tendencies. The tradition of dissident groups in the liberal field is real, but not relevant for explaining this case. The hegemonic tendencies of the National Liberal Party (PNL), both among the liberal-oriented parties and within the opposition, were not backed by significant political performance. Placed second, according to polls conducted in February and March 1990, its influence decreased continuously and generated the crisis of the party and the opening of successive fragmentations. A recent example of fragmentation, which might have important consequences, involved the Socialist Labour Party (PSM).

The legitimacy challenge

The transition from totalitarianism to democracy implies the rehabilitation of the public image of political organizations, which has been extensively compromised by the former dominant communist party. Temporarily hidden by the explosion of political participation immediately after the collapse of communism, the issue of the legitimacy of party pluralism and of each individual political organization became decisive for the prospects of democracy. Being representatives of definite interests, the parties must provide reasons for loyalty accepted by the target groups.

After December 1989, two different stages in terms of party dynamics and the population's attitude can be identified. The first is dominated by party building and high levels of expectation and participation. The influence of different parties depended upon general programmatic statements which, related to concrete actions, gave their basic and relatively stable image. The second stage is characterized by a decrease in the emergence of new parties and efforts to consolidate the existing ones. Regarding the population, the major features are the decline of trust in political institutions, the increase of political absenteeism and the orientation towards economic issues. Several surveys conducted by CSOP-Gallup International in this period show an increasing pessimism of the population; the dominant expectations are negative and refer to a worsening individual standard of living and economic decline. The political parties actively used several legitimative strategies and sources. The analysis of their specific content and impact is relevant for the actual political power distribution.

1. The historical legitimacy focuses on the long existence of the party and has two dimensions. The retrospective one emphasizes the role and contribution of the party in decisive moments of national history; the prospective one considers these elements as a guarantee of efficiency and credibility. Only three parties could use this theme: the National Peasant Party-Christian Democratic (PNTcd), the National Liberal Party (PNL) and the Romanian Social Democrat Party (PSDR). Because not all the previous activities of the

party could be converted into a positive background, several favourable selections were made. This generated major opportunities for delegitimization attempts. Owing to this internal tension, the historical legitimization had contradictory effects and now has a much lower profile.

2. The charismatic legitimization is related to the overpersonalization of the political parties. The post-communist mobility and renewing of political elites produced this typical feature of political system-building in Central and Eastern Europe. Its role was important in two situations, the common case of party building by individuals and the identification and evaluation of the party by means of their leaders' public image. The general lack of the most powerful legitimacy source (organization of the 1989 revolution) was compensated by interest in attracting prominent participants. Being successfully associated, in the public perception, with the 'revolution makers', the National Salvation Front (FSN) was the main beneficiary and consolidated its dominant position in the first half of 1990.

In many Central and Eastern European countries, Romania included, the dependence of parties and, generally, of public institutions on their current leaders is a potentially major weakness for the reforms process. It produced important opportunities for the anti-reformist forces and is one notable cause for the actual deadlock in some of the former communist countries. Jowitt (1992) adequately emphasized that institutions and a constructive individualism, not charismatic leadership, are the main challenges and urgent needs facing Romania.

This source also has ambivalent consequences because it generated counterattacks focused on the leaders' biographies. Although all the politically relevant persons were involved in such events, the contestation had different effects on their authority and prestige.

3. The doctrinaire legitimization focuses on the projection of future Romania and has several complementary dimensions: (1) teleological (strategic goals, general objectives); (2) axiological (central and peripheral values, accepted and rejected values) and (3) practical (operationalization of the strategy in sectoral programmes, solutions and priorities). It is important for the self-definition of the party on the left–right scale and for its ideological roots. Most parties tried to avoid the negative connotations of both left and right and place themselves in the centre. There are also many claims for representing the same ideological orientation, the most attractive being liberal and social-democratic doctrines. The overlapping generated the need for choosing among basically identical approaches. It was the image of the party and its perceived force which gave comparative advantages to some competitors and influenced the selection and final option. The main representative for each ideological field limited the growth of a social basis/support for other parties sharing a similar orientation.

This source of legitimacy provides elements for a typology of Romanian political parties. The first group includes the reductionist parties. They emphasize one issue considered to be of major importance and decisive for the other ones. They are also associated with unilateral solutions. The main representatives are the extremistic parties like the Greater Romania Party (PRM) or the Movement for Romania (MPR). The second group includes the integrative parties, which basically offer complex solutions for the different relevant issues.

A separate case is represented by the Democratic Union of Hungarians of Romania (UDMR), which shares specific features of both groups. Being focused on ethnic issues, it is a reductionist-type party; this has costly effects on its allies from the Democratic Convention for Romania (CDR). The extremist tendencies and representatives from both the Romanian and Hungarian communities and political organizations provide reciprocal reinforcement and mobilization of the radical options. At the same time the UDMR proved interested and introduced genuine offers related to basic issues of economic, institutional, political and social reforms.

The changes which occurred in the population's attitude towards politics, mainly the growing interest in pragmatic approaches, produced a reorientation of the parties. Most of the major parties tried to adapt to this new environment and to present themselves as being focused on problem-solving. In a survey conducted by CSOP-Gallup International in April 1994 on a national representative sample, the respondents were asked which party is the best at solving problems like economic recession, unemployment, inflation or corruption. Although the image of the parties reflects the respondents' political options, the distribution of answers confirmed the increase of pessimism and discontent (around 30 per cent answered 'don't know' and 15 per cent 'none').

In both the 1990 and 1992 elections, the 'shock therapy' programmes were less successful than the gradualist ones. The electorate was also more favourable to the paternalistic approaches (the case of the FSN and the PDSR).

4. The party-activity-based legitimacy promises/provides material or symbolic rewards for its social basis, both groups and individuals. It has several dimensions: (1) its significance is related to the place held by the respective issue in the population's individual agendas; parties focused on marginal themes did not gain support (the case of monarchist restoration, union with Bessarabia or revision of the constitution); (2) activism refers to the frequency and geographical distribution of activities; many parties virtually disappeared in the period between elections; (3) efficiency is related to the output of activities and the party's capacity for attaining the proposed goals; the credibility of the party is involved so that the failures are costly (for example, this perspective was avoided by the leadership of the National Union of Romanians Party/PUNR,

which finally obtained changes in the government and the promotion of its own members).

Local government (and the central one for the ruling party) and parliament are crucial from the point of view of this legitimization source. The decline in trust and satisfaction with these institutions represent a stable tendency. In the 1992 local elections a major comparative disadvantage of the National Salvation Front (FSN) was the actual experience of the population with its representatives and their poor performance. After the split in the FSN, the leaders of the newly emerged Democratic National Salvation Front (FDSN/PDSR) managed to disengage themselves from the costly negative image of the former government and successfully competed in the legislative elections.

5. The interest-representation legitimization aims to create a stable relationship between the party and a social group. Since even the historical parties lost their social basis, this concern was general. To some extent the request is less active in the case of ethnic-based parties (the UDMR). The relation developed from heterogeneous representation and support towards a more specific one. But even now the social basis of some parties is basically contradictory and this feature produces greater vulnerability (the PDSR provides the most relevant case). The different segments of the Romanian population are generally aware of their specific interests and seek adequate representatives (it is an entirely different problem if these interests are compatible with the need for global and sectoral changes). So the outcome of the 1990 and 1992 elections was not related to the 'blindness' of major parts of the electorate, but corresponded to the specific social structure of Romania. They represented rational choices based on high expectations of protection-focused political offers. In both cases the party which promised lower social costs was identified; also, the employees gave greater support to parties, like the former FSN or PDSR, favourable to the maintenance of large state prerogatives regarding property, employment, health and education.

The social cleavages have a growing influence on the political affiliation. Some parties are explicitly built on old or emerging cleavages. The Socialist Labour Party (PSM) focuses on class cleavages (rich–poor, owner–employee). Nationalistic parties like the PRM strengthen the importance of ethnic differences.

The capacity to address the relevant problems of the population is decisive for the consolidation and development of the party's social basis. A common feature in all the East and Central European countries is the centrality of concerns regarding prices, unemployment, income, public order and corruption. These themes give the population's interpretation of the legitimate and rational political/national agenda and also indicate its main expectations. They do not exclude ambivalence and internal contradictions, as the accurate description given by Tamas (1992) shows:

All the surveys and polling data show that public opinion in our region rejects dictatorship but would like to see a strong man at the helm; favours popular government but hates parliament, parties and the press; likes social welfare legislation and equality, but not trade unions; wants to topple the present government, but disapproves of the idea of a regular opposition; supports the notion of the market (which is a code word for Western-style living standards), but wishes to punish and expropriate the rich and condemns banks for preying on simple working people.

6. The institutional legitimization is connected with the direct or mediate support given to parties by various organizations. In these cases the credibility and influence of the institution is transferred to the party. Although there are legal provisions for the political neutrality of some major institutions (the mass media, army, courts and ministries), these have been the main targets. For example, the Democratic Agrarian Party of Romania (PDAR) developed a network within the Ministry of Agriculture. The influence of the ruling party (PDSR) and its allies in major institutions is also evident.

The lack of social control over public institutions, due to the underdevelopment of civil society, stimulates these attempts at domination. On the other hand, their supporters argue for the rationality of this explicit or mediate influence in order to achieve a 'coherent government'.

7. External legitimization is related to the credibility of the party abroad. The dependence upon foreign funding and the process of European integration increase the objective importance of this theme. With the significant exception of the nationalistic parties, which develop an autarchical project and present the outside world (especially the West) as a major threat, this theme has played a minor role in the political affiliation of the population.

Political cleavages and party system structure

The Romanian party system has already developed a significant cleavage, not entirely compatible with the traditional left–right one: the stabilization of two competitive political fields, both regarding the affiliation of the politically involved/interested segments of population and the parties themselves. This tendency has been identified in several polls conducted by CSOP-Gallup International, IMAS or IRSOP. The zonal fidelity means that the eventual redistribution in political choices/options first and foremost takes place within each field and that the direct migrations from one camp to the other are less frequent and less numerous. In this context, the redefinition of political support probably has a first phase of political absenteeism. The first political field corresponds to the governmental coalition and the second one to the Democratic Convention for Romania (CDR). Not all the relevant and relatively stable parties (which gained more than 1 per cent of the votes in the local and general elections) belong to one of these political fields. But the cost for this exterior placement is a greater vulnerability and probability of decline (the case of the National Liberal Party/PNL after the decision to leave CDR is relevant).

Each political field has its own central party, which plays the same hegemonic role but for different reasons. The distribution of incentives and rewards is the main source for the dominant position of the PDSR within the governmental coalition. As for the National Peasant Party–Christian Democratic (PNTcd), its status is based on its larger social basis, the support of civic organizations affiliated to CDR and the authority of its leader.

The leading position, which is the subject of internal contestation, does not mean total autonomy. The dependence of the PDSR is stronger; for reinforcing the cohesion of its own political field it has to accept the increasing demands of its allies for direct political influence. On the other hand, there is a dependency of each party upon its own political field. So, loyalty is an important element and the sanctions are very efficient (the cases of the PNL and the PDAR, which faced strong attacks coming from the former allies, are relevant). The central party of each field is also the main target for the outside contestation.

Both political fields are heterogeneous in terms of social basis or territorial coverage. Moreover, mainly in the case of the Democratic Convention for Romania (CDR), the alliance has a protective function for some of its members which have no significant social basis of their own (the Ecologist Party of Romania/PER, the National Liberal Party-Democratic Convention/PNL-CD and the Romanian Social Democratic Party/PSDR).

A project of the Centre for Political Studies and Comparative Analysis developed a theoretical framework for the identification and location of the different Romanian political parties on the reformist/counter-reformist scale (Sandor and Musetescu 1993). The following criteria have been used in order to achieve an extensive evaluation: (1) configuration of the proposed changes (content, direction, complexity, rhythm); (2) resources used for achieving the intended changes (the various social groups interested in the success of each project, institutions, ideology/programme, persons); (3) mechanisms of change (relevant indicators for this dimension are described by such polar pairs as autonomy–centralization, innovation–conformism, competition–egalitarianism, individualism–collectivism; (4) consequences of the change process (effectiveness, emancipation from the former political system and its rules, social reactions); (5) compatibility of the proposed changes with the existing international and domestic environment (model/pattern, adaptation).

References

Arendt, H. (1974) *Vies politiques*. Editions Gallimard.

Chirot, D. (1991) 'What happened in Eastern Europe in 1989' in Chirot, D. (ed.) *The Revolutions of 1989*. Washington: University of Washington Press.

Dahrendorf, R. (1993) *Reflections on the Revolution in Europe* (Romanian translation). Editura Humanitas.

Heller, A. and Feher, F. (1994) *From Yalta to Glasnost* (Romanian translation). Editura de Vest.

Jowitt, K. (1992) 'Romania are nevoie de individualism, nu de charisma' ('Romania needs individualism not charisma'), interview published by '*22*' *Weekly*, 27 (128), 10–16 July.

Munteanu, C. (1993) 'Pathological gradualism: the trap of the Romanian reform', '*22*' *Weekly*, 10–16 June.

Sandor, D. and Musetescu, A. (1993) 'Gramatica schimbarii' ('The grammar of change'), *Sfera Politicii*, no. 3.

Serbanescu, I. (1994) *Reforma economica. Jumatatile de masura dubleaza costurile sociale (Economic Reform. Half-Paces Double the Social Costs)*. Editura Staff.

Tamas, G. (1992) 'Socialism, capitalism and modernity', *Journal of Democracy*, vol. 3, no. 3.

Tismaneanu, V. (1993) *Reinventing Politics*. Bucharest: The Free Press.

Vosganian, V. (1994) *Contradictii ale tranzitiei la economia de piata (Contradictions of the Transition to Market Economy)*. Editura Expert.

4 Economic Change in Bulgaria since the Fall of Communism

Michael Wyzan

Introduction

The first four-and-a-half years of post-communist economic reform in Bulgaria have seen their share of successes and failures. On the asset side of the ledger, the macroeconomic stabilization programme inaugurated in February 1991 has to a large extent realized its goals of liberalizing prices and foreign trade, wiping out the monetary overhang, diminishing the importance of the state in the economic sphere and keeping current account problems within tolerable limits. A deal was at last cut in July 1994 with the London Club of commercial creditors, to which the country owed over $8 billion, providing Bulgaria access once more to international capital markets. In terms of structural change, the growth in the numbers and significance of private enterprises has been rapid, the country now boasts a number of substantial private banks, the first large privatization deals, some involving foreign capital, are finally starting to take place and a mass privatization programme is in the offing.

Despite these achievements, however, economic policy has been less purposeful and coherent, and economic performance poorer, than in Central Europe. Recent success stories notwithstanding, less headway has been made in privatizing major industrial concerns than in virtually any other East European nation. State commercial banks whose assets consist of bad loans to dying state enterprises dominate banking; attempts to solve this problem, including a fairly ambitious scheme at the end of 1993, have failed to do so. Moreover, there are signs that the accomplishments on the stabilization front are brittle. It has proved difficult to sustain monthly levels of inflation below 4–5 per cent. While foreign exchange crises, hikes in administratively set energy prices or agricultural difficulties are generally blamed for the periodic bursts of even higher inflation, the villain is undoubtedly rapid monetary growth resulting from financing budget deficits and ailing state commercial banks. Finally, looming on the horizon in the medium term is the burden of servicing the debt instruments issued under the London Club agreement.

This chapter examines economic policy and performance in Bulgaria from communism's demise up to 1994. The second and third sections analyse macroeconomic stabilization and structural policy in turn. The concluding section tries to put the Bulgarian experience into comparative perspective and to suggest reform priorities.

Macroeconomic policy and performance

The February 1991 stabilization programme: content and success

The collapse of CMEA trade and the inertia on economic matters of the regime of Todor Zhivkov's immediate successor were largely to blame for very poor economic performance during 1990. Table 4.1 portrays the large declines in output and investment, the start of significant inflation (even before price liberalization), the rising real wage and the emergence of serious fiscal imbalances. The data on the balance of payments in Table 4.2 depict the worsening trade and current account deficits.

Bulgaria filed a Letter of Intent with the IMF in February 1991, after joining it and the World Bank in September 1990. The 1991 stabilization programme's nominal anchors were domestic credit and incomes policy, but not the exchange rate. The Bulgarian National Bank (BNB)'s reserves were too small to intervene in the foreign exchange market, Bulgaria had no access to international capital markets (after its unilateral spring 1990 moratorium on interest and principal payments on foreign debt) and no one offered to finance a stabilization fund (Wyzan 1992b, 1993b; OECD 1992: 34–45; BNB 1991b). The stabilization programme had a number of successes: 'the monetary overhang was eliminated; prices and trade were liberalized; hyperinflation was avoided; budgetary adjustment was undertaken; wages were kept under control; and external balance was obtained' (OECD 1992: 74). Even so, 1991 economic performance (as revealed in Tables 4.1 and 4.2) was worse than expected, especially with respect to retail price inflation, the decline in real wages, the rise in unemployment, the fall in foreign trade and the nominal depreciation of the lev. The decline in GDP and the (cash) budget deficit were as expected, while the figures for the foreign reserves and the current account deficit were surprisingly good.

The stabilization package included a number of measures: price liberalization; the creation of a market-determined, floating and unified exchange rate plus the decontrol of most current account transactions; a slowing of the

Table 4.1 Recent Bulgarian domestic macroeconomic indicators

	1989	1990	1991	1992	1993	1994
GDP (leva 1000m)	35.6	45.4	131	195	286	460[1]
GDP ($1000m)[2]	17.6	6.9	7.5	8.4	10.4	8.6[1]
GDP per capita (dollars)	1957	769	836	990	1226	1019[1]
Share of private sector in GDP (%)	n.a.	9.1	11.8	15.3	19.4	n.a.
Unemployment (1000s; end-period)	0	65	419	577	626	514[3]
Unemployment rate (%)	0	1.6	10.8	15.5	16.0	13.4[3]
Average monthly wage[4]						
leva	274	378	1012	2047	3145	4211[5]
US dollars	136	58	58	88	114	89[5]

Percentage changes

	1989	1990	1991	1992	1993	1994
Real GDP	−1.9	−9.1	−11.7	−5.7	−4.2	−2.0[1]
Gross industrial production	−1.1	−16.8	−22.2	−15.9	−6.9	n.a.
Gross agricultural production	0.8	−6.0	−0.03	−12.0	−18.2	n.a.
Gross fixed investment	−0.5	−25.1	−15.6	−26.3	−21.6	n.a.
Consumer price inflation[6]	10.0	72.5	338.9	79.6	64.0	98.5[7]
Producer price inflation[6]	n.a.	n.a.	284.0	24.9	15.3	64.4[8]
Growth of nominal average wage[4,6]	8.7	38.0	167.7	102.3	53.6	n.a.
Broad money[6]	n.a.	n.a.	124.8	41.1	52.6	79.1[7]

Percentage of GDP[9]

	1989	1990	1991	1992	1993	1994
Budget revenue	57.9	52.8	41.0	42.1	36.7	34.0
Profit tax	23.2	17.9	13.1	7.0	5.7	4.6
Budget expenditure	58.5	57.7	44.8	47.4	48.1	40.1
Interest payments	3.1	9.5	14.2	6.7	9.8	8.5
Social security benefits	10.4	12.0	13.5	13.9	15.8	13.7
Subsidies	15.5	14.9	4.0	1.9	2.3	1.3
Cash budget balance[10]	−0.6	−4.9	−3.8	−5.3	−11.4	−6.1
Overall budget balance[11]	−0.6	−9.2	−15.7	−13.6	−15.0	n.a.

Notes:

1 Prognosis.
2 Converted at average annual official exchange rate; for 1994 the rate for 30 June is used.
3 As of end of July 1994.
4 State sector only, not including women on maternity leave.
5 For March 1994; dollar wage calculated at average daily exchange rate for March.
6 On end-of-period basis.
7 September 1993 to August 1994.
8 August 1993 to July 1994.
9 All figures in this section of the table refer to the consolidated state budget.
10 Excludes unpaid interest on foreign debt.
11 Includes unpaid interest on foreign debt.

Sources: Angelov (1994); BNB (1994: 26); Nenkova (1994); NSI (1990: 80); NSI (1993: 16); NSI (1994a: 89, 114, 115, 117, 130, 156); NSI (1994b); OECD (1992: 52); Wyzan (1993b: 127); Ministry of Finance.

Table 4.2 Bulgarian balance of payments (US$m)

	1989	1990	1991	1992	1993	1994 I and II
CURRENT ACCOUNT	−1306	−860	−77.0	−360.5	−523.3	277.4
Trade balance	−1199[1]	−757[1]	−32.0[1]	−212.4[2]	−329.7[2]	193.8[2]
Exports	3138[1]	2615[1]	3737.0[1]	3956.4[2]	3971.2[2]	1563.2[2]
Imports	4337	3372	3769.0	4168.8[2]	4300.9[2]	1369.4[2]
Services, net	−179	−211	−114.0	−191.0	−230.5	−4.8
Shipments, net	108	51	−13.8	−2.5	−53.2	−35.7
Travel, net	169	78	−84.2	−98.7	50.5	13.7
Interest, net[3]	−555	−396	−28.1	−95.6	−192.3	−87.5
Other, net	108	56	12.1	5.8	−35.5	104.7
Transfers, net (private)	63	108	50.0	39.7	36.9	88.5
Inter-official unrequited transfers	0	0	19.0	3.1	0.0	0.0
CAPITAL ACCOUNT	596	−135	115.0	760.9	127.6	271.6
Direct foreign investment	0	0	55.9	41.5	55.4	25.1
Medium- and long-term loans, net	712	−414	−48.1	42.1	−46.3	127.7
Drawings	3042	n.a.	108.0	232.4	97.2	65.8
Repayments	2330	n.a.	156.1	190.3	143.5	32.0
Loans extended, net	−167	299	294.9	307.6	347.3	102.6
Developing countries	n.a.	n.a.	92.4	23.4	35.0	9.1
Yamburg pipeline[4]	n.a.	n.a.	202.5	284.2	312.3	93.5
Short-term debt	51	−20	−187.7	−147.6	−0.1	29.4
Deposits and loans	n.a.	n.a.	−85.2	53.0	−68.1	29.6
Clearing accounts	n.a.	−102.5	−197.5	−200.6	68.0	−0.2
Unclassified capital	n.a.	n.a.	n.a.	517.3	−228.7	−7.8
Errors and omissions	276	127	26.2	−151.3	34.5	−62.2
OVERALL BALANCE	−434	−868	64.2	249.1	−361.2	398.3
Change in reserves	n.a.	n.a.	−64.2	−249.1	361.2	−398.3
Gross reserves/BNB	n.a.	n.a.	−358.0	−575.1	232.2	−430.1
Gold/BNB	n.a.	n.a.	0.0	0.0	0.0	−4.4
Reserves/BFTB[5]	n.a.	n.a.	−70.9	−18.2	19.4	−90.9
Reserves/commercial banks	n.a.	n.a.	−213.4	−45.2	33.5	−129.0
Credit from IMF	n.a.	n.a.	385.6	217.2	44.1	191.9
Loan from EC	n.a.	n.a.	192.5	172.2	0.0	0.0
Loan from EFTA	n.a.	n.a.	n.a.	0.0	32.0	33.4
Exchange rate differences/ BNB reserves	n.a.	n.a.	n.a.	n.a.	n.a.	30.8
Exchange rate (leva/$)[6]	2.02	2.84	21.81	24.492	32.711	61.001

Notes: 1989–91: foreign economic activity in convertible currency only; for 1992–93: all such activity.

1 Based on foreign trade activity reflected in payments operations of commercial banks.
2 Based on foreign trade activity reflected in customs statistics; payments data gathered from commercial banks show $5093.0 million in exports and $4608.5 million in imports in 1992; $4700.6 million in exports and $4567.1 million in imports in 1993; and $3934.1 million in exports and $3740 million in imports in the first half of 1994.
3 Includes only interest actually paid, not that falling due.
4 Includes repayments by former USSR in the form of natural gas.
5 Bulgarian Foreign Trade Bank.
6 End of period; for 1994 that on 27 September.
Sources: BNB (1991a: 100, 103); BNB (1993: 151); NSI (1994: 107); Wyzan (1993b: 128); other BNB sources.

growth of nominal wages among state employees; the placing of nominal limits on the budget deficit, while beginning a restructuring of revenues and expenditures; and a tightening of monetary/credit policy via large hikes in nominal interest rates and the setting of bank-specific credit ceilings based on the share of a bank in total credit at the end of the previous year. The details were as follows:

1. As to price liberalization, the prices of goods making up 10 per cent of trade turnover in 1991 were subject to state intervention, including margin controls for basic foods, drugs and oil products, and direct control of various energy prices. Even these last were subject to large one-time price hikes bringing them closer to international levels.

2. Since 1 February 1991 Bulgaria has had a liberal foreign exchange system based on a unified exchange rate and the decentralized allocation of foreign exchange on an inter-bank market. Every working day the BNB determines a central exchange rate against the dollar after observing events on the inter-bank market the preceding working day. In the realm of trade policy, quantitative import restrictions were abolished; import-licensing requirements were limited to very few products, mostly with a military orientation; and export bans, licensing requirements and ceilings were applied to only a small number of product categories. Enterprises were allowed to engage freely in foreign trade activity.

3. Incomes policy would be realized through ceilings on state enterprise wages funds, enforced via a tax on wage increases above the ceiling. During the first half of 1991, these ceilings and policies, which aimed to protect workers with low wages, led to significant declines both in the average real wage and in wage differentials.

4. In the monetary sphere, the BNB has maintained high nominal interest rates, although when inflation appears to be declining, the exchange rate stable and foreign reserves rising, it has reduced its refinance rate (e.g. in summer 1992 and spring 1993). Margins between borrowing and lending rates at commercial banks, with their portfolios full of bad debts, are as high as 20 points. The system of credit ceilings on bank lending proved effective in 1991 in cutting real credit and the real broad money supply, while raising the income velocity of money. However, this system came to be seen as providing only partial control over the money supply, and was replaced in August 1994 by one based on the setting of targets for the growth of reserve money. One consequence of the application of credit ceilings was that most lending to non-government (e.g. 88 per cent in 1992) went to state enterprises, leaving few funds available to the expanding private sector.

5. The programme's fiscal targets were to reduce the cash budget deficit to 3.5 per cent of GDP, to reduce government debt to the banking system, to reduce the percentage of GDP accounted for by both expenditure and rev-

enue and to bring price subsidies down from 16 to 3 per cent of GDP. A number of changes were made to the social safety net, including increasing spending on unemployment compensation, financed by hikes in contributions by enterprises, and reinforcing job training and job search services.

The Bulgarian public sector has shrunk relative to GDP more than that in any other former member of the Soviet bloc. The cuts in expenditure, while partially reflecting a policy shift, have been necessitated by the precipitous fall in revenue, which has gone from 57.9 per cent of GDP in 1989 to an expected 34.0 per cent in 1994 (see Table 4.1). Profits tax collections are now under 5 per cent of GDP, compared with over 23.2 per cent in 1989. The most promising source of revenue is the value-added tax, introduced in April 1994, and accounting for some 37 per cent of state tax revenue by mid-August 1994. In the first two years of stabilization, the cash budget deficit remained under control (4 to 5 per cent of GDP), but that deficit grew rapidly in 1993, surpassing 11 per cent of GDP. While the revenue side continued to shrink, a change in the wage-indexation method, mounting social spending and surging domestic debt service (the result of repeated deficits and high and lately rising interest rates) made deeper expenditure cuts impossible (AECD 1993: 7–20). Social security programmes are especially worrying: although their share of total spending is not unusually high, it will continue to rise, in view of Bulgaria's elderly population and low retirement ages (OECD 1992: 19–20). Despite these disturbing trends, however, there has been great progress in cutting subsidies, so that they reached 1.2 per cent of GDP in 1992, the level at which they have largely remained, making Bulgaria the stingiest country in this regard in the region.

By 1993, approximately 30 per cent of deficit finance was derived from selling government securities, rather than printing money. None the less, these bonds are bought largely by commercial banks, for whom they serve as collateral for Lombard loans from the BNB. Since these banks may borrow in this manner up to 60 per cent of their government security holdings, thereby directly increasing the monetary base, this method of deficit finance is highly inflationary (Miller 1993a: 53–5).

The distinguishing feature of exchange rate policy, a topic that has stirred considerable controversy in Bulgaria, is that that rate is generally viewed as a floating one. Of course, the BNB has intervened so as to build up the foreign currency reserves (which went from $125 million at the beginning of 1991 to more than $900 million at the close of 1992: see Table 4.1) and on certain occasions to try to stabilize the foreign exchange market. Until late 1993, the Bulgarian foreign exchange market was characterized by a remarkable stability in the nominal value of the lev and an attendant sharp rise in the real effective exchange rate. This rise must have been at least partly responsible for the rise in the trade and current account deficits in 1993. Other factors included the UN-sponsored embargo against Serbia/Montenegro and the EU's procrastination in ratifying its association with agreement with the country.

In the labour market arena, real wages declined in 1991 by 39 per cent, using the consumer price index as the deflator (see Table 4.1). In 1992 the goal was for enterprises' wages funds to remain unchanged, so that those reducing their staffs would be able to increase their average real wages. The method of wage indexation employed in 1992 tied wages at state enterprises to projected price inflation. During that year there was an increase in the real average monthly wage of nearly 13 per cent (almost 52 per cent in dollar terms, given the real appreciation of the lev). In 1993 the real average monthly wage fell by about 6 per cent, but again its dollar equivalent rose substantially. An early 1993 agreement (promulgated by the newly installed non-party regime of Lyuben Berov) corrected wages at state enterprises quarterly by up to 90 per cent of the previous quarter's inflation. Criticized by the international financial organizations for creating such a pro-inflationary mechanism, in 1994 the government returned to basing wage adjustments on projected inflation (*168 Hours BBN*, 14–20 February 1994, p. 11[1]).

It is clear from the data in Table 4.1 that the last few years have been harsh for the economy. While the decline in GDP is levelling off and may end in 1995, if the projection for 1994 proves accurate, it will have fallen by 30.3 per cent during 1989–94. If we make the same supposition about the behaviour of industrial output during 1994, this variable will have dropped by fully 51.9 per cent over the same period.

Recent macroeconomic developments

After two rather uneventful years for the macroeconomy, Bulgaria has in 1994 been rocked by instability, demonstrating the fragility of the gains in the stabilization sphere. Ironically, these problems have arisen at a time when relations with the IMF are back on track (a third stand-by agreement was signed in April after the parties failed to reach one in 1993), the fiscal situation has improved relative to 1993, agreement has finally been achieved with the London Club and the country has its longest-ruling government since Zhivkov.

The extent to which matters have gone astray in 1994 is seen by comparing the parameters of the IMF-approved macroeconomic framework for 1994 with what has transpired. Consumer price inflation was to be 30 per cent for the year, whereas the country will be lucky to remain in double-digit territory; the exchange rate was supposed to be 35–40 leva to the dollar, while it is currently at 61.1 (and reached 64.9 on 31 March); and the BNB's base interest rate was to be 35 per cent, compared with the actual 62 per cent for much of 1994 (raised to 72 per cent in early September). Two other predictions seem to be faring better: a cash budget deficit of 6.2 per cent of GDP and zero growth of GDP (BNB 1994; *168 Hours BBN*, 11–17 July, pp. 1, 3).

The macroeconomic framework for 1994 drawn up in early autumn 1993 has proven so unrealistic largely due to three periods of intense exchange rate depreciation, the first of which occurred late in 1993. These episodes are frequently blamed by observers in Bulgaria, such as the Agency for Economic Coordination and Development (AECD 1993: 20–2; a local macroeconomic think-tank), on the inaction of the BNB in the face of speculative pressures. Yet it cannot be denied that the lev had undergone a significant real appreciation during 1992 and 1993, so that some correction was overdue. It is, of course, not easy to explain the timing of the first episode (November 1993). However, the growth of the budget deficit during the second half of 1993 and the public position of BNB Governor Todor Vŭlchev that the BNB should refrain from supporting the overvalued lev (combined with a fall in its refinance rate in August) were important factors in this connection.

Two more periods of severe depreciation of the lev occurred in January and March 1994, resulting in its losing almost 50 per cent of its value over one quarter. The debate continued between those who saw these events as a stimulus to exports and those who saw them as lacking an objective basis and blamed the BNB and speculators. This time the uneasiness on the foreign exchange market was to a large extent related to the approach of the agreement with the London Club. The deal would require the BNB to buy some $750 million in US government securities to secure the Bulgarian government obligations issued to the foreign banks holding the debt; in the meantime, the foreign reserves had shrunk dramatically, from $1.095 billion in October 1992 to $593.2 million in February 1993.

On the heels of these foreign exchange developments, inflation increased markedly, the consumer price index growing by 7.5 per cent in March, 21.7 per cent in April and 7.9 per cent in May. The proximate causes of April's poor price performance were the depreciation of the lev, the introduction of the VAT and an increase in the price of electricity, the last two both occurring on 1 April (*168 Hours BBN*, 9–15 May, pp. 1, 15). The origin of this acceleration in inflation must ultimately be sought in monetary growth. March 1994 saw broad money grow by 21 per cent, but this was entirely the result of evaluating foreign currency deposits at the higher exchange rate; broad money fell in April and grew by under 3 per cent in both May and June. None the less, there remains concern that the lev money supply is growing too rapidly, this time not so much to finance the budget deficit as to refinance one or two ailing state commercial banks.

Moreover, while budget fulfilment through the first half of 1994 exceeded expectations, largely due to strong revenues, there are danger signals on the horizon. Interest expenditures on domestic debt had by 17 August reached 99 per cent of the projected figure for 1994. It will be an enormous challenge to achieve the primary surplus of 5 to 6 per cent of GDP necessary to stay within the fiscal targets agreed with the IMF in the face of this rise in interest expenditures. Problems with non-interest spending may appear as a result of wage indexation for government employees (although the government has so far been able to stick to the mechanism tying such indexation to projected price inflation) and of the growing deficit in the social insurance fund.

The macroeconomic outlook is at the moment unclear. Monthly consumer price inflation had returned to a more normal 4.1 per cent by June and hit a post-stabilization low of 0.63 per cent in July, due to seasonal declines in fruit and vegetable prices, before rising again to 5.2 per cent in August. After being stable for several months, in August and September the lev began to weaken rapidly again. Although this time the decline does not follow a significant real appreciation, there is one similarity with previous episodes – the BNB's foreign reserves have fallen to $629 million by 31 July (*Standart*, 9 August 1994, p. 15) from their peak of $1.16 billion on 30 June (*168 Hours BBN*, 11–17 July, pp. 1, 3), owing to the purchase of US securities under the London Club deal, making large-scale BNB intervention impossible. Still, there are promising signs: the decline in unemployment over January–June 1994, the fact that the fall in GDP has slowed to the point of almost stopping and the continuing rapid rise in the size and scope of the private sector (*168 Hours BBN*, 1–7 August 1994, p. 5).

The London Club and Paris Club agreements

On 29 June 1994 a 'Brady' deal was reached with the London Club after years of negotiations (and ratified by parliament on 27 July). The deal's most favourable aspect is its 47.9 per cent principal reduction (from $8.124 billion), similar to the 49.5 per cent reduction agreed by the Club with Poland in 1994 (*Demokratsiya*, 30 August 1994, p. 4). On the other hand, domestic critics have pointed to the deal's small recourse to buy-back, the most favourable method of debt reduction: 12.9 per cent of the debt is to be so treated, compared with the hoped-for 19 per cent – and the 25 per cent received by Poland (*Demokratsiya*, 30 August 1994, p. 4) – at 25.1875¢/$. The other options involve the issuing by the Bulgarian government of $5.137 billion worth of such instruments as past-due interest rate bonds, front-loaded interest reduction bonds (so-called FLIRBs) and collateralized discount bonds; the last two instruments may be used to buy objects up for privatization. The initial payment is $756 million, much of it for the purchase of US government securities to guarantee the instruments (*168 Hours BBN*, 4–10 July 1994, pp. 1, 3; *168 Hours BBN*, 1–7 August 1994, pp. 1, 4; *Pari*, 11 July 1994, p. 4). While such purchases have greatly reduced the BNB's foreign reserves, $500 million in international support for the deal is expected in 1994 (*Demokratsiya*, 30 June 1994, p. 4).

For the rest of the century, the need to service the instruments of the London Club deal and other debt (e.g. to the Paris Club and international organizations) will impose a heavy burden: annual outflows (peaking in 1997) of $250–300 million to the London Club debt and $500–1300 million in total (Angelov 1994). It is this burden, plus the low recourse to buy-back and the assertion that a better deal could have been reached when the UDF was in power, that led many in the UDF to oppose the deal (Mihaylova 1994). The agreement's supporters point to the need to restore access to international capital markets and that the deal can be a spur to carrying out long-delayed structural reform.

As to the Paris Club (official creditors), holders of 15 per cent of the debt, rescheduling deals were signed in April 1991, December 1992 and April 1994. While these deals all cover payments coming due over the succeeding twelve months, those in 1991 and 1992 stipulated repayment over a decade and six-year grace periods; the 1994 deal provides for an eleven-year repayment schedule and a seven-year grace period (*168 Hours BBN*, 18–24 April 1994, pp. 1, 3).

Structural reform

The perception both inside and outside Bulgaria is that little structural change has occurred these last four or five years. Discussions with the World Bank on a $150 million Financial and Enterprise Sector Adjustment Loan (FESAL) have dragged on for several years. The second ($100 million) tranche of a 1991 Structural Adjustment Loan (SAL) worth $250 million from the same body was not released until March 1994 owing to the Bank's displeasure with the slow pace of structural reform. Bulgaria has lacked major structural reform programmes in the manner of Czech/Slovak mass industrial privatization or the Polish integrated strategy to recapitalize and privatize state banks (Bonin 1994). The one case in which an ambitious, distinctive approach was attempted, restituting agricultural land to its former owners, has proven complex, contradictory and protracted, and agriculture finds itself in deep crisis. In other instances, such as dealing with the bad loans at state commercial banks, approaches have been piecemeal, necessitating further, likely multiple, revisits to the same problems.

On the other hand, it is wrong to imagine that there has been little structural change since communism's demise. If labour market trends are indicative, Bulgaria is a fast mover. Unemployment rose faster between early 1991 and late 1993 than virtually anywhere else (except Albania and Slovakia) and has fallen unusually quickly during 1994 (see Table 4.1). Private sector growth has been impressive: it now employs 900,000 and accounts for 19 per cent of output, so that it has a significant impact on macroeconomic performance (AECD 1993: 38; *168 Hours BBN,* 1–7 August 1994, p. 5). There are now 16 private banks, with 16 per cent of bank assets (AECD 1993: 39), some of which will be participating financial intermediaries on loans from the World Bank and other bodies.

Foreign investment

Bulgaria has had less success in attracting foreign direct investment (FDI) than the Central European countries. Through mid-1994, $500 million in FDI had been received, 41 per cent of which came from Germany, followed at a great distance by Holland (10 per cent), Switzerland, Belgium, the US, the UK, Austria and Greece (*168 Hours BBN,* 29 August–4 September 1994, p. 11). Looking at the balance of payments (Table 4.2) reveals a total from the beginning of 1991 through 30 June 1994 of only $178 million (Bŭklova 1994a). The extent of such activity is likely to be significantly underestimated relative to Central European lands owing to the substantial presence of small, unregistered Greek, Turkish and Middle Eastern ventures.

None the less, the level of FDI in the country is undoubtedly comparatively small. The slow pace of the chosen market method of privatization (so that potential investors must still deal with ministries) and the restitution of land to its former owners have proved to be obstacles to attracting FDI. Foreign investors frequently complain about the delays caused by the manner of work of the bureaucracy and the legal system. At the local level legal problems abound concerning the ownership status of land involved in joint ventures or privatized enterprises and there is a general lack of co-operation from the authorities. At the national level, where more than one ministry or agency is involved, these bodies often give contradictory indications as to whether there is an interest in a certain proposed venture. The provisions of legislation, such as those stipulating duty-free import by foreigners of machinery and raw materials used to produce goods for export, are often not implemented in practice. The instability of the lev and deficiencies of the banking system should also mentioned as obstacles facing investors (Bŭklova 1994a; Harizanova 1994; Todorov 1994). Ironically, these difficulties are occurring in the country with arguably the most liberal legislation on foreign investment in Eastern Europe (Wyzan 1992a).

Privatization: market, mass, spontaneous

From its inception large-scale privatization has eschewed the use of mass methods in favour of market forms of disposing of state property. The law regulating this process was passed in April 1992, during the reign of the UDF,
which, despite seeing itself in the ideological mould of Václav Klaus, opposed
mass privatization. Such opposition, which runs deep in Bulgarian society, is
partly an outgrowth of a scepticism towards grandiose reform programmes
inherited from the days of Todor Zhivkov. Indicative is the remark by the
former head of the Privatization Agency, as paraphrased in Bŭklova (1994b),
that the 'scheme [for mass privatization] proposed and passed by parliament
resembles the collective irresponsibility from the time when Zhivkov made
the workers proprietors (*stopani*) of [state] property'. Only very recently has
the notion of mass privatization gained support, and doubters still abound.

Every year the Privatization Agency (PA) comes up with a list of enterprises slated for privatization; given that they usually contain a very large
number of enterprises, these lists have proven to be far too ambitious. Under
the current (amended) rules, the determination to privatize a state-owned
enterprise is made by the Council of Ministers (or a state organ appointed
by it, usually a ministry) for enterprises with up to 70 million leva (about
$1.1 million at the current exchange rate). The PA makes such decisions for
larger state enterprises, while municipal councils do so for the firms that they
own. One problem with this method is that since ministries or municipal
councils retain ownership of enterprises until the latter are privatized, they
have an incentive to hold on to the more profitable ones.

The law sanctions many market methods of selling the shares of firms being
privatized, including open sales, public auctioning of shares, publicly-invited
tenders, negotiations with parties expressing an interest in buying them, purchase of all or part of an enterprise by its staff and any combination of these
methods. There are provisions for preferential participation of current and
former staff and pensioners: such persons may purchase up to one-fifth of the
shares (in total) at a discount of 50 per cent, but no one may receive a total
preference exceeding two years' gross salary. Although in its original conception the law avoided the use of vouchers, and thus did not stimulate the creation of investment funds, a so-called Mutual Fund was to be created. This
fund would receive 20 per cent of the shares of privatized enterprises and 20
per cent of the proceeds from privatization, to be used for financing social
insurance and compensating former owners.

By 31 December 1993, only 115 objects, most small ones, had been privatized, 98 of them entities forming part of enterprises (NSI 1994a: 211).
However, a number of major deals have recently been made, so that the market
method may finally be bearing fruit (*168 Hours BBN*, 8–14 August 1994, p.

12). After a procedure that lasted almost a year, in mid-July 1994 the German trucking company Willy Betz purchased for $55 million a 55 per cent stake in Bulgarian haulier SO MAT, agreeing to settle SO MAT's debt of $16 million and invest a further $48 million. Another important deal, this time without foreign participation, was the sale in June 1994 for the equivalent of $9.4 million of a 49 per cent stake in the Grand Hotel Varna to Multigroup, a Bulgarian private holding company; 20 per cent of the shares will be sold at half price to the employees and the remaining 31 per cent are to be sold to the public in two offerings through the State Savings Bank and Post Bank (*168 Hours BBN*, 20–26 June 1994, p. 12; *168 Hours BBN*, 15–21 August 1994, p. 12).

In order to speed up the process, and to broaden popular support and participation, the Berov regime has come up with a mass privatization scheme, which is contained in amendments to the privatization law passed by the parliament in June 1994. Between 1 September and 14 October all adult citizens will be eligible to obtain for 500 leva a book of investment vouchers valued at 25,000 leva; they may buy additional vouchers at 5000 leva apiece. The vouchers may be used to purchase shares in 340 enterprises on a special list (one-third of which are profitable) containing 25 per cent of state industrial firms. The coupons may also be used to join a co-operative licensed to transact in securities or entrusted to an investment fund. The auctions, which are expected to take place between mid-October and mid-December, are to have four rounds, while general meetings of new shareholders will be called during February–April 1995. Employees may acquire up to 10 per cent of the shares in their firms gratis or at a preferential price. It is expected that 3.5–4 million people will participate (*168 Hours BBN*, 8–14 August 1994, pp. 1, 12).

There is much opposition to this programme – the president was urged (to no avail) to return the law to parliament – from the trade unions, managers of state and large private enterprises, the PA and the UDF. One source of complaint has been that the listed firms are mostly loss makers, so that the population is not being offered something of value; indeed, there is a stigma associated with finding oneself on the list, and a number of firms have been attempting to get themselves taken off of it. Representatives of private business have criticized the fact that the vouchers are non-negotiable and that the interests of small-scale entrepreneurs are not protected. The lack of clarity in the relationship between mass and market privatization has been attacked by the PA's leadership (fearful of undoing deals already in train) and by the UDF, which sees the method as overly bureaucratic. Valentin Karabashev, formerly one of Berov's deputy prime ministers, views the changes to the privatization legislation as unconstitutional. He is referring, for example, to the stipulations that foreigners may not participate in mass privatization and that objects obtained through privatization may not be sold or leased outside the country for five years (Karabashev and Sŭbev 1994). There is also controversy over the rules governing the investment funds, which will play an important role in the process (Markov 1994; *168 Hours BBN,* 29 August–4 September 1994, p. 8). Despite all this, the programme is apparently supported by the World Bank (*Pari,* 10 July 1994, p. 6).

Mention should also be made of the 'hidden' or 'spontaneous' privatization of large numbers of state assets, including entire firms. No figures can, of course, be found for the extent of this phenomenon. Note, however, the great divergence between the rates of inflation as measured by the consumer price index and the producer price index (Table 4.1). One possible explanation is that this divergence may reflect the business practices of the managers of state enterprises who have spontaneously spun off private firms. Such a firm is said often to buy the production of the state enterprise at an intentionally low wholesale price and then sell that production at a much higher retail price (Miller 1993b).

Space limitations allow only brief mention of several other aspects of privatization. With respect to the restitution of small-scale urban property, 56.5 per cent of all relevant objects (83 per cent of shops and restaurants) had been restituted to their former owners by 30 June 1993 (NSI 1994a: 206). According to official statistics, by 25 January 1994 40.5 per cent of the eligible farm land had been returned to its former owners, mostly based on land distribution plans rather than within original borders (*168 Hours BBN,* 7–13 March 1994, p. 7). However, others, including the president, cite much lower figures.

Banking reform

After modest programmes of converting the bad loans in the portfolios of state-owned commercial banks into state obligations in 1991 and 1992, in December 1993 a larger-scale attempt was made to address this problem. The law passed at that time transformed the loans made by such banks before the start of 1991 but not serviced for 180 days into long-term state obligations. There are separate approaches, and types of state bond, for the affected 32 billion leva in domestic currency-denominated debt and the $1.808 billion in foreign currency debt. These obligations have 25-year maturities and five-year grace periods. To minimize the budgetary impact of the programme, the lev bonds pay one-third of the BNB's basic interest rate in years one and two, one-half of it in years three and four, two-thirds of that rate in years five and six and finally reach 100 per cent of it in the seventh year; the foreign currency bonds have the same arrangement but pay the LIBOR. The state securities in question may be held by the banks, traded with other banks, transferred to other persons, used as collateral for BNB refinancing or employed in debt–equity swaps (*168 Hours BBN*, 20–26 June 1994, pp. 1, 4). The programme may be criticized for not covering enough debt to clean up banks' portfolios, for using below-market interest rates and for leaving unresolved whether this procedure will have to be repeated in the future, given the large and growing volume of bad debt not covered by it. Little thought has been given to the nexus between bank privatization, enterprise privatization and the bad debt problem.

Conclusions

It remains to provide an evaluation of Bulgarian post-communist economic reform. Bulgaria is not easy to categorize, falling between such successes as the Czech Republic or Poland and disasters like Ukraine or Georgia. Judged in terms of economic stabilization, Bulgaria can be ranked behind Central Europe (including Slovakia and Slovenia) and Estonia and Latvia, but ahead of the other Balkan states and former Soviet republics. In terms of privatization, it has moved slowly and without clear purpose, losing time and allowing state assets to be plundered. However, a ranking on the scope of the private sector would put it higher than a ranking on privatization, a characteristic reminiscent of Poland.

The progress made on macroeconomic stabilization is considerable and, while 1994 has been distressing, it is highly unlikely that the country will deteriorate markedly from its current position. Like all countries in the region that have succeeded in avoiding the worst forms of economic instability, the officials in charge of monetary and fiscal policy have displayed considerable competence under extremely difficult circumstances.

The problem in Bulgaria, in addition to a number of exogenous shocks not faced by countries to the north of former Yugoslavia, occurs precisely at the dividing line between stabilization policy and structural reform. The budget problem is exacerbated by the need to solve the worst bad-debt problem in Eastern Europe and by trying to fund an exceedingly complex and expensive method of land reform. The failure to install profit-oriented management at state enterprises and to let those firms go bankrupt when necessary makes the domestic supply response to the new market conditions negligible.

In the end, however, Bulgaria is not so much a country without structural change as one where structural change has not been, and perhaps cannot be, managed in an orderly fashion. Bulgarians have an anarchistic streak that distrusts grandiose government programmes and in general is suspicious of authority; orderly Czech voucher privatization or even the Russian version by state order may not work. In the meantime, there is a thriving private sector and large private capital has already made its appearance, albeit in the form of large industrial groupings often run by individuals with dubious pasts and questionable business practices. One way or another state industrial giants will die and new private sector activities will appear to replace them; it is just that the Bulgarian method of getting to that point is particularly roundabout, disorderly and slow.

Given the situation just described, what items should receive the highest priority on the reform agenda? One task that seems particularly important is to make some fundamental decisions about the order in which certain actions should be taken, especially the privatization of banks and industrial enterprises. Another is to develop a strategy toward the new private industrial empires. Less attention should perhaps be devoted to the origin of their money and more to employing tax and anti-trust policy to make certain that these groups adhere to the rules of a competitive market economy. Finally, some effort should be devoted to identifying inexpensive actions that would prevent further erosion of the public's faith in the reform process. A good start in this direction would be made by improving the transparency with which the public sector at all levels operates.

Acknowledgements

The views expressed here are the author's own and do not necessarily reflect those of the US Department of the Treasury or the Bulgarian Ministry of Finance. He thanks Anders Åslund, Valerie Gregory, Ian Jeffries, Ivan Krŭstev, Deyan Kyuranov, Tsvetan Manchev, Krasen Stanchev, Ognyan Pishev and Petya Tsaneva for their comments and various other forms of assistance, with the usual absolution from responsibility.

Note

1 Throughout this chapter non-attributed articles in daily or weekly Bulgarian publications are treated as in this citation of *168 Hours BBN*; attributed articles may be found in the list of references.

References

AECD [Agency for Economic Coordination and Development] (1993) *The Bulgarian Economy in 1993: Annual Report*. Sofia: AECD, December.

Angelov, I. (1994), 'Makroikonomicheski izmereniya na sdelkite po dŭlga', *Pari*, 28 June, pp. 4–5.

BNB [Bulgarian National Bank] (1991a) *Annual Report.* Sofia: BNB.

——(1991b) 'Letter of Intent of the Bulgarian Government to the IMF', *News Bulletin*, no. 4 (16–29 February), pp. 2–34.

——(1993) *Godishen otchet.* Sofia: BNB.

——(1994) *Informatsionen byuletin*, no. 2. Sofia: BNB.

Bogetić, Z. and Fox, L. (1993) 'Incomes policy during stabilization: a review and lessons from Bulgaria and Romania', *Comparative Economic Studies*, vol. 35, no. 1.

Bonin, J. (1994) 'On the way to privatizing commercial banks: Poland and Hungary take different roads', *Comparative Economic Studies*, vol. 35, no. 4.

Bŭklova, A. (1994a) 'Za privlichaneto na kapitali e nuzhna politicheska volya', *Pari*, 26 April, p. 5.

——(1994b) 'Skeptichno za masovata privatizatsiya', *Pari*, 13 June, p. 2.

Harizanova, T. (1994) 'Byurokratsiyata goni i malkoto zhelaeshti da investirat u nas', *Standart*, 6 July, p. 18.

Hristova, C. (1994) 'Prinudata na sdelkata s kreditorite e moshten lost za reformi', *Pari*, 26 July, p. 5.

Jackson, M. (1986) 'Recent economic performance and policy in Bulgaria' in Joint Economic Committee, US Congress, *East European Economies: Slow Growth in the 1980s*, vol. 3, *Country Studies on Eastern Europe and Yugoslavia.* Washington, DC: US Government Printing Office (26 March).

Karabashev, V. and Sŭbev, G. (1994) 'Osnovni pravni zabelezhki po prietite ot NS izmeneniya i dopŭlneniya v zakona za preobrazuvane i privatizatsiya na dŭrzhavni i obshtinski predpriyatiya', *Pari*, 20 June, p. 5.

Kopeva, D., Plamen, M. and Howe, K. (1994) 'Land reform and liquidation of collective farm assets in Bulgarian agriculture: progress and prospects', *Communist Economies and Economic Transformation*, vol. 6. no. 2.

Markov, T. (1994) 'Hibridni strukturi shte izvurshvat privatizatsiya', *Pari*, 20 June.

Meurs, M. (1993) 'Incentives, risk and economies of scale: household decisions about organizational form during the agrarian transition'. American University, Department of Economics (mimeo).

Mihaylova, P. (1994) 'Sdelkata po dŭlga s Londonskiya klub e neponosima za Bŭlgariya', *Demokratsiya*, 20 June, pp. 1, 4.

Miller, J. (1993a) 'The Bulgarian banking system'. University of Delaware, Department of Economics, Working Paper no. 93–12, October.

——(1993b) 'The price index gap: A window to understanding the Bulgarian economy'. University of Delaware, Department of Economics, October (mimeo).

Nenkova, S. (1994) '13.4% e bezrabotitsata za yuli', *Pari*, 18 August, p. 2.

NSI [Natsionalen statisticheski institut] (1990) *Statisticheski godishnik na Republika Bŭlgariya 1990.* NSI, 1990.

——(1992) *Bezrabotni v Republika Bŭlgariya Kŭm 4.12.92 godina.* Sofia: NSI.

——(1993) *Naselenie.* Sofia, NSI.

——(1994) *Statisticheski spravochnik 1994.* Sofia: NSI.

OECD (1992) *Bulgaria: An Economic Assessment.* Paris: OECD.

PlanEcon (1992) 'Bulgarian foreign trade perfomance in 1991: trade collapses to less than one-half the 1990 level', *PlanEcon Report,* vol. 8, no. 32, 14 August.

Rangelova, R. (1994), 'National accounts for Eastern European Countries: a case study for Bulgaria in an international perspective'. Paper presented at seminar on 'Comparative Historical Accounts for Europe in the 19th and 20th Centuries', Groningen, the Netherlands, June.

Todorov, V. (1994) 'Byurokratichni prechki spirat chuzhdestrannite investitsii', *Pari,* 15 April, p. 5.

Wyzan, M. (1991) 'The Bulgarian economy in the immediate post-Zhivkov era' in Sjöberg, Ö. and Wyzan, M. (eds) *Economic Change in the Balkan States: Albania, Bulgaria, Romania and Yugoslavia.* London, Pinter.

——(1992a) 'Bulgarian law lowers foreign investment barriers', *RFE/RL Research Report,* vol. 1, no. 13, 27 March.

——(1992b) 'Bulgaria: shock therapy followed by a steep recession', *RFE/RL Research Report,* vol. 1, no. 45, 13 November.

——(1993a) Bulgaria: the painful aftermath of collective agriculture'. *RFE/RL Research Report,* vol. 2, no. 327, 17 September.

——(1993b) 'Stabilisation policy in post-communist Bulgaria' in Somogyi, L. (ed.) *The Political Economy of the Transition Process in Eastern Europe.* Aldershot: Edward Elgar.

——(1994) 'Bulgaria: a Country Study' in Joint Economic Committee, US Congress, *East European Economies in Transition.* Washington, DC: US Government Printing Office (forthcoming).

5 Problems of the Transition in Albania, 1990–94

Gramoz Pashko

Introduction

In almost all East European countries, including Albania, the collapse of communism was accompanied by a profound economic paralysis. Its most obvious consequences were a dramatic fall in production, a vast increase in unemployment and a rocketing upwards of inflation (Kornai 1994). Albania's NMP was 46.7 per cent lower in 1992 than in 1989 and the cumulative fall of gross industrial output over the period 1989–92 was 79.7 per cent (IMF 1994: 41). Unemployment in the state sector at the end of 1992 reached 39 per cent, while annualized inflation increased by 236.6 per cent from its 1991 level. This crisis was caused by the collapse of the socialist economy, while the economic imbalances themselves were a result of the accumulated structural distortions of the command economy (Pashko 1991a). The economic chaos into which Albania's economy plunged preceded a political breakdown. However, it is against the dismal record of its orthodox communist past that the transition should be assessed. In this respect, Albania's post–war history has two central characteristics: (1) endemic backwardness and (2) virtual isolation from the rest of the world, which led to extreme autarky.

The main aspects of the collapse of the communist economic system

Albania's starting point was very low. However, due to massive foreign assistance from Soviet Union until the 1960s and then China during the 1960s and 1970s, Albania enjoyed rapid growth during the period 1950–70. The average annual growth of NMP was 8.2 per cent in the period 1951–60, 6.7 per cent in the second decade 1961–70, and 5.1 per cent in the period 1971–80. Massive investment of approximately 30 per cent of the NMP ensured the maintenance of full employment as well as a steady increase in personal consumption (which was higher than the population growth rate). This averaged 2.4 per cent per year throughout the post-Second World War period (*Statistical Yearbook of Albania*, various issues).

It is equally clear, however, that the causes of the extraordinary malfunctioning of the Albanian economy during the 1980s can be summarized as follows:

1. Despite relatively high (although declining) rates of investments in the economy the marginal productivity of capital was negligible (Blejer *et al.* 1992: 11). GDP growth rates began to stagnate at 1.5 per cent in 1981–85, becoming negative (–1.3 per cent) in the second half of the 1980s. The ratio of net fixed investment during the 1980s was an average of 24 per cent of GDP, but as long as the GDP (GNI: Gross National Income) growth rate was decreasing and fluctuating by an average of –0.1 in the first half of the decade and –2.5 in the second half, the productivity of such huge investments was very low. According to a recent IMF study, there was virtually no increase in capital productivity during the period 1981–90 (0.04 per cent was the average annual rate of increase). Bulgaria had a substantially higher GDP growth of 3.5 per cent per year, with capital productivity increasing 0.23 per cent while devoting 10 per cent less of its GDP to capital investment. Czechoslovakia had a lower real NMP growth rate compared with Albania, but it also devoted 10 per cent less of its NMP to investment. Albania needed to invest more than any Eastern European country to compensate for lower productivity (Blejer *et al.* 1992: 25). At the same time the depreciation of fixed investments has been dramatic. The average consumption of fixed capital averaged 2.6 per cent during the 1980s. Therefore, the investment increase failed to replace fixed capital, being aimed instead at expanding employment. As Table 5.1 shows, there has been a remarkable increase in employment, which as an average has overtaken economic growth as well as labour productivity. A serious deterioration of the situation can easily be observed in the second half of the 1980s.

2. A second underlying cause leading to further distortions was the industrial structure. There was rapid growth of the heavy industry sectors, particularly mining and energy. Manufacturing was mainly restricted to intermediate production, but heavily dependent none the less on the import of other intermediate goods. For instance, Albania imported coke to produce steel and then spare parts to produce coal, some of it for export. In addition, Albania imported phosphates to produce fertilizers and exported raw tobacco. Engineering was also developed, but merely as a supplier of spare parts to other industries. Albania's industrial sector accounted for 58.4 per cent of national income. The only enterprises which were export-oriented were in the mining and energy sectors. They alone represented 75 per cent of the country's total FOB exports at the end of the 1980s, when their share in gross industrial output

Table 5.1 Average annual growth rates of economic productivity

	1950–60	1960–70	1970–80	1980–85	1985–90	1950–90
Population	2.8	2.9	2.3	3.1	2.0	2.5
Employment in the state sector	7.3	6.8	4.2	3.2	3.3	6.1
Gross National Income	9.1	7.4	4.6	1.5	−1.1	5.4
Labour productivity per worker	7.4	1.4	2.7	−0.6	−2.6	2.5

Source: Statistical Yearbook of Albania.

was less then 26 per cent. In contrast to this, manufacturing accounted for 74 per cent of gross industrial output in 1990, although it represented only 13 per cent of the country's total exports, or 23 per cent of the FOB exports from the whole industrial sector (*Statistical Yearbook of Albania* 1991: 296–7; Directory of Statistics, provisional data for 1992). The purchase of spare parts and other industrial inputs accounted for 61 per cent of total imports. Imports of machinery and equipment in 1990 were 31 per cent of the total with some slight variations during the 1980s (*Statistical Yearbook of Albania* 1991: 298–9).

The vulnerability of an economy heavily dependent on export earnings to pay for machinery and inputs (Pashko 1991a: 138–9) led to the collapse of foreign trade. The collapse in foreign trade was partly due to exogenous factors, such as the limitations of CMEA area for Albanian goods (the area accounted traditionally for more than half of Albania's exports). In 1990 exports to the CMEA countries decreased by one-third. Secondly, a fall in export revenues from raw materials due to the world recession was observed in the second half of the 1980s. In total, exports declined 25 per cent in 1990 and the emergence of a newly created foreign debt paralysed the country's ability to borrow from commercial banks, with corresponding restraints on imports. Consequently, industry's ability to import inputs, spare parts and raw materials became increasingly limited. The state planners estimated that $500 million (or more than twice as much as the value of exports in the same year) was needed to operate the existing industrial base at full capacity in 1990.

It is very interesting to observe the rapidity with which foreign debt built up from the second half of 1989 until the beginning of 1991. It was mainly due to the Central State Bank of Albania's speculating in the international spot exchange operations. The Bank ended up with a huge debt owed to more than fifty international banks.

In the absence of a well-defined property law (Åslund and Sjöberg 1992: 140), the maintenance of a high level of employment as well as the rate of personal consumption became a prime political issue. This combined with a relaxation of coercion and various controls (including those 'which had been hitherto employed against the industrial workforce to ensure adherence to plan directive': Schnytzer 1992: 338) to provoke a dramatic decline in labour discipline. This was perhaps only to be expected in a structure which ruled out incentives at all levels, resulting in little except shortages. Even if the nominal increase of wages had been marginal during the last fifteen years, real effective earnings rose by 14 per cent during the 1980s (Blejer *et al.* 1993: 32), mostly as a result of the increase in employment (thus as an increase in the gross wage fund), but also because of the increase in social security contributions. In response, labour productivity decreased by 15.2 per cent (*Statistical Yearbook of Albania* 1991: 81). As Table 5.3 shows, apart from some fluctuations, there was constant increase in the number of workers in the state sector (the annual average of which has been overwhelmingly higher than annual investment rate, particularly in industry).

As Albania plunged into total isolation after the mid-1970s (even the inflow of foreign savings was banned in the 1976 Constitution), high expenditures via domestically generated funds were required to safeguard the pre-existing level of investment. This effort sharply eroded the fiscal balances. The increase of expenditure took place at a time when revenues were falling slightly but continuously. Government expenditure rose from 48.8 per cent of GDP in 1986 to 63.6 per cent in 1990. At the same time total revenues in GDP

Table 5.2 Albania's balance of payments and foreign debt (in $ million)

	1990	1991	1992	1993
Exports	227	72	70	91
Imports	380	281	524	560
Commercial debt in convertible currencies	268	447	501	558
Trade balance ratio to real GDP (%)	−11	−22	−67	−40
Debt ratio to GDP (%)	11	75	65	43
Debt ratio to exports (%)	145	556	1069	861

Sources: Bank of Albania, December 1992; IMF Monthly Economic Statistics, Albania, December 1993; IMF 1994: 72, 76, 77.

terms decreased from 48.7 per cent to 47 per cent (*Statistical Yearbook of Albania* 1991: 330–1).

The simultaneous increase in nominal personal consumption was not related to the increase of labour productivity. Instead, economic growth was artificially maintained through budget financing by direct subsidies to enterprises or by indirectly subsidizing the differences between costs and retail prices. The total of direct subsidies to enterprises through the state budget in the second half of the 1980s rose by almost three times, from 5.7 per cent of the GDP in 1986 to 16.1 per cent in 1990. The latter figure is almost equal to the fiscal deficit in the same year, namely 16.6 per cent of GDP (data from the Ministry of Finance).

Two other forms of subsidizing the economy increased in importance during the 1980s: (1) the subsidizing of relative prices by artificially maintaining a very high value of exchange rate, and (2) food price subsidies caused by heavy lending to co-operative farms (short-term credits to them increased annually by 8.4 per cent and obviously they were never paid back).

An overview of reforms during the 1990–94 period

A number of reform proposals announced in early 1990 by the then-communist government did little to improve the situation. Although the Albanian Party of Labour won the first reasonably democratic elections to take place in Albania since 1924 in the spring of 1991, their efforts at stabilization came

Table 5.3 Annual rate of growth of some main macro indices (in %)

Years	1985	1986	1987	1988	1989	1990
GDP	1.8	3.1	−0.8	−1.4	9.8	−13.1
GDP/capita	0.1	1.1	−2.7	−6.0	7.7	−11.5
Gross wage fund	1.8	5.5	3.4	1.3	3.7	4.6
Number of workers	1.5	4.0	3.8	2.7	3.4	3.1
Personal consumption	0.8	4.6	3.4	1.1	8.9	2.0
Investment in industry	21.1	−3.6	8.2	1.9	12.2	−22.6
Machinery and equipment	27.3	1.7	8.6	1.5	31.3	−26.2
Exports	18.5	0.0	2.4	18.8	25.0	−45.8

Sources: Statistical Yearbook of Albania 1991; IMF 1994: 40.

to nothing (for an assessment of political developments during 1990–91, see e.g. Milivojevic 1992). Efforts made to reform the state enterprise sector and attempts at stabilization proved abortive. None the less, the communist government should be credited with introducing the freedom of entrepreneurship. With hindsight, no matter how reluctant the government seemed to be at the time the decree was introduced in response to the first refugee crisis, when Western embassies in Tirana were invaded by 5000 or so prospective emigrants.

Popular protest against communism started during the last part of 1990 and led to the founding of the country's first, legal, anti-communist opposition (the Democratic Party) in December 1990. The period after the elections of March 1991 marks the real beginning of the transition period. There was massive resistance to the communist victory in the urban areas, reflected in widespread civil unrest and politically motivated strikes. As a result, the government survived for just five weeks. Talks with the opposition led to the establishment of a coalition government on 11 June, called the Stability Government.[1] In March 1992 elections were held again and the communists were overwhelmingly defeated.

The Stability Government launched an ambitious programme aimed at stabilizing the economy. This meant divesting the state sector of a sizeable share of its assets and generally increasing the scope for foreign and domestic entrepreneurs (Åslund and Sjöberg 1992; Kaser 1993: 306–11). The pillars of the economic programmes, as set out in June 1991, were as follows: (1) the liberalization of external economic relations (trade, foreign investment, currency regulations etc.); (2) the introduction of a social security system; (3) the liberalization of prices and of the domestic economy in general; (4) the privatization of state assets (including institutional reform, e.g. in banking and agriculture); and (5) macroeconomic stabilization. A more coherent programme was adopted by parliament in October 1991 (Pashko 1991c), designing the axes of the reform until May 1992. A start was thus made, but as the government made more progress in some areas (economic liberalization, land reform and small-scale privatization) than in others (e.g. macroeconomic stabilization and large-scale privatization), many issues were left hanging in the air at the end of this government's short existence. At the beginning of December 1991, it was replaced by Ahmeti's caretaker government and most measures were frozen in anticipation of the elections of 22 March 1992. Only in April 1992, following the establishment of the first non-communist government of the post-war era, were the reforms resumed and a comprehensive programme adopted.[2]

The years 1991 and 1992 were ones of instability and populist pressures, which affected daily politics. So it proved difficult to establish and develop coherent reforms, even if some important measures were taken and a degree of continuity was sustained. Price liberalization, which started in October 1991, aimed at the full elimination of subsidies. By November 1993 all previously controlled prices were included. All administrative measures regulating exchange rates were banished by permitting the lek to float on the free market and by dissolving the state monopoly of foreign trade. The stabilization programme included a sharp reduction in government expenditure and various subsidies. A simple system of taxes and excise duties was also introduced to create a source of revenue for the budget, but without very much fiscal discipline. It included a turnover tax and a profit tax. At the same time the single banking system began to be restructured through the creation of three universal independent banks: the Agricultural and Development Bank, the Savings Bank and the Import–Export Commercial Bank.[3] Laws that ensured the clear separation of the Central Bank from the commercial banks were introduced together with the clause that the Central Bank should no longer automatically cover the budget deficit.[4] The Central Bank was charged with dealing only with monetary policy under strict guidelines for issuing money.[5] But implementation of a tight credit policy only began in July 1992.

Privatization was initiated in August 1991. The first rapid step was taken in retail trade, either through auctions or direct sales. By January 1992, almost 75 per cent of retail trade and small services was operating in private hands. The programme envisaged private ownership rights and the privatization of the existing state property via a National Agency ordered to use auctioning as a general practice. Small-scale privatization was achieved through transference by direct sale to tenants in most cases or leasing to them with a postponement of payments for six months, after which date the shops were scheduled to be auctioned off to the general public.

The most important achievement was in land privatization. Agriculture accounted for 35.9 per cent of GDP in 1990 and employed 49.4 per cent of the total workforce of Albania (World Bank – European Community 1992: 165). Preparations for land reform were made during July–August 1991. Co-operatives were dismantled and land began to be distributed by September 1991. In principle the land previously held by co-operatives was distributed with title of ownership to peasants using proportional criteria for all residents in the co-operatives until 1 July 1991. The law did not recognize restitution to former owners and a scheme of compensation was set up. For the first year new owners were compelled to use the land only for agricultural purposes. The sale of land was prohibited.[6] By Spring 1992 almost 80 per cent of the agricultural land formerly within the co-operative system had been distributed to approximately 400,000 families. Families received an average of 1.4 ha.

After land distribution began in 1991, the situation in agriculture was marked by an improvement, starting in 1992 (World Bank – European Community 1992). Further progress is now held up by delays in settling full entitlements of land property rights (needed to attract investors as well as making possible the concentration of fragmented small plots into larger farms). Nevertheless, the rights to lease and sell land still remain absent in the legal framework. The claims of former land owners, both urban and agricultural, have been increasing, creating a big bottleneck in the further sequence of reforms, such as developments in mortgage, credit and financial markets, as well as for foreign investments.

The electoral campaign of 1992 interrupted the reform process, leaving many aspects incomplete. The banking law was not implemented until June 1992. The law on enterprises concerning the public sector did not come into force until 1 January 1992. Furthermore, implementation of the law on social assistance was postponed and was not fully functioning until July 1992. Subsidies to loss-making enterprises continued. Budgetary constraints were eased and the government became extremely generous, expanding budget spending as well as bank credits at a time when revenues were collapsing (see Tables 5.6 and 5.7).

The economic situation deteriorated extensively during the first half of 1992, even after the first steps towards reform. Inflation increased and peaked at more than 300 per cent at an annualized rate. GDP continued to decline, exports fell by another 45 per cent and industrial unemployment reached 50 per cent.

The only two sources of revenue were (1) food aid (provided by G-24 donors), which amounted to more than $600 million in 1991–92, a sum equivalent to 63 per cent of real GDP and (2) remittances from Albanian emigrants mainly in Greece and Italy evaluated annually at approximately $350 million. Taxes on imports and counterpart funds from selling food aid together became the main sources of state revenue: 37 per cent of budget revenue (11.6 per cent of GDP) came from food aid, while tax revenues were 53 per cent of total state revenue, or 17 per cent of GDP in 1992.

The major macroeconomic stabilization reforms, which had been brought to an abrupt halt in December 1991, restarted only after July 1992 under the Meksi government. This government developed a standard stabilization programme which was supported by an IMF stand-by arrangement in August 1992. It introduced some important monetary and fiscal measures in the period June–July 1992, which included raising interest rates up to 40 per cent, adjusting the exchange rate to the daily market rate, the liberalization of remaining prices, and adjusting to the cost level those few items subject to monopoly (such as electricity and PTT tariffs). Secondly, it eliminated totally direct subsidies to enterprises, introduced tough credit ceilings and amended the laws raising the turnover tax, while the profit tax was extended and personal income tax was introduced (approved at the beginning of July 1992). Domestic credit to finance budgetary expenditures and enterprises was cut drastically in GDP terms as Table 5.6 shows.

Most importantly, the tight budgetary policy has witnessed a reduction in government expenditure and increase in revenue. Budgetary austerity in the second half of 1992 replaced the budgetary laxness of the first half of the year. Direct subsidies were no longer provided to state firms in the second half of 1992. They decreased from 13.2 per cent of GDP in the first half of 1992 to 4.5 per cent in the second. Farm price subsidies accounted for 58 per cent of the subsidy total. The costs of unemployment benefit were calculated to be covered by a social assistance fund, which accounted for 4 per cent of GDP. Defence and spending on the police remained very high, running at 14.4 per cent (8.8 per cent alone is spent on defence) of total government expenditure, which is the highest for the past ten years. But in terms of GDP, defence remains constant at 5.5 per cent, showing only a slight decrease over the 1990 figure.[7]

In essence the policy was oriented more toward redressing slumping revenue than restructuring expenditure. Revenue increased from 26.9 per cent of GDP in 1992 to 28.6 per cent in 1993, while the figures for expenditure were 44.2 per cent and 38.9 per cent respectively.

It was mainly tax increases, especially from private companies, as well as strengthening state control over the state sector of the economy, that restored the fiscal balance. The tax share as a percentage of GDP was 17.1 per cent in 1992 and increased to 24.5 per cent in 1993. Turnover tax and levies together accounted for 64 per cent of total state revenue, from which only 14 per cent has been deducted from state enterprises.

Table 5.4 Main economic and monetary indicators 1990–93 (in %)

	1990	1991	1992	1993
GDP growth	−13	−28	−10	11
Industry	−20	−37	−60	−10
Agriculture	−4	−21	18	14
Inflation annual average	0	36	226	85
Broad money (ratio to GDP in %)	23	104	153	75
Public sector balance (commitment basis)	−15	−31	−22	−16
Broad money	37	69	58	45

Sources: Bank of Albania; IMF.

Taking into account the magnitude of money in circulation, the government was successful in slowing the increase in the inflation rate. In the last quarter of 1992 inflation started slowing down. The end-year inflation rate (consumer prices) fell from 236.6 per cent in 1992 to 30.9 per cent in 1993.

But a programme of substantial structural reform involving investment deregulation and medium and large privatization has not yet been introduced, even through a programme of public investments for the 1994–96 period was presented by the Meksi government in April 1994. Instead, there have been efforts to regain control over the state sector by rectifying the 'Enterprises Law'. The rationale is to re-establish the state's ownership rights which had been assumed by firms following the 1991 liberalization. But investment independence and flexibility of response of enterprises to structural shifts have not yet been relaxed sufficiently to facilitate a response to market signals. Once again the boards of directors for enterprises are to be appointed by the respective ministries and municipalities. The initiatives with regard to establishing joint ventures as well as privatization remain with the ministries (in the case of enterprises of national importance) or with municipalities (in less important cases). Of considerable importance is the introduction of measures concerning how enterprises use profits and also measures dealing with the system of wages. Henceforth, restrictions are to be placed on how enterprises can invest or distribute profits. A mandatory system requires that enterprises use profits for the creation of capital reserves, reserves for development and other reserves. After such expenditures have been satisfied, only then can enterprises distribute the funds to profits.

Table 5.5 Aid and other disbursement to Albania (in $ million)

	1991	1992	1993
Counterpart funds	40	57	62
Grants	137	538	160
Medium- and long-term loans	21	165	241
Total disbursement	158	695	402
In % of current GDP	23.9	105.2	36.3
In % of GDP constant prices	12.3	63.3	33.0
Real GDP per capita			
US$ (1989 = 583.5)	368.4	342.9	380.7
Nominal GDP per capita	199.7	200.0	334.9

Source: Ministry of Finance.

Table 5.6 Domestic credit

	1992	1993
Domestic credit (% GDP)	60.8	37.8
To government	37.3	25.6
To state enterprises	20.6	11.8

Source: Bank of Albania; IMF.

On the other hand, the average wage for each enterprise is set by the respective ministry. If the enterprise raises the average salary more than 5 per cent of this average wage the punishment will take the form of the confiscation of 100 per cent of the same amount from profits. The lack of VAT (value-added tax) and the cascade effect generated by the turnover tax increases the burden of taxation. Together with inflexibility in the wage system this has inhibited economic growth and fresh investments. The consequence is that even potentially efficient enterprises are penalized. Many more opportunities should be given to potentially competitive state enterprises which can increase productivity while shedding excess labour. The hesitant steps towards large-scale privatization and restructuring when tight macrostabilization policy is in

Table 5.7 Budgetary main indicators

Year	1989	1990	1991	1992 (1st half)	1992 (full year)	1993
(in million lek)						
Current receipts	9003	7630	6786	3575	13,309	32,202
Current expenditure	10,603	10,331	9120	10,845	21,911	43,869
Current balance	−1600	−2709	−2427	−7274	−8602	−11,667
(in %)						
Growth of revenue	−0.5	−12.6	−34.3	—	95.5	242.1
Growth of expenditure	7.9	40.6	30.4	—	240.6	200.4
In % of GDP						
Revenue	48	45	49	—	26.9	28.6
Tax revenue	44	44	27	—	17	21
Expenditure	57	61	66	—	44.2	38.9
Balance (cash basis)	−9	−16	−31	—	−17	−11

Source: Ministry of Finance.

place has created a real threat in the shape of a build-up of inter-enterprise arrears, compromising the anti-inflationary policy in the next stage. Examples of excess inter-enterprise credits, resulting from the first step of stabilization programmes in Poland and Yugoslavia, demonstrate that it will be virtually impossible for Albania to avoid the same fate (Corricelli and Rocha 1991). The decline in real wages consequent upon price liberalization and the wage adjustment policies introduced indirectly reflects the elimination of the inflationary subsidizing of enterprise losses. But the inability of the authorities to initiate bankruptcy procedures is reflected in a massive build-up of inter-enterprise indebtedness. It can be seen that broad money grew in 1992 from 11.4 billion leks to 25.4 billion leks and reached 50.1 billion leks in 1993, when total domestic credit grew from 18.9 billion leks to 42.5 billion and 90.2 billion in 1993, a large part of which are bad debts. In 1992 broad money flow continued to increase by 150 per cent in GDP terms. So at the end of 1992 the estimate of nominal broad money to nominal GDP remains very high at 58 per cent (Albanian Central Bank data). The firms continue to ask for further investments from the government and when they do not get it they borrow at negative interest rates. Managers and workers can easily get to a compromise by avoiding paying taxes to the authorities, in order to maintain their existing salary levels.

Fighting inflation in the first period, even if it gives short-term positive results, should not be attempted without policies to achieve a supply-side response. Very little can be saved from what remains of Albanian industry, so structural adjustment by state investments is misguided. Hence, restructuring state enterprises by investment deregulation linked with a programme encouraging privatization is vital and urgent. If its implementation is delayed, shocks resulting from price liberalization and the abolition of subsidies will be a real danger for the continuity of the fight against inflation. Hesitation with respect

Table 5.8 Budgetary revenues in % of GDP

	1989	1992	1993	1994 (provisional)
Tax revenues	44.2	17.1	24.5	20.6
Turnover tax	22.6	4.9	4.4	4.0
Profit tax	11.1	2.7	4.7	4.0
Social security	4.9	3.4	2.8	3.8
Excise duties	0.0	2.5	3.9	4.6
Personal income tax	0.0	0.0	0.04	0.4
Small business tax	0.0	0.0	0.36	0.6
Import duties	0.0	3.0	3.2	3.8
Non-tax revenues	4.0	2.2	3.0	0.9
Total revenues	48.2	26.5	28.6	28.1

Source: Ministry of Finance.

to restructuring and privatization is still manifestly evident. One reason given for the delays is a widely publicized fight against corruption. Wide-scale privatization has been further arrested since March 1992 due to policies of holding back and controlling what has been privatized up to the present. The propaganda of fighting corruption seems to inhibit further reform, particularly in industry and commerce.

The big challenge, the solution of which still remains unclear, is how the country will find a balance between interventions to stop inflation and those policies promoting growth, that is, between a tight monetary and fiscal policy and structural changes able to introduce market incentives. And it looks as though economic recovery must wait for a while. Tight monetary policy and fiscal control in abolishing subsidies and stopping inflation are accompanied by rapidly rising unemployment (Sjöberg 1994).

Just as with other transformation examples in Eastern European countries (Corricelli and Rocha 1991), the reform in Albania looks like being paralysed just when continuation is needed most, particularly in the case of the restructuring of the state sector. Inflexibility in investment policies remains, as well as delays in bringing market managerial incentives and competitiveness to the state sector, and the lack of bankruptcy procedures is also critical. Albania, as I have tried to show, had one of the most severe recessions of its history. But the country has survived, partly because of abundant aid from EU countries (as shown in Table 5.5) but also partly owing to an important inflow of hard currency remittances from Albanians working mainly in Greece and Italy (which provided the country with a considerable source of hard currency).

Some remarks about the 'philosophy' of transition

As in other communist economies, the structural crisis generated by the distorted socialist system has resulted in shortages, poverty and lack of freedom. Breaking away from Europe's most ruthless communist dictatorship, setting Albania on a transition course, has made the country a battleground of ideas that will affect, for better or worse, the future of society. The developments of the past four years have seen Albanian society trying to get to grips with the transformation process and the introduction of a new system of values. But it is still far from mastering a point of symmetry between freedom and truth, civil values and decommunization, national identity and European orientation, and free-market-oriented reforms and state command. Transition from totalitarianism to a free democratic society has produced a real ideological vacuum and there have emerged serious socio-psychological dilemmas. In the appearing void the question is how a new system of values can be set up, how widely it can be sustained and how the new political class can make

it legitimate. Even if the systemic change happening in Albania in its principles is not too distant from what has been experienced in the former East
European communist countries, focusing on some of the particularities will
help gain a better understanding of the meaning and the outcome of a challenging process of transition.

There are three main particularities to be focused on regarding the Stalinist
legacy and its impact on the present state of transition in Albania: (1) the
almost complete absence of a democratic tradition prior to communism; (2)
total isolation from the outside world; and (3) backwardness and poverty without precedent in the rest of Europe.

1. Unlike most Central European former communist countries Albania suffered from an almost complete lack of democratic tradition before the communists took over after the Second World War. The country won its
independence from the Ottoman Empire in 1912 and this was followed by a
chaotic and unstable situation until 1924, when power was seized by Ahmet
Zog (who subsequently was proclaimed King of Albania in 1928). Astute
politician, liberal in his economic policy but authoritarian in eliminating opposition to him, Zog did not leave behind him any consolidated political structure with sound democratic elements in it. So the political vacuum was filled
fully and comfortably by the communists during the war of liberation. The
communists did not face any substantial political resistance immediately following the liberation and therefore every vestige of democratic opposition was
easily annihilated. Probably assisted by the fact that Albania was marginalized
from the attention of the West during the 45 years of their rule, the Albanian
communists never abandoned orthodox Stalinism and never agreed with any
tendency either to create socialism with a human face or to tolerate any kind
of divergence from Stalinism, such as happened in most Central European
communist states.

2. Albania did not become part of the wider socialist world, but, on the
contrary, totally isolated itself. In the beginning it was briefly dependent upon
Yugoslavia, but quickly broke with Tito in 1948. It then became a blind satellite of the Soviet Union, with which it subsequently broke totally in 1961,
withdrawing from Comecon as well as from the Warsaw Pact. China then
became the third big communist ally, a romance that endured rather longer
than the two previous ones, but which ended in 1978. This last alliance gave
to the country access to fresh foreign Chinese aid, but also it heavily affected
the country ideologically, committing the leadership to plunge into complete
isolation and economic autarky.

But at the same time Albania perpetuated a distinct socialism, a hard-line
command economy, nationalistic ideology and political totalitarian rule. The
paranoid ruling ideology kept its distance from both East and West, for both
worlds were considered enemies, not so much of socialism but of Albania

itself. Isolation gradually built up a Third World revolutionary ideology, a blueprint of the Chinese cultural revolution heavily marked by populism, egalitarianism and xenophobia, which completely replaced Soviet internationalism and Marxist messianism. It fused naturally with the traditionally paternalist mentality. The ideal of the oppressed classes trying to conquer the world was replaced by the self-imposed defensive psychology which combined with the ideal of the oppressed nation trying to survive. The 1976 Constitution legitimized this ideology and codified a socialism based on the principle of self-reliance. Foreign credit or investments were banned (in the penal code these were explicitly considered high treason) and religion as an alternative ideology was totally forbidden. During this period Albania even refused to join the Helsinki Final Act.

3. Albania remained the most economically backward country in Europe and the most egalitarian society. Per capita GDP in the 1980s was on average $725. On average in the same period the country was exporting less than 10 per cent of its GDP. Some 65 per cent of the population was left in the countryside working in the co-operative system. But backwardness was widely accepted as a general condition, legitimized by the equality of sharing it. The Albanian constitution was even explicit in specifying that wage differentials between workers and high officials should not be larger than 1:2.5. Compared with many other former communist countries in which some private property was maintained, in Albania it was absolutely forbidden. This was not because private ownership creates a different system of wealth, but because of incompatibility with the system, since it creates individualism and destroys the sense of community.

Both these two features, egalitarianism and isolation, combined to build up a communist populism mixed with a particular kind of nationalism. But the fact that Albania did not even test any marginal shiftings from Stalinism during the communist era had an important consequence in the fact the new political thinking was built up after the fall of communism, that is to say parallel to the reform process. So communist populism was reversed during the revolution of 1991 into a new populism, this time anti-communist. Populist pressures have not been less successful in inhibiting the government's policy. On the contrary, they have forced the government to make significant concessions detrimental to the deepening of the reforms and constraining it to be driven by daily policies. After liberalization and a relatively successful stabilization policy, populism remains in place to provide fewer opportunities for fundamental capitalistic values and related institutions to prosper. Thus, many aspects of reform have ended in a spontaneity which jeopardizes further progress.

The other important issue is the relation between expectations and results (Wolfson 1992). In the beginning it is not difficult to persuade ordinary people to rise up against the collapsing system. But then responsibilities are transferred to those who lead the reform, and they have to answer for the painful sacrifices. Many setbacks to the present transition in Albania can be explained by such factors which are not directly related to economic issues.

The economic distortions which appeared in Albania in the 1980s had obvious similarities with other Soviet-type economies (Winiecki 1986). They produced and generated major problems, but were socially quiescent until the political collapse of communism. Price stability was artificially maintained, nominal wages even increased, unemployment benefit following lay-offs was consistently maintained. It created a growing absenteeism among working people. Then, the requirement for change was more an inner need to replace the corrupt and incompetent ruling class than a need for radical change of system. Even change was somehow accepted in principle, but not its painful consequences. The reforms were supposed to stabilize and, at the same time, transform.

The inevitable collapse of communism has become obvious to almost everybody and the country has opened up, self-imposed isolation has been destroyed and freedom achieved. So in the beginning most people agreed that reform was needed as an alternative to socialism, against which most of the population had turned. But I still believe that people in the former communist Albania are more anti-communist than pro-capitalist. It is almost illogical to argue that they approve capitalism's basic principles, of a free society with equal opportunities but unequal results, while at the same time generations have been educated for many decades to accept a society of unequal opportunities but equal results.

Moreover, the total absence of private ownership and related institutions, as well as the people's attitude considering economic society from an egalitarian starting point, makes the transformation only partially acceptable (as a small-scale privatization; as a bakery-style capitalism rather than as a system in itself). Unlike other former soviet economies Albania had no private sector at all during the communist era. Industry was fully nationalized and mostly created during after the war. The collectivization of agriculture started early and by the mid-1960s all economic activities were socialized. Small plots and small livestock permitted until then for personal use by the peasants were also forcibly collectivized at the end of the 1970s. The 1976 Constitution served such a purpose. In Hungary, for instance, less than 10 per cent of land was nationalized and 35 per cent was occupied by co-operatives (Szekely 1993). Moreover, after 1968 they were also market-oriented and in 1990, prior to post-communist reforms, 90 per cent of prices were already liberalized. In Poland there existed more or less the same situation (Lipton and Sachs 1991: 234). In these countries the main controversy has been over the privatization of large-scale industry.

An existing, albeit limited, private sector prior to reform is very helpful because it creates and maintains the general idea that in principle private ownership performs far better than state ownership. In such a situation everybody has an equal opportunity to begin with. In the total absence of private ownership, as in Albania's case, the country faces two cultural difficulties. First, people ask the state to save their jobs, salaries etc., and gradually, especially after the shock of macroeconomic interventions, they become hostile to privatization. Secondly, there is the risk that privatization becomes very politicized and very complex. The politicization of the process of privatization means that authorities give preference to those who demonstrate loyalty to the ruling party, excluding as much as possible the so-called 'reds'. This was to be expected, given the legacy of a system based mostly on favours and privileges.

In Albania a major problem arises because of small-scale privatization. The country has been traditionally a paternalistic society. Mostly it was agrarian with small and very fragmented ownership of land. In the cities private property before the communists came to power was mostly in small shops or artisan workshops. The 1991 privatization of land and retail trade created an emerging class of small owners, but also stimulated a reaction to it in the form of large claims for restitution. This pressure forced the Democratic Party, the ruling political force of the country, to delay further the law on restitution and compensation of former owners. The law was passed when almost all land in agriculture and almost all small services in the cities were already privatized. Thus it further inhibits the government's firmness in building a strategy for further privatization or for investment until land problems are definitively resolved, with the risk that the overall process of transformation will be further compromised.

4. Privatization is not an important issue for ordinary people in the beginning, but it becomes very important after the liberalization of prices, when some people become rich (principally through commerce), and anyone can become rich in the newly emerging private retail trade. Everyone is tempted to become a private dealer, not because of the future but because of the present (everybody expects to lose if they remain in the public sector). The reform process then became a question of inter-relations between credibility and expectations. Expectations increase and they are reinforced by the easy profits made in trade, even without consistent reform (Dewatripont and Roland 1992).

5. Related to the latter is the political context. In the beginning, anti-communist populist movements confuse rational and coherent reform programmes by impoverishing their content. Albania, like other East European countries challenged by transition, faced similar political instability, or at least has been trying to avoid it by shifting towards authoritarian rule. There have been constitutional shifts of powers between the President and the government,

fragmentation of decision-making, and a weak and indecisive parliament. All these phenomena diminish the strength of the government to act and strengthen the populist forces obstructing the reform process. As time passes without important developments the reform becomes heavily politicized, affecting and distorting the correct timing of intervention. A short-termist orientation starts to prevail within the leadership as a consequence of the 'technicalization' of the government. On one hand the leadership wants to maintain the prevailing situation because substantial reform may expose it to a risky situation. On the other hand, among common people the need for reform appears less and less as a genuine principle related to democracy and freedom and more and more as a question of a possible and immediate solution to the recession provoked by the collapsing previous socialist leadership. People have a very superficial impression of the market economy, of its basic structures. They think that a capitalist society means luxury cars, a lifestyle shown in advertisements etc., but they do not accept profit and other aspects of the price mechanism. So after the first traumatic period, especially of high prices, the risk is that people then oppose capitalism itself.

Political instability and inconsistency in the programmes of the emerging political forces in Albania hamper further major reforms. This has resulted in a delay between macroeconomic stabilization, price liberalization and privatization. Privatization is delayed sufficiently to resurrect an anti-capitalist mentality. Populists rise up against capitalists, price determination, unemployment and all consequences of the macroeconomic measures. So the government has both less opportunity and less commitment to deepen reform.

Affected by the burden of a precarious situation in the Balkans and the legacy of its past, Albania lost many good opportunities at the beginning of a new era to make genuine, rapid and determined economic reforms. It seems that the country will now face a long transition. This transition will be filled with difficulties which will hinder the straightforward path to freedom, a long path after which we may judge if we were wrong or right.

Notes

1. This was the so-called Stability Government under Ylli Bufi, which only remained in power for six months. It was replaced by a caretaker administration under Vilson Ahmeti during the period preceding the elections on 22 March 1992.
2. The continuity between the macrostabilization policy of the October 1991 programme and that of the Meksi goverment was assured through the appointment of Genc Ruli as Minister of Finance in both governments.
3. The package of laws transforming the State Bank into a new central bank, named Bank of Albania (free from commercial activities), as well as laws restructuring the

entire banking system were prepared together with the reforms of October 1991. These, however, were only approved by parliament at the end of April 1992 and only implemented in the early summer of 1992.

4. Article 32 clearly prohibits the Bank of Albania from providing credits to the budget of more than a ceiling of 10 per cent of the previous year's revenue (*Fletorja Zyrtare* 1992, no. 2: 69).

5. Article 40 sets out strict rules for the Bank of Albania in issuing the currency.

6. This clause was included in the hope of preventing disputes among old and new owners. Since then amendments permitting the sale of land have been discussed.

7. Defence spending was 11.8 per cent of total budgetary expenditure in 1980, 11.4 per cent in 1985 and 9.1 per cent in 1990. The ratio of spending on defence to GDP was 5.6 per cent in 1980, 5.5 per cent in 1985 and 5.9 per cent in 1990.

References

Åslund, A. and Sjöberg, Ö. (1992) 'Privatization and transition to a market economy in Albania', *Communist Economies and Economic Transformation*, vol. 4. no. 1.

Blejer, M. *et al.* (1992) *Albania: from Isolation Toward Reform.* IMF Occasional Paper no. 98. Washington, DC, September.

Calvo, G. *et al.* (ed.) (1993) *Financial Sector Reforms and Exchange Arrangements in Eastern Europe.* IMF Occasional Paper no. 102, February.

Corbo, V., Coricelli, F. and Bossak, J. (eds) (1991) *Reforming Central and Eastern European Economies: Initial Results and Challenges.* Washington, DC: World Bank.

Coricelli, F. and de Rezende Rocha, R. (1991) 'Stabilization programmes in Eastern Europe: a comparative analysis of the Polish and Yugoslav programmes of 1990', *The Economics of the Market*, Prague, May–June.

Dewatripont, M. and Roland, G. (1992) 'The virtues of gradualism and legitimacy in the transition to a market economy', *Economic Journal*, March.

Fletorja Zyrtare e Republikës Shqipërisë (Official Journal of Republic of Albania) (1992–94, various issues).

Friedman, M. (1991) 'In Eastern Europe: the people versus the socialist elite', *The Wall Street Journal*, 9 May.

IMF (1994) *Albania.* Economic Reviews, no. 5. Washington, DC.

Kornai, J. (1990) *The Road to a Free Economy.* New York: Norton.

—— (1994), 'Transformational recession: the main causes', *Journal of Comparative Economics*, vol. 19, no. 1.

Lipton, D. and Sachs, J. (1991) 'Creating a market economy in Eastern Europe: the case of Poland', *Brookings Papers on Economic Activity*, vol. 1.

Milivojevic, M. (1992) *Wounded Eagle: Albania's Fight for Survival.* London: Institute for European Defence and Strategic Studies.

Pashko, G. (1991a) 'The Albanian economy at the beginning of the 1990s' in Sjöberg, Ö. and Wyzan, M. (eds) *Economic Changes in the Balkan States.* London: Pinter.

—— (1991b) 'Strukturprobleme und Reformen in Albanien', *Osteuropa*, heft 4.

—— (1991c) *Programme for the Transition to a Free Market of the Albanian Economy.*

Tirana (October).

—— (1993a) 'Inflation in Albania', *Communist Economies and Economic Transformation*, vol. 5, no. 1.

—— (1993b) 'Obstacles to economic reform in Albania', *Europe and Asia Studies*, vol. 45, no. 2.

Sachs, J, (1992) 'Building a market economy in Poland', *Scientific American*, vol. 266, no. 3.

Schnytzer, A. (1982) *Stalinist Economy in Practice: the Case of Albania*. Oxford: Oxford University Press.

—— (1992) 'Albania: the purge of Stalinist economic ideology' in Jeffries, I. (ed.) *Industrial Reform in Socialist Countries: from Restructuring to Revolution*. Aldershot: Edward Elgar.

Sjöberg, Ö. (1991) 'The Albanian economy in the 1980s: coping with a centralised system' in Sjöberg, Ö. and Wyzan, M. (eds) *Economic Change in the Balkan States*. London: Pinter.

—— (1994) *The Regional Effects of Economic Transformation in Albania: towards an Assessment*. Bucharest.

Smith, A. (1991) 'The implications of change in East Central Europe for the Balkan socialist economies' in Sjöberg, Ö. and Wyzan, M. (eds) *Economic Changes in the Balkan States*. London: Pinter.

Statistical Yearbook of Albania (1991). Tirana.

Szekely, I. and Newbery, D. (eds) (1993) *Hungary: an Economy in Transition*. Cambridge: Cambridge University Press.

Winiecki, J. (1986) 'Are Soviet-type economies entering an era of long-term decline', *Soviet Studies*, vol. 38, no. 3.

——(1990) 'Obstacles to economic reform of socialism: a property-rights approach', *Annals of the American Academy of Political and Social Sciences*, vol. 507, January.

Wolfson, M. (1992) 'Transition from a command economy: rational expectations and cold turkey', *Contemporary Policy Issues*, vol. 10, April.

World Bank – European Community (1992) *An Agricultural Strategy for Albania*. Washington, DC.

6 The Regional Effects of Economic Transformation in Albania: Towards an Assessment[1]

Örjan Sjöberg

Introduction

The reforms launched by the 'Stabilization Government' in mid-1991 and the adoption a year later of a programme of reform under the watchful eyes of the IMF, have had a breath-taking effect on the Albanian economy and society. Given the precarious state of the Albanian economy at the time of the fall of communist power and the subsequent breakdown of whatever industrial capacity was left in place, the efforts to introduce measures not only to stop but also to reverse the collapse were, of course, a dire necessity. This should not, however, be allowed to conceal the resourcefulness and imagination of the officials in charge and Albania today indeed owes something to the determination of its first generation of post-communist politicians and economists.

It should, nevertheless, be kept in mind that irrespective of the degree of success and irrespective of the preferred method or sequencing of reform the effects across the territory of the reforming economy are likely to show considerable variation on some counts, less so on others. This is also reflected in the burgeoning literature on the geography of the transition, in which the existence of 'a daunting set of regional problems, a relatively poor record of dealing with them under socialism, and some implied pessimism about the ability of the nations of Central and Eastern Europe to successfully address them in the future' (Berentsen 1992: 339) are recurring themes. There is little to indicate that Albania is an exception in this regard and time has, therefore, come to chart the geography of economic transformation in this Balkan state.

Such a venture faces a number of obstacles, foremost among which are the inadequacy of existing theory and the lack of reliable, regionally disaggregated data. Existing theory is by and large normative, in addition to which it has shown a propensity to change as previously cherished notions have been found wanting (witness, for example, the openminded 'reordering of priorities' proposed by Kornai 1994: 57). This is a problem of some magnitude, since normative theory should also possess at least a minimum of coherence and stability in the face of moderately changing circumstances. In view of the varying experiences of the formerly centrally planned economies, neither does positive theory provide much by way of guidance (but see, for example, Åslund 1994). Equally challenging, the testing of theory (and hypotheses deduced from it) requires data of a quality and scope not yet available.[2] And even should all of these challenges be met, current theory relating to the transformation process has little to say on regional development *per se*.

The lack of appropriate theory and data in turn implies that the efforts reported here by necessity are explorative and only represent the first steps towards an assessment of the regional effects of economic transformation in Albania. For no other reason than expediency, then, I shall confine myself to those aspects of the transition that fall within the compass of the attempts made to increase the share of private sector in the national economy. No attempt will be made to arrive at anything but tentative conclusions; the study only strives to identify some of the patterns created by the processes that evolve rather than the final outcomes that can be expected as reforms are successfully implemented.

On the other hand, and on a less modest note, it can be argued that the significance of the Albanian case goes beyond that of enhancing our understanding of the least developed among the former socialist states of Europe. Although Albania's economic structure and its low level of development may frustrate any attempt to generalize from its experience, the country's outstanding Stalinist credentials[3] ensure that, in some respects, it nevertheless serves as something of a benchmark case. At the very least, despite the expectation that Albania may in fact benefit from being highly agrarian,[4] it has arguably the farthest to go before reaching anything remotely resembling an average European industrial economy. Therefore, the impact of the transformation is likely to be as clearly spelt out as anywhere else in Eastern Europe.

The pre-reform economy

Although Albania may seem small and homogeneous enough to warrant being treated as but one geographical unit, it can be shown that regional disparities have been and remain pronounced. In no small part this stems from the basic features of central planning, but obviously regional patterns of development also owe something to the history and geography of Albania itself. Without going into detail, I shall consider both of these factors in turn below.[5]

The economic system

To most intents and purposes, following the consolidation of communist power, Albania embarked on the road towards the introduction of a standard, unreformed version of central planning. However, it moved slowly in the world of top-down investment and production planning, material balances being the height of planning sophistication throughout the communist period. The number of state industrial enterprises were few (on average they were also rather small in size) and a very traditional system of plan indicators detailed the targets of these enterprises (Pashko 1991: 131–2). The urban private sector was abolished by the late 1960s, while the final vestiges of private farming (the peasant market and the household plot, uncollectivized farming no longer existing post-1967) were dealt severe blows in the opening years of the 1980s.[6] A significant share of the meagre resources available (a substantial part of which was provided in the form of Soviet aid and subsequently by China: Schnytzer 1978) were invested in mining and basic metallurgy, much of it embodying technologies already obsolete by the date of the commissioning of the plants. As for the rest, most state enterprises were to be found in light or food industry branches (Schnytzer 1993: 320). Parallel with the intensifying state domination in all spheres of the economy, by the early 1970s local administration lost whatever meagre resources it still controlled (Banja, Hilima and Koli 1988: 15–16), while previous efforts at regional planning were quietly terminated (Sjöberg 1991a: 100–4). Thus, save for some token copying from China during the 1960s and early 1970s, there was little or no hint of reform, leading Brus (1986: 228) to conclude that 'it is unwarranted to call the institutional changes in the decade 1966–75 an "economic reform", or even to discuss them in these terms'. Although there are indications of a change of heart with respect to development priorities by 1983 (Schnytzer 1993: 335–7), only in May 1990 were the first reluctant moves towards economic reform actually taken (Pashko 1991: 139–42; Kaser 1993: 304–6).

To the extent that Albania deviated from orthodox central planning, it was mainly on account of its low degree of development.[7] Allowing for that, all the trappings of the traditional shortage economy (Kornai 1980) were in place with the expected patterns of economic behaviour and low productivity levels to match. In short, Albania like other centrally planned economies squandered resources, mainly at the expense of its own citizens.

Regional development

This antiquated system of central planning combined with history and an unusual disregard not only for national but also for regional comparative advantages to produce the least prosperous country of Europe. All districts were urged to achieve extraordinarily high levels of local autarky, only a limited number of agricultural products and food items being shipped across district (*rreth*) boundaries. With such a disregard for prevailing conditions, natural or otherwise, incomes at the district and sub-district levels were highly dependent on the local resource endowment. Statistically, districts with a rather small share of agriculture in their local economy would seem to be far better off, average incomes being higher there. However, in the dichotomized urban–rural world of Albania this would make little difference to the individuals concerned, unless of course rural dwellers could circumvent the controls which prevented them from enjoying the benefits of being state employees (Sjöberg 1993: 494, 499–501).

Albania was early on observed to provide as good a case as any of polarized industrial and economic development (Mihailović 1972: 37). Albanian scholars themselves were not loath to admit as much, and Luçi in particular (1970: 55) was critical of a situation where by the beginning of the 1970s the five least developed districts were said to account for a mere 0.5 per cent of total industrial production, the top five districts sharing as much as 80 per cent of the output between themselves. By the late 1980s, regional disparities may have been reduced, but they did remain very substantial (Yzeri 1988; Directorate of Statistics 1991: 171).

Sivignon (1987) has argued that whatever regional disparities may exist in Albania are the consequences of topography and natural environment on the one hand and history in the form of old social structures, including religious differences, on the other (Daniel 1989). The strategy of development and the manner in which scarce resources were allocated under central planning are crucial to our understanding of Albanian economic development, however, and these factors go a long way towards explaining why topography and natural environment would be important in the first place. Two remarks are in order here. Firstly, centrally planned economies are highly resource-dependent, not least because they have emphasized 'material production' (especially at the heavy end of manufacturing), but also because they have proven inept at improving resource allocation and utilization rates. Conversely, they have by and large tended to discount the importance of taking factor proportions into account, both nationally and regionally. Secondly, because of the nature of the strategy of development adopted (it being very orthodox and highly autarkic in the case of Albania) and the inherent logic of central planning, both the preservation of locational patterns and the fragmentation of geographical space have been promoted. As a result, regional economic development became the hostage of local natural resource endowment.

Although there is no doubt that environmental factors are important, this is a result of, and to a considerable extent compounded by, the policies pursued. This is especially true, as Wildermuth (1989: ch. 5; 1993: 361–2) convincingly argues, of agrarian and agricultural policies. Piedmont and upland areas were made to substitute crop production for animal husbandry, no matter what the absolute and comparative advantages of the two were. As a consequence of their inability to produce only minimal quantities of grain (which, one may add, higher procurement prices did little to compensate for), mountain areas and in particular the north-eastern part of Albania quickly fell behind the rest of the country. In many districts, low levels of agricultural output severely restricted the development of the food industry, which could conceivably have provided the basis for industrial expansion in previously non-industrialized areas. Throughout much of the period of central planning only the expansion of mining and forestry and the construction of a network of hydro-power stations provided alternative sources of industrial growth and employment generation (Yzeri 1988: 223; Sjöberg 1987 and 1991a: 122).

While the dependence on localized resources may appear commonplace with respect to agricultural production and rural development, it must be recognized that the type of policies imposed from above carried an opportunity cost of some magnitude. This is as true for industry as for agriculture. In the non-agricultural sector the preferred strategy of development and the manner in which the economy was managed also led to sluggish growth (Sandström and Sjöberg 1991; Blejer et al. 1992; Schnytzer 1993). Furthermore, the inherent logic of planning and enterprise behaviour under central planning served to reinforce the initial pattern of investment. Enterprises, forced into the substitution of labour for capital (Kornai 1980), and with soft budget constraints at least in priority sectors (Kornai 1986; Ericson 1988), are much given to in situ employment expansion, with regions not the base of priority industrial development unlikely to be compensated by new investment funds or additional employment opportunities. The few exceptions from this dismal pattern are a policy-induced shift into raw material extraction typically associated with the early stages of the construction of a socialist economy or with the efforts to absorb labour released through the collectivization of agriculture (Mihailović 1972; Ronnås 1984 and 1988). As Albanian politicians, planners and scholars recognized by the late 1980s, there was some merit in trying to moderate the heavy-handed impact of sectoral policies by introducing a measure of regional coordination (Sjöberg 1991a: 103–4; a map of the four regional planning units thus devised can be found in Bërxholi 1991: 95). Despite the fact that the proposed system of regional planning was never fully implemented, it is doubtful whether this would have had the envisaged effects, since it was a measure that did not transcend the logic imposed by central planning.

The emerging pattern of the regional impact of reform

Agriculture and rural change

Agricultural production was as badly hit by the chaotic conditions prevailing during the late 1980s and early 1990s as industrial production. The full range of problems from incentives to technological backwardness to the lack of imported inputs found in industry were also present in agriculture. As has been forcefully established throughout much of the centrally planned world, agriculture was inherently ill-suited to detailed production plans handed down from above. In addition to this, a wave of vandalism swept through parts of the countryside, destroying much of the fixed assets not previously rendered useless through mismanagement. By and large, the co-operatives ceased to exist as operational units, a standstill made the longer by the, no doubt necessary, introduction of radical land reform (Wildermuth 1993: 363–7; Wyzan and Sjöberg 1992: 13–21).

In Albania's case this was compounded by a rapidly growing population and a shortage of land that could be converted to agricultural use when attempts to increase the productivity of the land failed. Because of the rather successful, if administratively enforced and highly unpopular, rural retention policies of Albania (Sjöberg 1990: 179–86; 1991a: ch. 3; 1994), rural densities are often very high. In 1990 a rural population of 2.08 million had 704,000 ha of arable land (or 0.338 ha per capita) at its disposal for agricultural production (Directorate of Statistics 1991: 35, 178–9). Even if calculated in terms of land per agricultural worker, the average Albanian peasant or agricultural labourer has no more than 1.5 ha at his disposal (World Bank 1992: 173). Under these circumstances it goes without saying that the farms resulting from land distribution are often very small indeed. This expectation is borne out by the map in Figure 6.1, where the projected average farm size by district is given.[8]

On average, the 376,000 farms expected to be created once land distribution is completed[9] will each have 1.36 ha at their disposal (1.44 ha in lowland districts and 1.22 ha in mountain districts). These figures vary considerably between districts, however, with peasants in the south generally being better off than those in the north. Thus, the biggest units are anticipated in the mountain districts of Kolonjë (2.81 ha), Përmet (2.15 ha) and Skrapar (1.92 ha), with the smallest ones to be found in equally mountainous Pukë (0.55 ha) and Mirditë (0.74 ha). Furthermore, these minuscule holdings are often

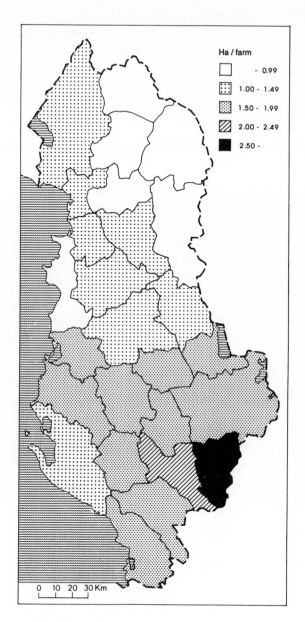

Figure 6.1 Land reform: projected size of farms (ha per family)

Source: World Bank (1992: 256).

further subdivided into two or three plots. Yet another problem is that in some regions the principle of equitable distribution has been violated, with a return to pre-communist farm boundaries being favoured in some highland areas of Shkodër, Tropojë and Kukës (*ATA Weekly Economic Report*, 16 August 1993). The obverse of this is that some families will have to contend with even smaller lots or perhaps no land at all.

To compound further the problem of small farms, land is of varying quality and much of it with a slope of 5–25 per cent (37.5 per cent of total arable land) or more (18.5 per cent of total arable land: World Bank 1992: 168). In response to the dismal outlook for many of the newly created family farms, the setting up of Western-type co-operatives has been suggested as a remedy. Although early reports claimed that a small number of former co-operativists 'have overcome their previous experiences with forced cooperativism' (World Bank 1992: 19) and formed a number of private farmers' associations, over-all results are not entirely encouraging. There were 57 of these co-operatives by August 1992, covering a total of 2383 ha in the lowlands and 576 ha in mountain districts, organizing a total of almost 2900 families (World Bank 1992: 177), the number of unions increasing to about 100 by the spring of 1994 (*ATA Weekly Economic Report*, 8 June 1994). Beyond this, and despite encouragement by the present government, little headway appears to have been made. In fact, reports also convey the impression of lacklustre performance on part of those farmers' unions already in existence, a mere 5 to 10 per cent of which are said to function normally (e.g. *ATA Weekly Economic Report*, 8 June 1994).

Another early outcome of the collapse of collectivized agriculture and land reform was a marked shift away from wheat and barley, either to maize or to non-grain crops such as beans and vegetables. Production of many industrial crops such as cotton, tobacco, sugarbeets and sunflower seeds has been given up by co-operativists turned peasants, only partly being compensated for by state farms increasing their production of these crops (World Bank 1992: 188; *ATA Weekly Economic Report*, 26 July 1993). Presumably, given the nature of the crops and previous cultivation patterns, wheat and barley lost out both in the plains and in mountain districts, in both instances on account of the difficulties the new farms experience in making a living by producing grains which have no natural advantage under conditions of small-scale, labour-intensive production. Furthermore, upland farms must have found these grains ill-suited to local physical conditions, reverting instead to the more traditional crop, maize.

While wheat has since made a partial comeback, cash crops are not likely to re-emerge on a significant scale until the industrial and export sectors have been reorganized, if at all. Meanwhile, with animal husbandry no longer being constrained by pressures to achieve self sufficiency in bread grains and by misconceived policies based on collective ownership of livestock, fodder production has assumed a new significance, seeing a 25 per cent increase in acreage from 1993 to early 1994 (*ATA Weekly Economic Report*, 11 May 1994).

Industrial restructuring and unemployment

One of the most striking features of centrally planned economies was, of course, the maintenance of high levels of employment. While there is a certain rationale to labour hoarding under the conditions prevailing in a shortage economy, this leaves all the former Soviet-type economies with a legacy that will be difficult to manage. As is frequently observed, the emergence of open unemployment and a change in the structure of employment have both been standard features of the transformation of the East European economies (e.g. Boeri and Keese 1992a: 147–50). However, the experience gained from the transition economies in East Central Europe reveals a considerable time lag before the disruption of the economic system and decline in output is reflected in falling levels of employment. Put differently, the growth of unemployment has generally been slower than might have been expected (Boeri and Keese 1992b: 384). One of the main reasons behind the delayed effect on employment of economic decline is that continued soft budget constraints and lack of effective competition have made it possible for enterprises to retain surplus labour, often accumulating huge and potentially destabilizing inter-enterprise debts in the process. Work sharing, reduced work hours and temporary lay-offs are often resorted to in order to avoid outright dismissals.

Albania is something of an exception in this regard. Not only did unemployment exist prior to the disastrous fall in industrial production towards the end of the communist era (Sandström and Sjöberg 1991: 935–6; Blejer *et al.* 1992: 28–9), but the ranks of the unemployed were quickly expanded as a result of industrial closures and the shedding of mostly white collar staff at various 'budgetary institutions'.[10] The 'Stabilization Government' not only made sizeable cuts in state administration staff levels, but also instituted a system of unemployment benefits and picked up a considerable part of the costs faced by enterprises forced to dismiss employees temporarily due to the fall in demand for their products or to a lack of critical inputs, both factors conspiring to compel many plants to decrease production sharply or to stop altogether.[11]

Thus, as is summarized in Table 6.1, by the end of 1992, out of a labour force of 1,066,000 excluding co-operativists and peasants, a staggering 394,000 (or 37.0 per cent) were unemployed. Out of these, 312,000 enjoyed unemployment or social security benefits (*ATA Weekly Economic Report*, 2 August 1993). Indeed, although not shown in Table 6.1, by mid-1993 the unemployment total reached 437,000 individuals, set against 555,000 employed, that is, an unemployment rate of 44 per cent in the non-agricultural sector.[12] Incomplete as statistics are, there is evidence to suggest that the highest level was reached by April or May 1993, since when the number of persons on the dole has decreased while the number of job seekers not eligible for such support has remained roughly unchanged (*ATA Weekly Economic Report*, 11 October 1993). Still more recent statistics put unemployment at 267,300 so registered individuals, 83,400 of whom received unemployment benefits (*ATA Weekly Economic Report*, 1 June 1994). While the latter piece of information can conceivably be used to call into doubt the success of the adjustment programme, it is likely that on closer inspection the higher figures in spring reflect seasonal fluctuation in labour demand and supply. On a more cynical note, variations in unemployment statistics may also reflect the poor state of statistics or outright manipulation by politicians.

It has also been noted that in many transition economies there is 'a wide variation in unemployment rates across regions' (Boeri and Keese 1992b: 390). For one thing, there is the issue of the regional impact of restructuring and divestment of state property (Ronnås 1991: 64; Burda 1991: 123; Barta 1992: 375–7; Kinnear 1992: 64). Given the objective of resource mobilization pursued by central planners, it comes as no surprise that the locational pattern of major industrial establishments reflects factor and resource availability (Ronnås 1984). Locations with pools of under-utilized urban and rural labour were often deliberately selected for large-scale industrial developments characterized by high capital intensity. Such locational decisions were typically taken with little regard for the spatial margins to profitability (Rawstron 1958) and these plants are therefore not very likely to survive in a marketized environment. Evidence from such countries as Hungary (Cséfalvay 1993: 39–41) and Slovakia (Bucek 1992; Pavlínek 1992: 365–6) strongly suggests that this rapidly translates into regionally differentiated unemployment rates. As the centrally planned economies frequently made the economic base of small and medium-sized towns rest on one or two large enterprises (e.g. Ronnås 1991: 64; Matykowski and Stryjakiewicz 1992: 155), the impact of closures on such badly diversified local and regional labour markets may prove a headache to any government.

To the best of my knowledge, no regionally disaggregated data on unemployment *rates* have been published for Albania. The reason seems to be the lack of reliable information on the size of the labour force (i.e. the number of individuals at work or willing to enter employment). Absolute numbers of registered unemployed by district do exist, however,[13] and a few observations can therefore be made:

1. Unemployment is largely but not quite exclusively an urban phenomenon. For the most part, peasants, including former members of co-operatives,

Table 6.1 Employment and unemployment in the non-agricultural sector, 1991–93

	December 1991	December 1992	October 1993
State sector	850,000	610,000	454,000
Private sector	40,000	62,000	101,000
Unemployed	74,000	394,000	243,000

Source: Gazeta Shqiptare, 28 January 1994.

may be underemployed, but they are not likely to be unemployed in a formal sense. Exceptions among rural dwellers include former state farm labourers and miners, loggers or sawmill workers and professionals once employed by the co-operatives. The latter group includes teachers, medical staff and various agricultural specialists, several thousand of whom have reportedly lost their jobs. These are relatively minor groups, however, and the implication is that, assuming that closures and the dismissal of redundant workers are evenly spread across urban centres, the larger the share of urban dwellers in the district population total, the higher the unemployment rate in that district. This would in turn imply that Tirana and a few other lowland districts (such as Durrës, Elbasan, Fier, Vlorë) are badly hit. However, there is nothing to indicate that this assumption is in fact justified. Rather, the sectoral composition of contracting industries and the degree of diversity of the local or regional economy can be hypothesized to be of critical importance, with plants originally set up with the needs of self-reliance in mind being particularly exposed. To quote but one example, by March 1994 the registered unemployed in Tirana numbered 35,300, while Elbasan (the site of some of the country's major metallurgical plants) saw the number of unemployed reach 26,600 (*ATA Weekly Economic Report,* 1 June 1994);[14] given that the urban population of Tirana is about three times the size of that of Elbasan, this clearly reflects the impact of local and regional industrial structure.

2. Albania has its fair share of local economies relying on but one major industrial employer;[15] compared to some of these also above mentioned Elbasan would seem reasonably diversified. Typically, they depend on mining or metallurgy, neither of which has been cushioned during the past few years of turbulent change. To a large extent these vulnerable settlements or localities are located in the mountain areas in the north-central or north-eastern part of the country; these are the regions where there is little prospect of productive agriculture and few other options to pursue. A few are to be found in the lowlands (Ballsh, Kuçovë, Laç, Patos), but they are perhaps less vulnerable on account of their more central locations and more favourable environments.

Generally speaking, long-established district centres with better diversified economies and with both industrial and agricultural linkages to be exploited (such as Korçë or Shkodër and of course Tirana) would seem to be in the best position in this regard.

3. Privatization, while an indispensable component of industrial restructuring, is not likely to increase employment in the short and medium term. On the contrary, privatization implies for the most part a trimming of operations in the firms concerned. After all, the vital exposure to competitive markets, which privatization and marketization are relied upon to achieve, requires the breaking up of monopolies and the introduction of pricing based on what the market will bear. In a competitive environment, or at least one in which soft budget constraints have been hardened, the retrenchment of workers rather than an expansion of the labour force is the order of the day. If additional labour is to be absorbed, existing enterprises and plants cannot be relied upon.[16] To the extent that services and amenities originally were allocated in accordance with population numbers (see Sjöberg 1991a: 149, for an inconclusive sifting of the evidence), the effects of privatization will be roughly the same throughout the country. The one factor that may militate against such a geographically neutral development is the uneven distribution of purchasing power across the population. In this case it is probable that retailers and providers of various services will be less likely to stay in business in those poorer areas, as indeed has been noted elsewhere among the economies in transition (Gács, Karimov and Schneider 1993: 82). Hence, as industrial restructuring is making progress, and unemployment at least initially increases, hopes have been attached to two phenomena previously almost unknown in post-war Albania. These are entrepreneurship (or the growth of the private enterprise sector through new start-ups) and new venture creation through foreign direct investment. To these two we now turn.

Entrepreneurship and foreign direct investment

If privatization is not the panacea sought, the means to generate new employment opportunities will have to be found elsewhere. Over the longer term, privatization is likely to contribute by making formerly state-owned enterprises more competitive and thus better equipped to withstand the pressures of the market. If this in turn translates into economic growth, employment should be more easily generated. But for the duration of much of the transition to a market economy, other means will have to be relied upon. Foremost among them are indigenous entrepreneurship and foreign direct investment. These also figure prominently in the attempts to restructure and rejuvenate the Albanian economy.

Once the straitjacket of central planning was removed, private entrepreneurial activities became a prominent feature of Albanian street scenes.[17] Although attempts were made, the communist regime never managed to wipe out all such activities. With the decision, in July 1990, to again allow private sector activities in handicrafts and services, previously held back or black market ventures established themselves in the open. The progress was slow, however, with licensing procedures often fraught with inordinate amounts of red tape, the severity of which varied between districts.

With the collapse of central planning and the advent of a regime bent on restructuring Albania's ailing economy along the lines of the advanced market economies, petty trade mushroomed. Thus, town officials have recently reported that about 10,000 individuals rent space from the municipality in order to trade in the official street markets of Tirana (*ATA Weekly Economic Report*, 22 June 1994). In addition, a considerable amount of petty trade can be assumed to go unrecorded (and untaxed). Although misgivings as to the ability of these entrepreneurs to move into the formal sector may appear to be justified, quite a few have made it on their own account or with help from relatives abroad. A report from late 1993 indicates that there were more than 10,300 privately owned shops, restaurants and bars in the capital alone (*ATA Weekly Economic Report*, 25 October 1993). The main difficulties arguably lay ahead, however, as the graduation from micro or small-scale enterprises to larger establishments is not easily accomplished. It is also an open question whether service sector entrepreneurs will move into other sectors, such as small-scale manufacturing. At present, there is little to indicate that this is the case.

Furthermore, as yet we lack information to evaluate the regional impact of the entrepreneurial energies as they unfold before our eyes. It is not being particularly bold to hypothesize, however, that there are pronounced differences between the various regions of the country. Presumably, densely populated lowland areas (and notably the capital city) gain more than most from these developments, with even forecasted tax revenues from private firms being overtaken by taxes actually collected (*ATA Weekly Economic Report*, 26 July 1993). Anecdotal evidence would also suggest that other areas gaining from the liberalization are to be found in the southern districts neighbouring on Greece, where a brisk border trade has been developed (not least by the Greek-speaking minority). Conversely, districts such as Kukës have found their geographical position, the peripheral qualities of which are reinforced by the ban on trade with what is left of Yugoslavia, much to their disadvantage.

The pattern sketched above also conforms to the experience of other economies in transition. In most of the formerly centrally planned economies, there are marked regional disparities in the number of private enterprises that have been established (Matykowski and Stryjakiewicz 1992: 151–2; Cséfalvay

1993: 37–41). Not only are market opportunities superior in centrally located and diversified areas as compared to other regions, but the dominance or even presence of major state industrial enterprises may serve to suppress the entrepreneurial culture of an area (as argued by, for example, Raagmaa 1993: 21–2). Additionally, beyond the realms of petty trading or regular retailing, small and medium-sized manufacturing enterprises are often dependent on subcontracting work from or on other more or less formalized relations with larger plants or companies. A lack of such linkages has been noted elsewhere among former Soviet-type economies (McDermott and Mejstrik 1992; Webster 1994) and there is little to indicate that Albania is able to break out of this mould with any measure of ease.

Much the same would appear to be true of foreign direct investment (FDI). Indications are that FDI favours some regions while shunning others. Similarly, foreign investors may not be easily talked into betting on former large-scale manufacturing enterprises, or establishing themselves locally with a view of entering into some co-operative agreement (such as subcontracting) with remaining or reconstituted state sector giants. Thus, in Poland it was noted at an early stage that the presence of and aggregate employment in foreign companies showed a distinctly different regional pattern than that fostered by Polish state industry (Szul 1989: 294, 297).

In Albania, where the corresponding processes unfold at a much reduced scale, something similar is indeed about happen. Apart from Tirana, which of course has been the economically dominant district all along, there is no or little evidence that FDI has been attracted to districts where mining, metallurgy or manufacturing industry dominate. The map in Figure 6.2 identifies all joint ventures and other foreign investment licensed as of 7 April 1993.[18] To date, 131 projects have been approved and of these 121 have been identified by district.[19] The map should be interpreted with a few caveats in mind, however. It neither indicates the value to the local community of the FDI (in terms of jobs created, for instance[20]), nor the medium- or long-term prospects of the venture as such. Furthermore, there is little to suggest that whatever benefits that may eventually accrue to Albania are localized, or localized in a pattern fully congruent with the originally selected sites.

The overwhelming majority of the FDI ventures licensed (54 out of 121) are associated with the capital and its immediate hinterland. Durrës registers twenty, with Sarandë a distant third with eight projects. Lushnjë (seven), Kavajë (six) and Gjirokastër (five) also stand out. Out of these, Gjirokastër and Sarandë are located in the far south, neighbouring on Greece and with a substantial part of their respective populations belonging to the Greek minority. As for the rest, there is a strong concentration to the central lowlands.

Another notable feature of the map in Figure 6.2 is the low level of interest in Shkodër (one) and Korçe (two) shown by foreign investors; both of these are densely populated and agriculturally favoured areas, the latter in addition having direct access to Greece and Macedonia (Shkodër, although adjacent to Montenegro, presently derives little or no benefit from border trade). In addition, both districts, and their major towns, have a diversified economic structure by Albanian standards. Districts dependent on mining barely enter into the picture and out of the two ventures registered in Dibër, for instance, neither is related to mining (the one located to Bulqizë, the site of Albania's largest chromium mine, intends to exploit locally available marble). As importantly, mining districts such as Kukës, Librazhd, Mirditë and Pogradec are altogether missing from the list.

However, to draw the conclusion from the above information that the distribution of FDI creates regional disparities or causes existing ones to increase would be premature. Not only does the map of the location of joint or foreign owned ventures say little about localized effects, but the information reported by Figure 6.2 should ideally be weighted in terms of population or the economic strength of given locations or regions. A first indication of what this may entail can be had by comparing Figures 6.2 and 6.3, the latter of which shows the variation in population potential (e.g. Stewart and Warantz 1968) over the territory of Albania.

At the present scale of mapping many of the finer details are of course lost (such as the very real influence of Albania's rugged topography and poor physical infrastructure on accessibility and economic opportunity), but the map should help put the information contained in Figure 6.2 in perspective. In particular, firms that are market-oriented or those dependent on a large and diversified pool of labour rather than localized inputs can be assumed to perceive the economic landscape in a manner conforming to that in Figure 6.3. Any activity facing transportation costs that are high relative to those of production may also find the population potential surface a reasonable guide.[21] Notable features of the two maps include the prominence, relative to the population potential, of FDI in some of the southern districts as outlined above. This can only be explained in terms of the effect of the opening of the border with Greece, which provides a obvious window of opportunity for these districts. One may also venture the guess that the opportunities conferred by the southern neighbour are also fuelled by the existence of substantial number of speakers of Greek capable of acting as something akin to 'cultural brokers' or a 'trading minority' (Hagen 1962: 60–1).

The main feature, however, is the high level of concentration of the population potential. As is often revealed by maps of this kind, the population potential weighs heavily in favour of a major centre, in this case Tirana, and its immediate surroundings. This may in turn shed some light on the resilience of major urban settlements in the central lowlands. Not only are they better 'shock absorbers' as the process of undoing previous mistakes and peculiari-

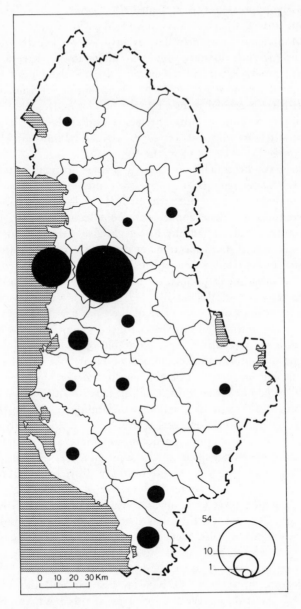

Figure 6.2 Foreign direct investment in Albania (up to and including April 1993)

Sources: ATA Weekly Economic Report, 29 January and 7 May 1993.

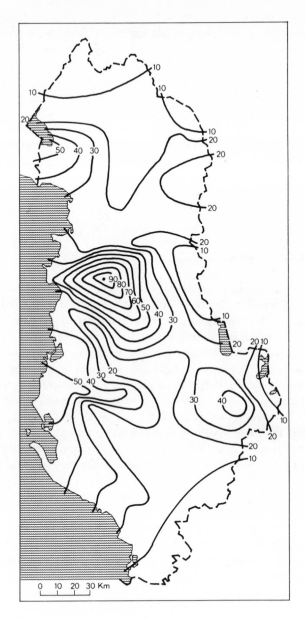

Figure 6.3 Surface of population potential, 1993 (Tiranë = 100)

Source: Author's calculations based on population statistics published in *Statistika*, no. 1, May 1993, p. 13.

ties proceeds, but above all they provide superior opportunities for new venture creation and employment. By the same token, as weighted by access or exposure to population, the geographical distribution of FDI clearly would seem to have a less adverse impact on regional equity than one would be led to believe on the basis of investment projects by districts alone. Rather, at this early stage of the transition it is perhaps equally plausible to hypothesize that, once adjusted for the adverse impact of the pre-transition industrial structure, FDI responds to, and reinforces, existing or emerging regional patterns rather than creating them in the first place. At the very least, then, it appears reasonable to conclude that regional inequality may possibly increase because of an inequitable pattern of investment, but not quite to the extent implied by Figure 6.2.

Outlook for future research

The information available at this rather early stage of the transition from a centrally planned economy, while scant and in many respects inadequate, provides some support for the argument that the impact of reforms is differentiated regionally. While it is too early to conclude whether this is a consequence of previously prevailing patterns of regional disparities or the result of emerging regional advantages or disadvantages, we need not doubt that a measure of regional realignment is indeed taking place as the economic transition proceeds. Similarly, although it is as yet not possible to determine whether regional disparities are increasing or diminishing as a result of the reforms, we can rest assured that the pattern will be different as compared to the recent past. To simplify prospective discussions concerning emerging trends, as hinted above it may be worthwhile to try to establish the relative impact of the 'undoing effect' (rectifying inertia and old mistakes) and the 'opportunity effect', which could be expected to approximate to the regional variation due to inherent or emerging factors.

As regional shifts of economic activities and outcomes crystallize, they are also made manifest through other societal processes. The patterns thereby created should ideally be analysed in their own right. From a geographical point of view, perhaps the most obvious is the migration resulting from economic restructuring within and among regions. Pre-existing variations in or the emergence of differences in the opportunities available to the inhabitants of the regions, and the burdens associated with life in poor, peripheral or environmentally degraded parts of the country, are the backdrop against which migration takes place. In a society where migratory movements were previously severely circumscribed, the breakthrough of democracy has provided openings hitherto unavailable to the average citizen. Most obviously, emigration in search of income opportunities has proliferated, to the extent that the population of Albania has fallen by a few hundred thousand since the beginning of the 1990s. In fact, despite a continuing high level of natural growth (1.8 per cent in 1992), most, if not all, districts have seen their population numbers decrease. This must not be allowed to conceal a not inconsiderable movement of people out of poorer regions (and the north-east in particular) to the western lowlands, with the capital and its immediate surroundings being the favoured receiving areas (Schmidt-Neke and Sjöberg 1993: 484; Karaj 1994).

Other effects are perhaps less apparent, but no less real. The changing structure of incentives facing farmers, for example, may lead to as distinct outcomes as land being left uncultivated or children dropping out of school to work as farm hands on the family farm. Anecdotal data collected during a recent trip to Albania (summer 1994) suggest that both of these outcomes may coexist. For instance, in southern Albania employment opportunities across the border appear to impose an opportunity cost of some magnitude on the proper cultivation of the land. One may well envisage a situation where members of Albania's Greek minority, because of their more favourable position in the labour market of Greece (language skills, cultural affinity, political considerations), find temporary emigration a more attractive proposition or a more easily attained goal than do their Albanian neighbours. In the heated world of Balkan ethnic politics, it requires little power of imagination to conjure up a situation where ethnic Albanians turn on Albanian Greeks because of the latter's greater propensity to let their land lay fallow when land is perceived to be in short supply. Simultaneously, north-eastern farmers, trying to eke out a meagre living from their small plots of land, often face incentives implying high levels of labour input. With the young and able migrating to the western lowlands, available labour for agricultural chores tends to be school children and the aged. The resulting high levels of drop-outs from basic education do not augur well for the future.

Such regionally differentiated incentives are matched by the difficulties faced by local authorities, the poorer of which find themselves in possession of a miserable tax base, one capable of providing but little in the way of revenue to be collected locally. Also allowing for the weaker base, recent newspaper reports indicate that inland districts tend to fall behind planned tax collection (e.g, *Koha jone*, 3 September 1994: 8). This, in turn, has implications for the new laws on local and national budgets currently being prepared, which, unless they include a measure of regional redistribution or cross-subsidization, may spawn further differentiation in attained levels and quality of schooling. The patterns of regional differentiation identified here, and many others of the same cast, hint not only at the costs of adaptation faced by individuals and society, but also at some of the traps attempts to devise policies aiming to 'fine tune' at the national level are likely to end up in.

102 ÖRJAN SJÖBERG

The above are just a few of a multitude of micro-level changes taking place in Albania today. While most reports tend to focus on national aggregates and the impact of reform as a national process of restructuring, this paper has attempted to add regional detail to the overall picture. Whether the process determining the patterns analysed here is helpful or unfavourable in the short run, it seems reasonable to infer that the emerging picture is more in line with local and regional comparative advantages than was the pre-reform pattern. Albania was, after all, the most orthodox among the socialist states of Europe, a country where the scant regard for economics as the science of allocation of scarce resources was a matter of policy and where regional development schemes were merely seen as the futile attempts of capitalist countries to postpone for a while the inevitable collapse of their outdated mode of production.

Notes

1 An earlier version of this paper was presented at the 25th National Convention of the American Association for the Advancement of Slavic Studies, Honolulu, HI, 19–22 November 1993. The author would like to thank Darrick Danta, Barry Ickes, Gramoz Pashko and Michael Wyzan for helpful comments.
2 As for statistical inputs, the restructuring of the Albanian Institute (formerly Directorate) of Statistics is not yet completed. For now, we shall therefore have to contend with the absence of the annual statistical abstract for 1992 and 1993. The first few issues of *Statistika* are a helpful but not fully up-to-date substitute.
3 See, for example, Schnytzer (1982 and 1993); Sjöberg (1991a and 1991b: ch. 4); Kaser (1993); Schmidt-Neke (1993b); and Pashko (1994) for details on strategies, policies and institutions.
4 If the experience of some of the reforming Asian socialist economies is anything to go by, an economy dominated by agricultural production appears to reduce some of the costs of the transition; this view is taken by, for example, Brabant (1992: 266), Sachs and Woo (1994: 105–13) and Dollar (1994: 374).
5 A description of the regional geography of Albania is not within the scope of this paper; publications introducing the subject include Bozgo (1984, 1985), Carter (1991), Lienau (1991, 1993) and Schappelwein (1991, 1993).
6 Peasant markets were closed down in 1981; at the same time, with a few exceptions remaining private livestock was 'collectivized', too. In a rather uncommon gesture to an unyielding reality, peasant markets were allowed to reappear by mid-decade. Similarly, the private plot, while no longer being universal or of the size previously permitted, was never completely done away with. For further details see Wildermuth (1989: ch. 4) and Sjöberg (1991a: 95–100, 129–35).
7 Hutchings (1989a) has argued that Albania displayed a development pattern quite distinct from that found in the Soviet Union of the Stalinist era and that the divergence from the original blueprint increased over time. But elsewhere he neverthe-

less notes that 'the Albanian economy diverges from Stalinism in circumstances and policy but not in structure; however, the worst diseases of a centralized system are not experienced' (Hutchings 1989b: 328). The latter of these two views, with some reservations about the final clause, is broadly consistent with the perspective adopted here (Sjöberg 1991b). After all, the observation that the 'practical implementation [of economic Stalinism] had become impossible' by the late 1970s (Schnytzer 1993: 331), while in all likelihood true, does not, as the same author points out, rule out 'a determination to persist with the Stalinist development strategy in the face of external difficulties' (p. 333).

8   The administrative division of the country used here is the one existing prior to the approval by the Council of Ministers on 23 July 1991 to separate Kavaje from Durrës. This is done for reasons of convenience, as in many cases statistics are yet to appear for the resulting set of 27 districts, not to speak of the 36 districts in use since October 1992. Figure 6.3, however, is based on population register data for the full set of 36 districts.

9   By the summer of 1993, an offical of the Ministry of Agriculture claimed that 95 per cent of former co-operative land had been assigned to their new owners (*ATA Weekly Economic Report*, 16 August 1993). In view of earlier success reports, some of which indicated that as large a share had already been distributed by early summer 1992 (e.g. Wyzan and Sjöberg 1992), this figure must also be taken with a pinch of salt.

10 An *institucion buxhetor* is a non-industrial or non-producing organization or institution financed from the state budget.

11 *Rilindja demokratike* (2 September 1993) claims that, by April 1992, 47 per cent of the state enterprises produced at reduced capacity with a further 28 per cent having ceased production altogether. Such statistics, which are unlikely to have improved much since, support the early impressions reported in, for example, Åslund and Sjöberg (1992: 140).

12 Much more appalling statistics have been circulated. However, it is likely that these higher percentages report urban rather than state sector unemployment, the latter being augmented (in 1990) by 197,000 state farm labourers (Directorate of Statistics 1991: 80). If the workers of the state farms are deducted, leaving about 870,000 employees in the state sector, the urban unemployment rate would be approximately 46 per cent. On the other hand, it also appears that only those on unemployment benefits or eligible for social security are actually considered unemployed. As a consequence, the Albanian government claimed that 350,000 were unemployed by mid-1993, which would yield a figure of about 39 per cent being unemployed rather than 44 per cent. Throughout the period covered by Table 6.1, another 450,000 to 500,000 can be estimated to have been engaged in agricultural pursuits outside state farms and some 200,000 to 300,000 or so to have left the country for work elsewhere.

13 As reported by, for example, *Statistika*, nos 1 (May 1993: 43–5) and 2 (September 1993: 29–31) not reproduced here.

14 These statistics, although in the present author's view plausible, must not be considered final, as other reports sometimes claim higher figures. Examples include

Transition (1994, vol. 5, no. 5, p. 21), imparting information to the effect that 113,100 are out of work. Reckoned as a percentage of Tirana's working age population, this corresponds to a 60 per cent unemployment rate. While said to refer to the conditions in the capital, the report is however, undated.

15 For a description of the functional profile of Albanian urban centres, see Sjöberg (1990: 195–7 and appendix).

16 According to the rather incomplete statistics provided by the Ministry of Finance (1993: 8), about 10,000 of these operated in the trading sector, 5000 in various services and 3500 in transport. A mere 32 were to be found in industry and construction.

17 A note of caution should be inserted at this point. The number of self-proclaimed entrepreneurs or small business proprietors is not a particularly good guide to the contribution of newly-created ventures to labour absorption, economic restructuring and growth, as Laky (1989) found with respect to the Hungarian economy.

18 More up-to-date listings were not available at the time of preparing this paper. This is of some concern, as 1993 appears to have marked a decisive improvement as regards FDI, with $291 million for 204 ventures pledged by year's end (*ATA Weekly Economic Report*, 10 January 1994). Lasting changes in the regional pattern of investment, while perhaps not likely, cannot therefore be completely ruled out.

19 The remaining ten either being footloose or impossible to identify by location. In case no location of the proposed activity is given, joint ventures have been assigned to districts on the basis of the domicile of the Albanian partner to the contract. Also note that the source material refers to approved, not necessarily actually started, projects. In addition, some of those that in fact did start operations may since have been wound up or withdrawn temporarily.

20 By the end of 1993 a total of 15,105 were employed in joint venture companies, 7400 out of which were engaged in the agricultural sector and 4700 in industrial pursuits (*ATA Weekly Economic Report*, 10 January 1994).

21 For analytical purposes it is desirable that the structure of the labour force (such as educational attainment and skills) and not only population numbers are taken into account. Similarly, rather than accepting population as a convenient measure, firms producing for consumer markets or being engaged in retailing may want to consider incomes and spending potential instead, as originally outlined by Harris (1954) in his measurements of market potential.

References

Altmann, F. (ed.) (1990) *Albanien im Umbruch – Eine Bestandsaufnahme*. Untersuchungen zur Gegenwartskunde Südosteuropas 28. Munich: R. Oldenbourg.

Åslund, A. (1994) 'Lesson of the first four years of systemic change in Eastern Europe', *Journal of Comparative Economics*, vol. 19, no. 1, pp. 22–38.

Åslund, A. and Sjöberg, Ö. (1992) 'Privatization and transition to a market economy in Albania', *Communist Economies and Economic Transformation*, vol. 4, no. 1, pp. 135–50.

Banja, H., Hilima, S. and Koli, R. (1988) 'Përsosja e mëtesjshme e përdorimit të disa levave të mekanizmit ekonomik e financier', *Probleme ekonomike*, vol. 35 (NS vol. 6), no. 4, pp. 11–18.

Barta, G. (1992) 'The changing role of industry in regional development and regional development policy in Hungary', *Tijdschrift voor economische en sociale geografie*, vol. 83, no. 5, pp. 372–9.

Becker, H. (ed.) (1991) *Jüngere Fortschritte der regional-geographischen Kenntnis über Albanien. Beiträge des Herbert-Louis-Gedächtnissymposions*. Bamberger Geographische Schriften 10. Bamberg: Fach Geographie an der Universität Bamberg.

Berentsen, W. (1992) 'Introduction to the special issue: regional problems and regional planning in Central and Eastern Europe', *Tijdschrift voor economische en sociale geografie*, vol. 83, no. 5, pp. 339–41.

Berry, B. and Marble, D. (eds) (1968) *Spatial Analysis: a Reader in Statistical Geography*. Englewood Cliffs, NJ: Prentice-Hall.

Bërxholi, A. (1991) 'Tendenzen und Probleme der demographischen Entwicklung in Albanien' in Becker (1991), pp. 83–114.

Blejer, M., Mecagni, M., Sahay, R., Hides, R., Johnston, B., Nagy, P. and Pepper, R. (1992) *Albania: from Isolation toward Reform*. IMF Occasional Paper 78. Washington, DC: International Monetary Fund.

Boeri, T. and Keese, M. (1992a) 'Labour markets and the transition in Central and Eastern Europe', *OECD Economic Studies*, no. 18, pp. 133–61.

—— (1992b) 'From labour shortage to labour shedding: labour markets in Central and Eastern Europe', *Communist Economies and Economic Transformation*, vol. 4, no. 3, pp. 373–94.

Bozgo, A. (1984) *Gjeografia e rretheve. Material ndihmës për vendlindjen* (1). Tirana: Shtëpia Botuese e Librit Shkollor.

—- (1985) *Gjeografia e rretheve. Material ndihmës për vendlindjen* (2). Tirana: Shtëpia Botuese e Librit Shkollor.

Brabant, J. van (1992) *Privatizing Eastern Europe: the Role of Markets and Ownership in the Transition*. International Studies in Economics and Econometrics 24. Dordrecht: Kluwer Academic.

Brus, W. (1986) '1966 to 1975: Normalization and conflict' in Kaser (1986), 139–249.

Bucek, M. (1992) 'Regional policy of the Slovak Republic in the period of transition' in Vaško (1992), pp. 1–14.

Burda, M. (1991) 'Labour and product markets in Czechoslovakia and the ex-GDR: a twin study', *European Economy*, special edition no. 2, pp. 111–28.

Carter, F. (1991) 'The economic and demographic development of Albania since 1945'. Paper presented at the conference on 'Demographic and Economic Development in the Mediterranean Area', Bari, Italy, 9–12 November.

Cséfalvay, Z. (1993) 'Die Transition des Arbeitsmarktes in Ungarn – Konsequenzen für die sozialräumliche Entwicklung', *Petermanns Geographische Mitteilungen*, vol. 137, no. 1, pp. 33–44.

Daniel, O. (1989) 'L'Albanie nouvelle: le développement d'une centralité et les problémes de la politique régionale' in Radvanyi and Rey (1989), pp. 21–7.

Directorate of Statistics (1991) *Vjetari i statistikor i Shqipërisë/Statistical Yearbook of Albania 1991*. Tirana: Drejtoria e Statistiksë, Ministria e Ekonomisë.

Dollar, D. (1994) 'Macroeconomic management and the transition to the market in Vietnam', *Journal of Comparative Economics*, vol. 18, no. 3, pp. 357–75.

Ericson, R. (1988) *Priority, Duality, and Penetration in the Soviet Command Economy*. RAND Note, N-2643-NA. Santa Monica, CA: RAND.

Gács, J., Karimov, I. and Schneider, C. (1993) 'Small-scale privatization in Eastern Europe and Russia: a historical and comparative perspective', *Communist Economies and Economic Transformation*, vol. 5, no. 1, pp. 61–86.

Grothusen, K. (ed.) (1993) *Südosteuropa-Handbuch/Handbook on South Eastern Europe*, Band/vol. VII, *Albanien/Albania*. Göttingen: Vandenhoeck & Ruprecht.

Hagen, E. (1962) *On the Theory of Social Change: How Economic Growth Begins*. Homewood, IL: Dorsey.

Harris, C. (1954) 'The market as a factor in the localization of industry in the US', *Annals of the American Association of Geographers*, vol. 44, no. 4, pp. 315–48.

Hutchings, R. (1989a) 'Albanian industrialization: widening divergence from Stalinism' in Schönfeld (1989), pp. 109–24.

—— (1989b) 'Albania' in Joint Economic Committee (1989), pp. 328–46.

Joint Economic Committee (1978) *Chinese Economy Post-Mao*, vol. 1, *Policy and Performance. Papers submitted to the Joint Economic Committee, United States Congress*. Washington, DC: US Government Printing Office.

—— (1989) *Pressures for Reform in the East European Economies*, vol. 2, *Study Papers Submitted to the Joint Economic Committee, Congress of the United States, October 20, 1989*. Washington, DC: US Government Printing Office.

Karaj, D. (1994) 'Demografia shqiptare përballe sfidave të tranzicionit. Interviste e nënkryetarit të Akademisë së Shkencave, Prof. Ylli Vejsiu', *Rilindja demokratike*, 21 June, p. 3.

Kaser, M. (ed.) (1986) *The Economic History of Eastern Europe 1919-1975*, vol. III, *Institutional Change within a Planned Economy*. Oxford: Clarendon Press.

—— (1993) 'Economic system' in Grothusen (1993), pp. 289–311.

Kinnear, R. (1992) 'Regional development challenges and problems in Central Europe' in Vaško (1992), pp. 63–88.

Kornai, J. (1980) *Economics of Shortage*, vols A–B. Contributions to Economic Analysis 131. Amsterdam: North-Holland.

—— (1986) 'The soft budget constraint', *Kyklos*, vol. 39, no. 1, pp. 3–30.

—— (1994) 'Transformational recession: the main causes', *Journal of Comparative Economics*, vol. 19, no. 1, pp. 39–63.

Laky, T. (1989) 'Vanished myths – wavering intentions (small enterprises revisited)', *Acta Oeconomica*, vol. 40, nos 3–4, pp. 285–306.

Lienau, C. (1991) 'Einige Grundzüge der Raumstruktur und Raumenentwicklung Albaniens' in Becker (1991), pp. 47–68.

—— (1993) 'Geographische Grundlagen' in Grothusen (1993), pp. 1–25.

Luçi, E. (1970) 'Shpërndarja racionale e forcave prodhuese në vendin tonnga pikëpamja territoriale', *Ekonomia popullore*, vol. 17, no. 1, pp. 54–9.

McDermott, G. and Mejstrik, M. (1992) 'The role of small firms in the industrial development and transformation of Czechoslovakia', *Small Business Economics*, vol. 4, no. 3, pp. 179–200.

Matykowski, R. and Stryjakiewicz, T. (1992) 'The adaptation of industry and its labour force to the changing economic system in Poland', *Erdkunde*, vol. 46, no. 2, pp. 149–57.

Mihailović, K. (1972) *Regional Development: Experience and Prospects in Eastern Europe.* Paris: Mouton.

Milor, V. (ed.) (1994) *Changing Political Economies: Privatization in Post-Communist and Reforming Communist States.* Boulder, CO: Lynne Rienner.

Ministry of Finance (1993) 'Programi afatmesëm i zhvillimit ekonomik 1993-1996'. Tirana: Ministria e Financave dhe Ekonomisë, October (Draft).

Pashko, G. (1991) 'The Albanian economy at the beginning of the 1990s' in Sjöberg and Wyzan (1991), pp. 128–46.

—— (1993a) 'Inflation in Albania', *Communist Economies and Economic Transformation*, vol. 5, no. 1, pp. 115–26.

—— (1993b) 'Obstacles to economic reform in Albania', *Europe–Asia Studies*, vol. 45, no. 5, pp. 907–21.

—— (1994) 'Albania: The transition from a command to a free market economy', *Südosteuropa*, vol. 43, no. 5, pp. 223–39.

Pavlínek, P. (1992) 'Regional transformation in Czechoslovakia: towards a market economy', *Tijdschrift voor economische en sociale geografie*, vol. 83, no. 5, pp. 361–71.

Raagmaa, G. (1993) 'New enterprises and regional development in Estonia'. Paper presented at the 'European Summer Institute in Regional Science', Joensuu, Finland, June.

Radvanyi, J. and Rey, V. (eds) (1989) *Régions et pouvoirs régionaux en Europe de l'est et en URSS.* Paris: Masson.

Rawstron, E. (1958) 'Three principles of industrial location', *Transactions, Institute of British Geographers*, no. 25, pp. 135–42.

Ronnås, P. (1984) *Urbanization in Romania: a Geography of Social and Economic Change since Independence.* Stockholm: EFI, Stockholm School of Economics.

—— (1988) 'Städtewachstum und Raumentwicklung in Rumänien', *Osteuropa*, vol. 38, no. 11, pp. 1008–21.

—— (1991) 'The economic legacy of Ceauşescu' in Sjöberg and Wyzan (1991), pp. 47–68.

Sachs, J. and Woo, W. 1994) 'Structural factors in the economic reforms of China, Eastern Europe, and the former Soviet Union', *Economic Policy*, no. 18, pp. 102–45.

Sandström, P. and Sjöberg, Ö. (1991) 'Albanian economic performance: stagnation in the 1980s', *Soviet Studies*, vol. 43, no. 5, pp. 931–47.

Schappelwein, K. (1991) 'Die wirtschaftliche Entwicklung Albaniens unter besonderer Berücksichtigung von Bergbau und Industrie' in Becker (1991), pp. 147–57.

—— (1993) 'Bergbau und Energiewirtschaft' in Grothusen (1993), pp. 376–90.

Schmidt-Neke, M. (1993a) 'Innenpolitik' in Grothusen (1993), pp. 57–85.

—— (1993b) 'Politisches System', ibid., pp. 169–242.

Schmidt-Neke, M. and Sjöberg, Ö. (1993) 'Bevölkerungsstruktur' in Grothusen (1993), pp. 464–90.

Schnytzer, A. (1978) 'The impact of aid on Albanian industrial development – China and the Soviet Union as major trading partners' in Joint Economic Committee, pp. 860–80.

—— (1982) *Stalinist Economic Strategy in Practice: the Case of Albania.* Oxford: Oxford University Press.

—— (1993) 'Industry' in Grothusen (1993), pp. 312–42.

Schönfeld, R. (ed.) (1989) *Industrialisierung und gesellschaftlicher Wandel in Südosteuropa.* Südosteuropa-Studien 42. Munich: Südosteuropa-Gesellschaft.

Sivignon, M. (1987) 'Les disparités régionales en Albanie', *Bulletin de la Société Languedocienne de Géographie*, vol. 21, nos 1–2, pp. 97–103.

Sjöberg, Ö. (1987) 'A contribution to the geography of hydro-electric power generation in Albania', *Österreichische Osthefte*, vol. 29, no. 1, pp. 5–27.

—— (1990) 'Urban Albania: developments 1965–1987' in Altmann (1990), pp. 171–223.

—— (1991a) *Rural Change and Development in Albania.* Boulder, CO: Westview.

—— (1991b) 'The Albanian economy in the 1980s: coping with a centralised system' in Sjöberg and Wyzan (1991), pp. 115–27.

—— (1992) 'Underurbanization and the zero urban growth hypothesis: diverted migration in Albania', *Geografiska Annaler*, vol. 74B, no. 1, pp. 3–19.

—— (1993) 'Social structure' in Grothusen (1993), pp. 491–504.

—— (1994) 'Rural retention in Albania: administrative restrictions on urban-bound migration', *East European Quarterly*, vol. 28, no. 2, pp. 205–33.

Sjöberg, O. and Wyzan, M. (eds) (1991) *Economic Change in the Balkan States: Albania, Bulgaria, Romania and Yugoslavia.* London: Pinter.

Stewart, J. and Warantz, W. (1968) 'Physics of population distribution' in Berry (1968), pp. 130–46.

Szul, R. (1989) 'The spatial structure of Poland's industry', *Osteuropa-Wirtschaft*, vol. 34, no. 4, pp. 290–302.

Vaško, T. (ed.) (1992) *Problems of Economic Transition: Regional Development in Central and Eastern Europe.* Aldershot: Avebury.

Webster, L. (1994) 'Private sector manufacturing in Eastern Europe: some cross-country comparisons' in Milor (1994), pp. 175–91.

Wildermuth, A. (1989) *Die Krise der albanischen Landwirtschaft. Lösungsversuche der Partei- und Staatsführung unter Ramiz Alia.* Wirtschaft und Gesellschaft in Südosteuropa 6. Neuried bei München: Hieronymus.

—— (1993) 'Land- und Forstwirtschaft' in Grothusen (1993), pp. 343–75.

World Bank (1992) *An Agricultural Strategy for Albania: A Report Prepared by a Joint Team from The World Bank and the European Community.* Washington, DC: World Bank, October.

Wyzan, M. and Sjöberg, Ö. (1992) *Agricultural Privatization in Bulgaria and Albania: Legal Foundations and Prospects.* Working paper 61. Stockholm: Stockholm Institute of East European Economics, October.

Yzeri, E. (1988) 'Tipare të shpërndarjes gjeografike territoriale të forcave prodhuese të industrisë në vitet 1960–80', *Studime gjeografike*, no. 3, pp. 215–27.

7 Problems of the Transition to a Market Economy in Romania, Bulgaria and Albania: Why has the Transition Proved to be so Difficult?

Alan Smith

Introduction

The purpose of this paper is to compare the progress of the transition to a market economy in the former centrally planned economies in the Balkans (Romania, Bulgaria and Albania) with that of the Central East European economies (Poland, Hungary and the Czech and Slovak Republics). The paper is divided into three parts: (1) the strategy of reform in Central Eastern Europe and the arguments for shock therapy and gradualism respectively; (2) a comparison of the economic performance of the Central East European economies and the Balkan economies since 1989; (3) a preliminary attempt to analyse why it has proved so difficult to implement 'shock therapy' policies in the Balkan economies.

The transition strategy in Central Eastern Europe

The essential elements of the transition

The transition strategy of the Central East European economies had the broad support of the IMF and was in part derived from the experience of stabilization and liberalization programmes adopted in Latin America in the 1980s. The strategy, which has been described as the 'Washington consensus', involved a number of measures, including the following: macroeconomic stabilization (incorporating tight fiscal and monetary policies to eliminate suppressed inflation and to prevent the emergence of inertial inflationary pressures); price liberalization (to remove the widespread distortions arising from administered prices); the removal of constraints to the development of a private sector *ab initio* in trade, services and small and medium-scale production; the privatization of existing state-owned enterprises; the decollectivization and privatization of agriculture; and measures to create an open economy, including the replacement of administrative and quantitative controls over foreign trade by market levers, the introduction of forms of convertibility and the unification of exchange rates.

The 'return to Europe' (the reorientation of trade away from the CMEA towards inter-war trade partners in Central and Western Europe) was seen by the new governments of Central East Europe as an essential political, as well as an economic, goal. It was recognized that it was necessary to replace the import-substituting model of development (which had been imposed on the economies through their participation in the CMEA and which had created excessive dependence on the Soviet market and Soviet supplies of energy and raw materials) by a more export-oriented philosophy to trade which actively encouraged foreign direct investment.

Although it was recognized that the transition to a market economy would involve significant transitional costs in the form of lost output, open unemployment, widening income inequality and the growth of poverty, the extent of these costs appears to have been underestimated. Both deductive reasoning and the experience of macrostabilization in Latin American countries indicated that the strict deflationary policies required to eliminate inflation would contribute to short-term falls in output, employment and income. These would compound the lost output and employment required by structural transformation and improvements in labour productivity. The resulting high levels of unemployment (much of which would be of long duration), and the continued threat of unemployment, would reduce demand for consumption during the transitional period, which would, in turn, reduce the short-term profitability of private investment in areas which had a long-term potential. Substantial price increases for foodstuffs, energy and housing following the removal of subsidies and price controls, combined with widening wage differentials, would also bring the threat of real poverty in economies that have depended on guaranteed employment and cheap prices for basic staple goods as the principal method of welfare provision. This would be expected to depress consumption still further. The majority of governments hoped (and even anticipated) that external assistance would help to alleviate some of the short-term costs of the transition and in particular the budget costs of welfare programmes. Similarly, it was hoped that measures to encourage foreign direct investment would lead to an inflow of foreign capital, which would assist in industrial modernization and stimulate the redirection of exports to the West.

The majority of economists who have studied the operation of the centrally planned economies of Eastern Europe accept that excessive centralization and state intervention were major factors contributing to the collapse of the communist economic system. The systemic problems were aggravated by populist budgetary polices in the 1980s, whereby the state attempted to buy off different interest groups by acceding to their demands for resources and expenditure, but was unable, or unwilling, to raise the revenue to pay for them. This resulted in growing, but suppressed, internal and external macroeconomic disequilibria whose impact on productive capacity and living standards was exacerbated by poor investment decisions.

Consequently, there is a broad consensus that macroeconomic stabilization, price liberalization, trade liberalization and the development of a thriving private sector are necessary features for the transition to a functioning market economy. Major disagreements have arisen between different schools of economic thought over a number of critical issues. These include the speed of implementation and the sequencing of the various components of the transition, the role of market forces in stimulating economic growth and recovery during and after the transition process, the degree of reliance that should be placed on privatization as means to achieve the essential restructuring of industry, the role of market forces and private capital in generating investment in infrastructure, and how extensive the role of the state should be in the process of transition.

Neo-liberals and shock therapy

Several of the more important economic portfolios in the new governments of Central Eastern Europe (particularly in Poland and the former Czechoslovakia) were occupied by neo-liberals, who combined a strong faith in the benefits of the free market and free trade with strict monetarist arguments, and who derived their economic inspiration from either neo-classical general equilibrium theory or the Austrian school of economic analysis. Both of these schools provide logical arguments in favour of a rapid transition to a market economy.

General equilibrium theory indicates that the 'first best' solution to the problems created by the transition is to minimize the economic distortions that will inevitably arise from the coexistence of mutually incompatible economic systems during the transition period by removing the source of the distortions as quickly as possible. This will prevent contradictory or inaccurate price signals resulting from the coexistence of mixed systems leading to incorrect decisions, which, particularly in the case of investment, will have lasting consequences. While many members of the Austrian School remain sceptical about the concept of market perfection, they are even more sceptical about claims that it is possible to predict and plan for the future with any certainty. Consequently, neo-liberals argue that private entrepreneurs who are capable of interpreting and responding to the changing signals sent out by markets are more able to react quickly and efficiently to rapidly changing circumstances. This argument emphasizes the need for the rapid development of a private sector, which requires the removal of constraints to the development of a private sector *ab initio* and measures to privatize existing industry (including large-scale industry) as the principal methods for improving enterprise efficiency and achieving structural transformation. This, combined with the rapid replacement of administrative controls by market clearing prices will remove opportunities for arbitraging, corruption and other rent-seeking activities and will weaken the hold of the old administrative elite (the *nomenklatura*) whose ability to circumvent shortages was a major source of their power.

Many neo-liberals accept that it is sensible to inform the population about the short-term costs and long-term benefits of the transition in order to increase support for unpopular measures. Others, of a more technocratic persuasion, argue that bargaining over proposals to alleviate the short-term costs of the transition may result in the adoption of measures which create greater social and economic problems in the long term than they are intended to solve in the short term. The latter tend to see economic transformation as a 'top-down' process which involves the implementation of what, in their view, is the only workable blueprint for reform. Opposition to this may be well-intentioned, but is seen to be misguided and to be resisted.

Both macrostabilization and structural adjustment require breaking the power of the former *nomenklatura* and preventing the emergence of power groups which will lobby for the preservation of their own authority and for continued financial favours. Political opposition to market-oriented policies by those who will be materially disadvantaged, by those who will lose power and by those who are genuinely ideologically opposed to marketization must also be expected. Neo-liberals are not alone in arguing that a 'clean political break with the past' is essential both to weaken organized opposition to reforms and to provide clear evidence to the population at large that genuine marketization will happen and will bring long-term benefits (Åslund 1994). This will bestow credibility and consistency on the process of transition and may not just weaken organized opposition, but may even persuade the former *nomenklatura* to support the transition process. This implies that it is important to utilize the 'window of opportunity' which will be open in the short term, when popular support for the transition is at its greatest, before tolerance to the social and human costs of the transition becomes exhausted. For these reasons neo-liberals espouse as rapid a transition to a market economy as can be sustained under the prevailing circumstances. This school of thought (which argues that the ability of the new governments to sequence and fine-tune the transition is extremely limited and involves giving power to the former *nomenklatura* and that the best solution is to move as fast as possible, on as many fronts as possible including macroeconomic stabilization, price liberalization and privatization, to achieve as much progress towards the ultimate goal of creating an integrated market economy in the shortest possible time) has become popularly known as 'shock therapy'.

Gradualism

Opponents of the neo-liberal approach are frequently described as 'gradualists' as their central point is that the various processes of transition should be (and more controversially can be) fine-tuned and sequenced according to the specific circumstances facing each individual country in order to minimize the human and social costs of the transition. This implies a slower pace of reform. A further distinction is that many economists who espouse a 'gradualist' approach to structural reform have less confidence in the ability of free markets to generate economic recovery without central guidance. They argue that the elimination of inflationary pressures, although necessary, is not a sufficient condition for stimulating economic growth and that the state should play a more *dirigiste* role in stimulating the growth of export-oriented industries. They also question the role of privatization of existing state-owned enterprises as the only, or even principal, method of stimulating industrial restructuring and argue that significant gains in economic efficiency could be realized by exposing enterprises to hard budget constraints while they remain under state control. Thus privatization of state industry tends to be seen more as a long-term objective than an immediate necessity which requires 'give-away' approaches.

Gradualists also support a social-democratic approach to the human and social costs of the transition. They attach greater importance to informing and educating the public about the potential short-term costs and long-term benefits of the transition and to responding to and assuaging popular anxieties about the process. Przeworski (1993) shows that one of the most important of these is the fear of unemployment which, in an economy that has only rudimentary welfare facilities and where the value of savings has been virtually eliminated by inflation, brings the immediate prospect of poverty and is a major factor contributing to popular opposition to reforms. Gradualists argue that genuine consultation is necessary to win popular recognition of the need for unavoidable but unpopular measures if they are not to be reversed by the democratic process (Bresser Pereira *et al.* 1993).

More specific economic arguments in support of a gradualist approach are that over-tight fiscal and monetary policies will lead to excessive falls in output and employment, which reduce the tax base and increase the pressure for expenditure on welfare. This will make it harder to reduce budget deficits which cannot be financed by government borrowing until more sophisticated instruments for funding government debt have been established. Tight monetary policies which necessitate high real interest rates will discourage private sector investment and tight fiscal policies will limit investment in infrastructure, both of which inhibit long-term growth. Finally, gradualists argue that deflationary policies reduce incomes below their long-term equilibrium level and reduce the demand for consumer goods industries which have long-term potential. It is also argued that enterprises that have the potential to survive in the long term may not be capable of withstanding exposure to foreign competition in the short term (the infant industry argument).

Gradualism and 'shock therapy' in Eastern Europe

Nuti and Portes (Portes 1993: 12), reviewing the early experience of the transition in Central Eastern Europe, demonstrate that the range of practical strategies available to Central East European governments was far more restricted than theoretical debates between 'shock therapists' and 'gradualists' suggest. In practice, those who espouse a rapid transition to a market economy accept that the process cannot be instantaneous (and in particular that structural change and privatization will take time to implement and to take effect) and that there will be a need for some sequencing. On the other hand, the threat of hyperinflation in some countries made macroeconomic stabilization an immediate necessity, while the collapse of the planning networks, information flows, central institutions and tax revenues and the spontaneous development of a private sector *ab initio* required urgent action and prevented any real possibility of a properly phased transition in the majority, if not all, the former centrally planned economies.

Nuti and Portes argue that only the former GDR can be considered to have followed an approach that could be described as true 'global shock therapy' as a result of monetary union and unification with the FRG. The first eighteen months of the transition in Poland (the Balcerowicz plan) involved a rigorous macroeconomic stabilization programme, together with price liberalization and the removal of consumer subsidies. Poland has subsequently experienced major difficulties in implementing its programme to privatize large- and medium-scale industry, although the pace of privatization of assets, as opposed to whole enterprises, has been relatively fast. Czechoslovakia also

implemented a tight macroeconomic stabilization programme, price liberalization (following a year of preliminary discussion and preparation) and a
scheme of rapid, mass privatization, based on a voucher system. 'Shock therapy' in Czechoslovakia was largely justified on the grounds that a rapid transition would substantially weaken the power of the *nomenklatura* (thus ensuring
a clean break with the past) and help to remove the microeconomic distortions inherited from communism. Hungary is often cited as an example of a
gradualist approach to the transition. Nuti and Portes argue that this reflected
a consolidation of the gradual progress that had been made towards the introduction of market mechanisms under socialism, which eliminated the need
for sudden shocks. Although the latter might be taken as evidence that gradualism is possible, there is little evidence that reforms in Hungary had reached
the critical mass under socialism whereby irreversible progress to a market
economy had been achieved.

Romania, Bulgaria and Albania were either unable or unwilling to pursue a
rapid strategy for the transition to a market economy in the immediate aftermath of the collapse of communist authority in Eastern Europe. Although the
precise nature of the transition has differed substantially from country to country, the general features have included the following: partial price liberalization
(including the phased reduction of price controls and retail price subsidies); the
continuation of measures to protect state industry from market forces, including a reluctance to submit enterprises to hard budget constraints; a slower pace
of financial reforms and restructuring; looser monetary policies (involving either
higher budget deficits or the expansion of state credits to write off enterprise
debts); difficulties in imposing positive real interest rates; and an opaque foreign exchange regime with limited or inconsistent attempts to introduce internal convertibility. In general, markets (retail, wholesale, labour and foreign
exchange) have been subject to more administrative regulation than in Central
Eastern Europe and have been cleared by prices to lesser degree than in Central
Eastern Europe, contributing to the continuation of the economics of shortage.

Although the Balkan economies have all implemented policies involving
the redistribution of agricultural land which have resulted in immediate gains
in output, the structure of land holdings has resulted in a large number of
small plots. This militates against agrarian investment and the development
of a market-based agrarian economy, while land titles in general remain con-
fused, thus preventing the consolidation of land holdings. Progress towards
the privatization of state industry has been slow, exhibiting a reluctance to
act against virtually bankrupt and obsolete industry. Finally Romania, Bulgaria
and Albania did not achieve a clean political break with the past in the very
early stages of the transition. As a result the transition was not pursued with
consistency. This deprived the process of much of its credibility, a topic to
be discussed in the conclusion.

Economic performance in Central Eastern Europe and the Balkans 1990–93

Problems of measuring the success of the transition

Bresser Pereira (1993) argues that the success of transition programmes to date has been judged on the basis of three simple criteria: (1) the 'continued implementation of reform measures' (p. 3); (2) the progress of stabilization and liberalization; and (3) the resumption of growth under democratic conditions. Bresser Pereira rejects the first two criteria. He argues that the first assumes that there is a single correct blueprint which should be slavishly applied to each and every country and that success can be simply measured in terms of degree of progress made, while deviations from the norm, for any reason whatsoever, indicate failure. The second implicitly assumes that economic growth will necessarily resume following the elimination of inflationary pressures and the removal of constraints to individual action and that this growth will be to the benefit of the domestic population not to that of foreign investors and creditors. Bresser Pereira proposes that the best test of success is the resumption of growth under democratic conditions and that until this has been clearly demonstrated it is necessary to maintain an agnostic position.

The 'resumption of growth test' has the advantage of being quantifiable, but it involves problems of definition and measurement. First, it can be argued that the level of output (in relation to the economy's potential output) needs to be taken into consideration, since an observed increase in output (which could be interpreted as the resumption of equilibrium growth) could merely reflect the rebound from an unnecessary and oversharp initial fall in output. Secondly, it is important that any observed growth is not temporary, but represents the beginning of long-run sustained growth. For this to be true, observed growth must satisfy the demands of end-users who must be capable of remaining in business and generating demand in the long run. In the case of the former centrally planned economies this means that output should not reflect excessive production for stockbuilding or be accompanied by abnormal levels of inter-enterprise debt.

Sustained growth will, therefore, require progress towards both macroeconomic stabilization and liberalization. High levels of inflation will distort (or impede the observation of) the relationship between relative prices and, when combined with exchange rate instability, the relationship between domestic prices and world market prices. This will lead to incorrect investment decisions and discourage foreign direct investment. Similarly, the prevalence of negative real interest rates in combination with high inflation destroys the incentive to save, which the experience of South East Asian economies indicates is an essential prerequisite to growth. Consequently, the removal of inflationary pressures (which would otherwise necessitate further monetary and fiscal tightening which would, in turn, restrict growth) is a prerequisite for sustained growth. This problem can be illustrated by the experience of Russia, where the initial fall in output before macrostabilization did not prevent further falls in output when controls over the money supply were tightened in the first half of 1994.

Finally, some essentially subjective judgements about the progress of macro-economic stabilization and economic liberalization are unavoidable. The continuation of controls over prices, foreign exchange, exports, imports, involves distortions which will impede rational investment decisions and hinder sustained growth. If the stated objective of the transition is to achieve a market economy, it is not purely metaphysical to measure the success of the transition in terms of the degree to which the economies concerned function in the manner of market economies (rather than centrally planned economies) and the extent to which the progress of marketization appears to be irreversible.

Consequently, I would argue that the resumption of growth under democratic conditions is a necessary, but not sufficient condition for declaring the transition to be a success. The resumption of growth must have been determined by market demand, must have taken place under stable (or relatively stable) macroeconomic conditions and must be accompanied by steady progress towards liberalization. If these conditions are not satisfied, any observed growth in output may not be long-lasting.

Table 7.1 Annual growth of real GDP (%)

	1990	1991	1992	1993	Cumulative
Poland	−11.6	−7.6	+1.0	+4.0	−14.3
Czechoslovakia	−1.8	−15.1	−7.1		
Czech Republic	−1.9	−14.5	−6.7	−0.3	−22.0
Slovakia	−1.3	−16.4	−8.0	−4.1	−27.5
Hungary	−3.5	−11.9	−4.5	−1.6	−21.1
Albania	−10.0	−27.7	−9.7	+11.0	−35.4
Bulgaria	−9.1	−11.7	−7.7	−3.8	−28.8
Romania	−5.6	−12.9	−13.6	+1.0	−28.2

Sources: National data; Economist Intelligence Unit; IMF (1994).

Table 7.2 Consumer price inflation (annual average)

	1990	1991	1992	1993
Poland	586	70	43	35
Czech Republic	8.4	61.0	12.7	20.8
Slovakia	8.4	61.9	9.9	23.2
Hungary	28.9	35.0	23.0	22.5
Albania	0	35.5	226.0	86.0
Bulgaria	21.6	333.5	82.6	72.3
Romania	5.1	161.1	210.4	256.1

Sources: National data; Economist Intelligence Unit; IMF (1994).

Table 7.3 General budget deficits as a percentage of GDP

	1990	1991	1992	1993
Poland	+3.1	−5.6	−6.8	−4.1
Czechoslovakia	+0.9	−0.6	−3.8	−1.1
Czech Republic				+0.3
Slovakia				−7.9
Hungary	+0.5	−2.7	−7.5	−5.8
Albania	−16.6	−34.0	−21.8	−15.5
Bulgaria	−9.2	−11.8	−14.0	−13.5
Romania	+1.0	+1.4	−5.5	−4.6

Note: + indicates general budget surplus.
Sources: 1992 and 1993: IMF (May 1994); 1990 and 1991: National data; OECD reports; IMF.

Table 7.4 Official recorded unemployment levels in Eastern Europe (% of labour force)

	1990	1991	1992	1993
Poland	6.3	11.8	13.6	15.7
Czechoslovakia	1.0	6.6	5.1	
Czech Republic		4.1	2.6	3.5
Slovakia		11.8	10.4	14.4
Hungary	1.7	8.5	12.3	12.1
Bulgaria	1.6	11.7	16.4	17.0*
Romania	—	2.7	8.4	10.2

Note: * = estimate.
Sources: OECD *Short Term Economic Indicators: Transition Economies;* national data.

Macroeconomic stability and the resumption of growth in Eastern Europe

Tables 7.1–7.4 provide basic data (taken from official sources) on the macroeconomic performance (inflation, growth and unemployment levels) of the East European economies from the end of 1989 to the end of 1993. There are, of course, considerable problems of reliability and comparability of data. The basic data suggest that although the performance of the Central East European economies has not been outstanding during this period, they have in most respects outperformed the Balkan economies.

The raw data in Table 7.1 indicate that the cumulative fall in GDP in each of the Central East European countries between 1990 and 1993 was below that of each of the Balkan economies. Estimated GDP fell by over 28 per cent in Bulgaria and Romania, and by 35.4 per cent in Albania, compared with 21–22 per cent in the Czech Republic and Hungary and 14.3 per cent in Poland. Poland alone among the transition countries provides strong evidence that the decline in real GDP has bottomed out and has been followed by sustained growth, with a small growth of GDP of 1 per cent in 1992 followed by 4 per cent in 1993. Elsewhere, the picture is patchy and any return to growth remains fragile. Economic performance in the Czech and Slovak republics in 1993 was adversely affected by the dissolution of the Federation. Industrial output fell for the fourth consecutive year in the Czech Republic, but preliminary figures indicate that this was offset by the growth in services (particularly tourism), which also helped to restrict unemployment to 3.5 per cent of the registered labour force. The Slovak Republic was the least successful of the Central East European economies. The continued fall in industrial production of 13 per cent in 1993 contributed to the fourth consecutive year of decline in GDP. Unemployment rose to 14.4 per cent of the registered labour force by the end of the year and continued on a rising trend in the first quarter of 1994. Industrial growth resumed in Hungary in 1993 after three consecutive years of decline, but the continued decline in agricultural output resulted in a fall in GDP for the fourth consecutive year.

In the Balkans, both Romania and Albania reported positive growth of real GDP in 1993 of 1 per cent and 11 per cent respectively. In the Albanian case this followed a cumulative fall of 42 per cent in GDP between 1990 and 1992, one of the largest falls in output recorded in a peacetime economy. The recovery of output in 1993 was concentrated in agriculture and the previously persecuted private services sector. Romania reported positive growth of both GDP and industrial output in 1993. Although industrial output started to recover on a monthly basis in the last quarter of 1992, the growth in output was initially accompanied by negative real interest rates, which encouraged stockbuilding, while the growth of inter-enterprise debt allowed potentially insolvent enterprises to continue production. Consequently, it will prove difficult to sustain this form of growth in the long term and further structural adjustments will be required. In Bulgaria industrial output continued to fall by an estimated 8 per cent in 1993, contributing to a fall in GDP of 3.8 per cent.

Table 7.2 indicates that the level of consumer price inflation in each Central East European in 1993 was below that of each of the Balkan economies. Average consumer price inflation was just over 20 per cent in Hungary and the Czech and Slovak republics and 35 per cent in Poland. Albania and Bulgaria were still experiencing consumer price increases in the range of 4–5 per cent a month in 1993, while inflation continued to rise in Romania in 1993, averaging 256 per cent and reaching 295 per cent on an end-year basis. Although inflationary pressures have been reduced to levels where the growth of retail prices does not directly threaten the social fabric, the growth of wage rates and wholesale prices was still sufficiently high to affect international competitiveness and prevent stabilization of the exchange rate, while a reduction in the existing level of inflation will necessitate tighter fiscal and monetary policies, which will have a negative impact on output.

All of the transition economies experienced difficulties in limiting the size of budget deficits in the face of falling budget revenues (following the transition to tax systems based on *ex ante* regulations in place of *ex post* confiscation) and increasing demand for expenditure on welfare payments (particularly unemployment benefits). Relatively undeveloped capital markets have complicated the problem of financing state budget deficits by public borrowing, requiring them to be funded by the printing press. There are major problems in interpreting intra-country comparisons of budget deficits, particularly as a high level of tax revenues may indicate the continued use of traditional means of *de facto* expropriation, which are indicative of a failure to implement market reforms rather than the successful implementation of reforms. However, the data in Table 7.3 indicate that the Balkan economies (where progress towards the creation of a tax system based on *ex ante* rules has been slower than in Central Eastern Europe) have also been less successful in containing consolidated budget deficits than the Central East European economies. Albania and Bulgaria have run budget deficits in excess of 10 per cent of GDP for most of the transition period, compared with single-digit rates in Poland, the Czech Republic and Hungary. Although Romania appears to have been relatively successful in containing the official budget deficit (partly as a result of the low level of external debt service), the low level of expenditure is largely accounted for by the exclusion of extra-budget and off-budget expenditures, while inflation taxes on enterprises have proved to be the main source of budget revenue (OECD 1993: 66). Inflationary pressures have been increased by the monetization of inter-enterprise debt and, until the end of 1993, by the prevalence of highly negative real interest rates which have destroyed any incentive to save. Critically, Bulgaria and Romania cannot claim both to have resumed demand-led growth and to have achieved a reasonable degree of price stability. Consequently, more stringent measures will be required to reduce inflationary pressures which will, in turn, inhibit economic recovery. Albania's return to growth followed an unprecedented fall in output and was accompanied by inflationary pressures in 1993.

Official statistics for the level of registered unemployment as a percentage of the registered labour force (which do not capture short-time working in the majority of countries and should be treated with caution) are shown in Table 7.4. All of the East European countries (with the exception of the Czech Republic, which benefited from significant growth in the service sector) experienced double-digit rates of registered unemployment in 1993. It is not possible to detect a significant difference in the levels of registered unemployment between countries that have pursued rapid transition strategy or those that have pursued a more gradualist approach on the basis of the available raw data.

Difficulties in implementing the transition to a market economy in the Balkans

General difficulties in implementing 'shock therapy' in the Balkans

The data in Tables 7.1–7.4 indicate that the former centrally planned economies in the Balkans experienced larger falls in GDP and industrial output, were less successful in controlling inflation and, at best, had no more success in avoiding open unemployment than the economies of Central Eastern Europe during the period from 1990 to 1993. In general, the performance of the Balkan economies, which pursued a gradualist strategy to the transition, was inferior to that of the Central East European economies which pursued a faster transition strategy. Furthermore, the Balkan economies were less successful in creating the institutions of a market economy and in generating structural change. It is necessary to examine whether the poorer economic performance of the Balkan economies can be directly attributed to differences in the transition strategy itself or to other factors specific to the region. Finally it is necessary to examine whether the quantitative and qualitative lag in development between the Balkan economies and the Central East European economies will be of a long-term nature, or whether the gap can, or will, be reduced over the medium to long term.

While it is clear that there are substantial historic, cultural, geographical and political differences between the Balkan and the Central Eastern Europe states (which are discussed in other chapters of this book), it is necessary to ask whether these factors are sufficient to explain the relatively poorer economic performance of the Balkan economies since 1989. This is an area that requires far more detailed research, which must await the publication of more reliable data. This section will examine three interrelated factors which appear to be important (but not exclusive) explanations of the poorer economic performance of the Balkan economies. It is argued in the conclusion that these factors increased the costs of the transition, thus creating greater popular support for politicians who advocate a gradual approach to reforms.

The lower level of industrialization at the onset of communism

The lower level of industrialization attained in the inter-war period and the greater dependence on agriculture for employment meant that the Stalinist policy of forced industrialization involved a greater departure from the pattern of development that would be determined by the long-run comparative advantage of the Balkan economies than was the case in Central Eastern Europe. This implies that a greater fall in industrial output will be required before the economy can adopt a stable pattern of demand-determined growth.

This has been reflected in the more rapid collapse in industrial production in the Balkans in comparison with Central Eastern Europe and the relatively faster recovery of the agricultural sectors in the Balkans (much of which may not be fully reflected in official statistics).

These problems were compounded in Bulgaria by the greater dependence on Soviet inputs of energy and raw materials and the Soviet market for industrial output, which contributed to a comparatively greater fall in demand for industrial production following the collapse of the CMEA. Although Romania was less dependent on the CMEA market for industrial goods, the domestic structure of demand was affected by the grandiose investment projects of the Ceauşescu era, which created a pattern of demand for construction goods (cement, iron and steel) that could not be sustained after the revolution. These factors were also present in the case of Albania (see Pashko's chapter in this book). As a result, the Balkan economies faced severe problems of de-industrialization, which will necessitate a lengthier and more complicated process of industrial restructuring than that faced by the Central East European economies.

The social problems associated with de-industrialization are complicated by the concentration of post-war industrialization in newly created (or greatly expanded) single company towns, populated by first and second generation migrants from villages with limited skills, who have little or no experience of job search and who have grown up in an industrial culture which has avoided the need for labour mobility and industrial retraining. Unemployment in these areas will be localized and of long duration. This will arouse strong opposition to structural change which has a direct impact on the locality, which will, in turn, strengthen the position of those members of the local *nomenklatura* who oppose structural change. At the same time the smaller size of the urban middle class and intelligentsia has reduced the political significance of the bourgeoisie, who could act as a catalyst for the further development of a private sector.

Lower incomes at the onset of the transition

The introduction of current account convertibility for residents at a fixed but substantially depreciated exchange rate (in comparison with purchasing power parity) in the initial stage of the transition was one of the most innovative and successful features of the Balcerowicz plan in Poland. The former centrally planned economies which succeeded in introducing a form of current account convertibility at a fixed or pegged exchange rate early in the reform process (including Latvia, Estonia and Slovenia), supported by the appropriate fiscal and monetary policies, also appear to have made greater qualitative progress towards the creation of a market economy.

The failure of the Balkan economies to stabilize the exchange rate must be chiefly attributed to loose fiscal and monetary policies. However, it can also be argued that the impact of combining price liberalization with currency convertibility at a depreciated rate on popular living standards will be greater in countries with a relatively obsolete capital stock, which results in lower initial incomes. Current account convertibility at a depreciated rate (by definition) makes domestic wage rates and incomes relatively low when converted into Western currencies at the prevailing exchange rate, while trade liberalization (in the absence of subsidies) means that the domestic price of imported goods will be driven up to the world market price, converted at the prevailing exchange rate. Similarly, unless the domestic price of potential exports approximates the world market price at the prevailing exchange rate, domestic producers will find it more profitable to export these goods, forcing the price of all tradeable goods up to world market levels at the prevailing exchange rate.

Consequently, full price and trade liberalization will result in the reduction and (eventual) elimination of significant differences between the 'dollar' prices of tradeable goods (including basic staples) between European economies. Relative wage rates and incomes will continue to be determined by productivity, which will, in turn, be determined by the capital stock, which will reduce average wage rates in economies that are capital-scarce (or have a relatively backward or obsolete capital stock). Average monthly wage rates in Central Eastern Europe approached $300 in Hungary in 1992 and $150–160 in Poland and Czechoslovakia, compared with $70–80 in Romania and Bulgaria. Estimates based on the prices of basic staple goods prevailing in the spring and summer of 1994 suggest that the time taken for a worker receiving the average wage to earn an equivalent amount of eggs, bread, potatoes and the cheapest cuts of meat was approximately three times greater in Bucharest than in Prague or Budapest. Employees whose wages are close to or below the average face a far greater prospect of poverty following trade liberalization and the removal of price controls. Similarly, as welfare benefits are directly related to wage levels, the threat of real poverty and the fear of unemployment is greatly increased. It would not be surprising if this resulted in increased popular resistance to price liberalization and to greater pressure for price controls and subsidies on basic staple goods during the transition period and strengthened the political position of those advocating price controls on humanitarian grounds. Controls on domestic prices, in turn, necessitate export controls on products whose prices are below those of world markets and/or import subsidies, which deprives the transition of consistency.

Geographic location and problems of redirecting exports to the OECD

Table 7.5 indicates that the per capita levels of Balkan exports to the OECD and exports of manufactured goods in particular were substantially below those of the Central East European economies. In 1992 per capita exports to the OECD from Hungary ($714), and Czechoslovakia ($590), were significantly

Table 7.5 East European exports to the industrialized West

	Exports to OECD in 1992			Exports of manufactured goods 1991		
	$m	volume 1989=100	per head ($)	$m	per capita ($)	per em-ployee* ($)
Poland	11,232	147	292	5488	143	1643
Czechoslovakia	9204	205	590	4931	316	2210
Hungary	7380	145	714	4118	400	4093
Bulgaria	1560	169	174	643	71	604
Romania	2388	77	105	1670	73	524

Note: * Per employee in manufacturing in 1991.
Sources: Columns 1 and 3 estimated from data in OECD *Monthly Foreign Trade Statistics: Series A*. Columns 2 and 4 from ECE *Economic Bulletin for Europe*, vol. 44, pp. 63, 140. Volume data exclude exports to former east German Länder. Employees in manufacturing industry from OECD *Short Term Economic Indicators*, Central and Eastern Europe.

higher than from Poland ($292), partly reflecting the larger population of Poland and lower degree of trade dependence. These figures all exceeded the per capita exports to the West from Bulgaria ($174), which has a population similar to that of Hungary, and Romania ($105). Bulgaria was the only Balkan economy to expand its exports to the OECD (by 69 per cent in volume) between 1989 and 1992, although this growth largely reflects the lower start-ing point of exports in 1989 and the greater dependence on the Soviet market at that date. The volume of Romanian exports to the West fell by 23 per cent. This can only partly be explained by the diversion of exports to the domestic market following the post-Ceauşescu shift in government strategy away from debt reduction as exports continued to fall in 1991 and 1992. Albania also experienced a fall in export volume of 50 per cent.

The failure to penetrate Western markets is more marked in respect of exports of manufactured goods (data referring to 1991). Per capita exports of manufactured goods in Romania and Bulgaria were just over $70 per head of the population, compared with a low of $143 per head in Poland and a high of $400 per head in Hungary. The figures for Romania and Bulgaria are comparable with those of the import-substituting economies of Argentina and Brazil in the 1980s, while per capita exports of manufactured goods to the OECD by the Central East European economies themselves are still substantially below the levels for Korea (over $1000), Taiwan (over $2500) or Singapore (over $7000). Column 6 in Table 7.5 indicates that differences between the weight of manufactured goods in total output are not the major factor explaining the difference between the level of manufactured exports from the Balkan economies and the Central East European economies to the OECD. Exports per employee in manufacturing industry in both Romania ($524) and Bulgaria ($604) were significantly lower than those of all their Central East European counterparts, which range from $1643 per employee in Poland to $4093 per employee in Hungary.

The relative failure of the Balkan economies to penetrate Western markets for manufactured goods (to compensate for the loss of the CMEA market) can be attributed to the relatively low level of development and lack of competitiveness of manufactured exports and to their less favourable geographic location compared with the Central East European economies. This has been exacerbated by the war in former Yugoslavia and the impact of UN sanctions which have complicated transport routes and deterred potential Western traders. The differential growth of exports from the two regions to the reunified Germany is most marked. Imports of the Federal Republic of Germany from the Central East European countries grew from $4659 million (excluding the eastern Länder which came to approximately $2500 million) in 1989 to $12,972 million in 1992 (including the eastern Länder); imports from Romania and Bulgaria only grew from $998 million to $1194 million over the same period, which did not compensate for the loss of the East German market of approximately $600 million. Furthermore the volume of Romanian and Bulgarian exports to the Central East European economies themselves also fell by more than 60 per cent between 1989 and 1991 (Smith 1994).

It can be argued that the use of OECD data (made necessary by the continued inaccuracy of East European data) overstates the problems facing Romania and Bulgaria since the latter are more favourably located for exports to non-OECD markets, including the Middle East and former Soviet republics (particularly the Central Asian republics), while Romania increased its exports to China in 1994. However, these markets will be slow to recover from the impact of the collapse of the Soviet economy itself. At the very least, the above data indicate that the Balkan economies will experience major problems in integrating their economies with Central Europe and an expanding European Union.

Conclusion: The problem of making a clean break with the past

In Central East Europe there was a brief transitional period in the 1980s during which power passed from the elderly leadership of the Brezhnev era to a younger generation of reform communists (Hungary) or anti-reformers (Czechoslovakia), while in Poland communists who had only retained power on the basis of martial law and the indirect threat of Soviet intervention were forced to share power. Economic reforms imposed during this period were subject to severe political constraints, which prevented genuine marketization. The failure of these policies to bring any improvement to economic performance effectively discredited market-socialist or 'halfway-house reforms' and paved the way for a radical approach, which embraced a commitment to introduce a form of capitalism without the co-operation of former communists.

One common feature of the reforms in Central Eastern Europe was that they were pursued with credibility and consistency in the initial stages after the collapse of communism, with the result that they were virtually irreversible even before the collapse of the Soviet Union itself. Public anxiety over the costs of the transition has been reflected in election results which have seen the return of governments dominated by former communists in Poland in 1993 and Hungary in 1994, and the break-up of the (then) Czech and Slovak Federal Republic. In all cases (with the possible exception of Slovakia, where the initial Meciar government opposed a rapid transition but was subsequently replaced by a more market-oriented government) the new governments have expressed their commitment to continued marketization and privatization, although possibly at a slower pace and with greater emphasis on welfare. Popular support for the transition remains strong in the Czech Republic.

In none of the Balkan states was there a clear transitional period between the end of 'ancien régime' communism and the beginning of 'post-communism'. Consequently, former communists were able to retain significant power and influence in the initial stage of 'post-communism', frequently with large-scale electoral support. This imposed constraints on the speed with which the transition to a market could be pursued, and contributed to a greater reluctance by the IMF and other financial institutions to provide assistance and become heavily involved in the transition process. Many observers argue that the inability of the Balkan states to make a clean political break with the past in the crucial initial stage of the transition process and to pursue the transition with credibility and consistency is the critical factor that distinguished them from Central Eastern Europe. Whether it will it be possible to make a clean break from the past is a political question. Some observers argue that Albania has now made that critical break, which contributed to the growth of output reported in 1993.

Hanson (1994) argues that macroeconomic stabilization is a form of collective good which benefits the population as a whole, but which bestows costs on individuals which they have an incentive to avoid whenever possible (the 'free rider' theorem). This can be extended to argue that the transition programme as a whole is a long-run positive-sum game, specific aspects of which impose significant short-run costs on large numbers of the population, some of whom will be permanently disadvantaged. Critically, there will be inter-generational and inter-class transfers of benefit from older workers (who face the loss of savings, employment, status and stable prices) to members of younger generations (who have the mobility and skills to profit from a market economy and will live long enough to reap the benefits). The deterioration of economic performance and the growth of shortages in the 1980s persuaded a sufficiently large proportion of the population in Central Eastern Europe that the long-run benefits could not be realized without bearing the short-run costs and that individuals must play their part. A rapid transition was intended to implement change while popular tolerance to unpleasant measures was high, and to break organized resistance to the transition.

The populations of the Balkan economies had, at best, a limited experience of 'halfway-house' reforms in the 1980s. This contributed to a greater tendency to blame the political leadership, rather than the economic system, for stagnating or deteriorating living standards and to underestimate the size of the changes necessary to bring real change. Consequently, the *nomenklatura* in the Balkan economies were not confronted with the political challenges that faced their counterparts in Central Eastern Europe. The greater probability that a rapid transition would destroy the existing industrial base, leading to higher levels of unemployment and a greater threat of genuine poverty for a larger proportion of the population, increased the popular appeal of a gradualist strategy in which the government (or the local *nomenklatura*) promised to protect the population from the harshest effects of marketization.

Will the basic features of a *nomenklatura*-dominated economy (including soft budget constraints, budget subsidies to loss-making industries, a lack of genuine privatization, the continuation of supply constraints and the economics of shortage and the associated bribery and corruption, protection from foreign competition, hostility to foreign investment and a tendency towards import-substitution rather than export orientation) prove to be enduring or purely transitional? Although a return to the old system of central planning seems improbable, the possibility of the emergence of an *ad hoc* 'third way', in which the economy is administered in a fashion that is neither fully capitalist nor fully communist cannot be ruled out. However this would result in growing international isolation and the prospect of a widening gap between the Balkan economies and the rest of Europe. It now appears more probable that the process of transition will accelerate, with greater support from external agencies, which will be made conditional on the implementation of structural reforms as well as macroeconomic stabilization. An optimistic scenario is that the period from 1989 to the mid-1990s will prove to be one in which the Balkan countries prepared themselves for change, while outside agencies came to appreciate the problems specific to the region. However, the scale of the economic problems facing the Balkan economies should not be underestimated.

References

Åslund, A. (1994) *Systemic Change and Stabilization in Russia*. London: Royal Institute for International Affairs.

Bresser Pereira, L., Maravall, J. and Przeworski, A. (1993) *Economic Reforms in New Democracies: a Social-Democratic Approach*. Cambridge: Cambridge University Press.

Economist Intelligence Unit, *Country Reports* (various issues). London.

Hanson, P. (1994) *Regions, Local Power and Economic Change in Russia*. London: Royal Institute for International Affairs.

IMF (1994) *World Economic Outlook,* May. Washington.

OECD (1993) *Romania: an Economic Assessment.* Paris.

OECD *Short-Term Economic Indicators: Transition Economies* (various issues). Paris.

OECD *Monthly Foreign Trade Statistics: Series A* (various issues). Paris.

Portes, R. (ed.) (1993) *Economic Transformation in Central Europe: a Progress Report*. London and Luxembourg: Centre for Economic Policy Research and European Communities.

Smith, A. (1994) *International Trade and Payments in the Former Soviet/CMEA Area*. London: Royal Institute for International Affairs.

United Nations Economic Commission for Europe (1993) *Economic Bulletin for Europe*, vol. 44.

8 The Economic Divergence of Yugoslavia's Successor States

Ivo Bicanic

Introduction

The five new national economies which emerged as Yugoslavia's successor states have accumulated five years' experience of designing, implementing, sidestepping, backpedalling and modifying transitional economic policies. In the first three years they accumulated this experience as part of Yugoslavia and the next two as newly independent national economies. Most of that experience is common and they share it with other economies in transition. But some of it is, of course, specific to the area and economies in question. The variety of policies attempted and experienced makes the area of former Yugoslavia an interesting 'laboratory' for studying the economics of transition. Of the many aspects of economic transition this paper deals with two. The two topics have been chosen because they reflect how some general features of economic transition have been reflected in the complex economic environment of Yugoslavia's successor states.

The first aspect to be discussed is the relationship between economic transition and the break-up, more precisely how the economics of transition developed during the disintegration of Yugoslavia. This allows a discussion of a wider topic, namely the importance of asymmetric policy effects during economic transition and the rising popularity of 'go-it-alone' policies. Citing the Yugoslav experience, it will be argued that economic transition is a major destabilizing process which itself breeds and leads to a greater popularity of 'go-it-alone' policies. Uniform economic policies in a heterogeneous economic environment have important asymmetric effects. Important among them is the generation of significant economic inequality, both among social groups and between regions. One of the results is a strong incentive to design regional economic policies which can be called 'go-it-alone' policies. Generally, such policies can be of two kinds. The first are pro-active economic policies designed and implemented to promote regional economic transition. The second are reflexive policies whose purpose is to prevent unfavourable redistributions or externally imposed transition paths. Both types of economic policies developed in Yugoslavia's constituent republics during the late 1980s and early 1990s. They led to economic divergence between regions and a segmented economic structure.

The second aspect concerns the divergent economic transition paths experienced once Yugoslavia's successor states became independent national economies. Each of the new economies chose a different set of policies to deal with economic transition. The differences concern both transition policies (such as privatization, marketization and restructuring), policies designed to deal with the repercussions of economic transition (e.g. macroeconomic stabilization and social policies) and policies aimed at establishing a new national economic space. As a result, the economic divergence which started during the build-up to the disintegration accelerated and increased with economic independence. Within months of achieving independence, regions which had for over seventy years been part of a uniform economic space became fundamentally different economies. By discussing these variations in the economics of transition in Yugoslavia's successor states, the section will address the wider topic of varying transition paths and the inadequacy of any prescriptive *a priori* solutions.

The economics of transition and Yugoslavia's disintegration

Economic transition started in Yugoslavia in 1988, two years before changes in the political system led to multi-party elections and three years before the country finally disintegrated into four new internationally recognized national economies and four unrecognized ones. The period can best be described as one of economic segmentation.

Economic segmentation

The three-and-a-half-year period from the middle of 1988 to the end of 1991 is one during which Yugoslavia disintegrated. At the beginning it was a uniform economic space and it ended the period by spawning new national economies. Before 1988 the Yugoslav economy was a uniform economic space and a common market. There were no internal trade barriers, there was one monetary authority, and constituent republics enjoyed the latitude permitted by fiscal and legislative federalism. In 1988, economic segmentation emerged and from then on grew. The trigger was the unilateral changing of the constitution of one republic (Serbia), which all but eliminated the autonomy (including economic autonomy) of its hitherto autonomous two provinces. Prior to that year, as in any economy, accusations were levelled of discriminatory and biased decisions at all levels of government. Even though their extent and importance has not yet been adequately studied these decisions were not rooted in the legal system, which guaranteed a common market and permitted only marginal differences in economic institutions. In this sense, prior to 1988 segmentation was covert. After 1988 segmenting decisions were backed by legislative change and the common market started dissolving. At the end of the period the Yugoslav economy had completely dissolved into the new national economies of the successor states. The first two successor states (Slovenia and Croatia) became internationally recognized in January 1992. This date thus marks the end of segmentation.

The federal transition path

Yugoslavia's economic transition started in 1988. It came after a decade-long 'maturing' process. This 'maturing' led the Yugoslav economy through two failed attempts at reforming socialism (in 1983 and 1986 respectively[1]) and three failed attempts at crisis management (three macroeconomic stabilization attempts failed in 1982, 1986 and 1988 respectively[2]). By the end of the 1980s this left the economy with hyperinflation, internal macroeconomic disequilibrium, external imbalances, a decade-long secular downturn and a rich experience of policy failures.

The transition package was made up of two policy clusters. One dealt with economic transition and the other with macroeconomic stabilization. Both were passed by the federal legislature and thus can be called the 'federal transition path'. The two clusters were not part of one general and overall plan; indeed, the policies in the transition cluster themselves did not represent a co-ordinated effort, while those of the stabilization cluster did. Finally, neither cluster was presented as part of a transition path; instead they were presented as a last ditch attempt to reform and save socialism.[3] In spite of these disclaimers and for reasons given below, it seems more justified to consider these two clusters as part of a transition rather than a reform effort.[4]

The transition policies of the 'federal plan' were composed of new legislation regulating property rights and their changes and extending marketization. The property rights legislation almost levelled the ownership playing field: it eliminated most of the institutional privileges of 'social ownership' and limitations on the private sector and defined possible privatization paths (based on enterprise initiative and government approved privatization) (Uvalic 1992). Marketization involved freeing market entry for private firms (allowing grass-roots privatization), extending markets to capital (markets for goods and services had existed since the 1950s) and liberalizing foreign trade (in the hope of promoting domestic competition). Most of the alterations in the legislature these changes implied, however, were not made in one sudden sweep or according to a thought-out plan. Instead, they are part of the maturing process which started legislating changes to the economic system in 1986. Due to this maturing process, laws were passed in a much more radical form than initially proposed. Previous legislation was frequently amended to legislate events after they had taken place (former legislation was not always mutually coherent).

These legislative changes, even though introduced under a different guise, do represent an economic transition and not reformed socialism. They fundamentally undermine the structure of a socialist economy. They remove the institutional underpinnings of socialist promotion (by almost equating all property rights and introducing capital markets) and socialist protection (by opening the economy to domestic and foreign competition and allowing privatization).

The macroeconomic stabilization policies associated with the 'federal transition path' started in late 1989.[5] Two phases were envisaged. The aim of the first phase was to stabilize prices and of the second to stabilize the economy. The first 'policy package' concentrated on inflationary expectations as the main generator of hyperinflation. Its primary goal was decisively and in one sweep to reduce inflationary expectations. It hoped to achieve this by introducing 'internal convertibility', extending foreign trade liberalization and providing psychological support to the plan's credibility with a new currency. In a less spectacular move it also changed some relative prices of government controlled products. The plan had the financial backing of the international financial community in the form of an IMF stand-by loan, the twelfth such loan approved for Yugoslavia (Stojanovic 1991).

In evaluating the federal transition path another important aspect must be taken into account. By 1990 political transition caught up with economic transition. During that year multi-party elections were held in all constituent republics, with very different results. In two republics (Croatia and Bosnia-Hercegovina) non-communists gained control of the presidency, parliament and government executive. In another two (Slovenia and Macedonia) there was a division, with parliament and the executive branch controlled by non-communists and leaders of the renamed communist party elected as president. In two (Serbia and Montenegro), the renamed communist party retained complete control. Multi-party elections in the republics had a limited impact at the federal level. While the Federal Assembly, elected in 1986 when the country was a one-party state, extended its mandate, the membership of the collective presidency reflected the outcome of the republican elections.

As a result, the political environment in which the federal transition path was implemented changed radically. It was conceived in 1988 in a one-party state after an extended maturing process. When the prime time of macro-economic stabilization and initial privatization came in 1990 it coincided with preparations for multi-party elections. Later, the policies were implemented in a dramatically different distribution of power which emerged after the elections. The shift was so big that during the first half of 1991 negotiations got under way to recontract the relations of the constituent republics.

Actual transition during segmentation

When tracing the transition path of the Yugoslav economy during segmentation (i.e. from 1988 to the end of 1991) two processes must be taken into account. The first is the implementation of the 'federal transition path'. The second is the increasing segmentation resulting from economic policy decisions in the constituent republics. The complex interrelationship of these two processes is best discussed in terms of the three dominant economic processes of the time: changing property rights, macroeconomic stabilization and market segmentation.

The success with which the 'federal transition path' changed property rights was very limited. The socialized sector underwent ownership restructuring in which socially-owned enterprises were reorganized as joint stock companies, i.e. as a shell of daughter companies around an unprivatized core enterprise. Overall, the plan's success in actually changing ownership through privatization was very modest and was confined to a few managerial and worker buy-outs of small and medium-sized enterprises. The federal government in reality admitted its failure in 1991 by extending for the second time the initial one-year deadline for preparing enterprise privatization plans. Since the implementation of the plan depended on the republican administrations, there were regional differences. Major divergences emerged as the new, post-election governments came to power in the republics during 1990. All the new republican governments reconsidered the federal privatization plan with varied results (Bicanic 1992). Slovenia suspended its application, but by not passing any privatization legislation of its own froze the process (Cvikl *et al.* 1993). Croatia, after freezing the federal plan in 1990, passed its own privatization legislation in April 1991 and applied it from June 1991 onwards. It chose to abolish socialized ownership and opted for state-controlled, revenue-oriented privatization with a deadline for enterprises submitting privatization schemes and extensive incentives for employees to become small shareholders (Bicanic 1993). Serbia passed new privatization legislation in August 1991 which reflected its choice of a state-dominated system which favours worker and managerial buy-outs and extensive state involvement. Institutional protection for socialized ownership remained (Bosnjak 1993). Macedonia and Bosnia-Hercegovina did not pass their own privatization legislation, but while the latter slowed down the application of the federal one the former accelerated it (Bicanic 1992). As a result, institutional segmentation emerged as firms in individual constituent republics increasingly faced a different institutional framework.

While the patterns of privatization were increasingly varied, the changing ownership structure due to market entry from new private firms was broadly similar. Grass-roots privatization was a result of liberalizing market entry which led to a mushrooming of new private firms in foreign trade, consumer services and trade.

The track record of the macroeconomic stabilization package had limited success as well. After briefly lowering inflation rates (which some attribute to the previous 'four anchors' stabilization policy) a new inflationary spiral started getting under way. The application of policies varied in constituent republics. Constituent republics (1) showed different degrees of enthusiasm in implementing monetary austerity (this they did by overlooking 'grey money expansion', i.e. inter-enterprise promissory notes, debts and loans); (2) had differing attitudes towards the unofficial economic activities of the socialized sector and government (regarding which there was an old and established strong nexus between business and government); (3) postponed imposing financial discipline (thus maintaining the soft budget constraint); and (4) continued to monetize republican and federal budget deficits. As a result of (4), fiscal reform did not get under way at either the federal or the republican level. Of course, these policies led to major regional policy-induced asymmetric effects and redistributions in which the slowest (and least interested) stabilizers gained.

The remaining aspect of segmentation concerns market segmentation proper, fiscal and legal discrimination and, finally, loss of control over the money supply. Market segmentation took the form of the erection of trade barriers to inter-republican trade (Uvalic 1993). The government of one republic (Serbia) followed up the consumer boycott it orchestrated in autumn 1989 with internal tariffs in October 1990 for goods from Slovenia and Croatia. Fiscal discrimination was more widespread and practised by most republics. It took the form of a refusal to transfer federal revenues collected by the republics to the federal budget (Serbia stopped transferring the sales tax in September 1990, while Slovenia and Croatia stopped transferring or paying federal taxes in February 1991), collection of tariffs (by Slovenia in 1991) and property tax discrimination (non-Serbian enterprises paid higher real estate taxes in Serbia than domestic firms). Legal discrimination was more widespread. This enabled many enterprises with plants in more than one republic to break up and become one-republic enterprises. Usually the break-up was a unilateral decision of plants to break away from a head office in another republic. Even though completely illegal it was tolerated and the new firm reregistered as a new one. The policy was most widespread in Serbia, but other republics followed in a more modest way. Sometimes enterprises from different republics organized plant ownership swaps, leaving them as one-republic enterprises (Bicanic 1992). The monetary system (Uvalic 1993) broke down in December 1990 when one republican bank (Serbia's) surpassed its credit limits in the National Bank of Yugoslavia by 50 per cent and thus started unilaterally following its own expansionary monetary policy. The independent supply of central bank credit by a republican central bank prevented any monetary policy and led to redistributions from the more to the less financially disciplined republics. The only resort was monetary independence. During segmentation this was chosen by two republics. Slovenia introduced its currency in October 1991 with the excuse of wanting to pursue its own macroeconomic stabilization policy (Mencinger 1993). Croatia introduced its currency in December 1991, stating that it had to defend itself from imported inflation and the redistributive drain to which the differential inflation rates were leading (Skreb 1994).

Macroeconomic divergence

Increasing market, fiscal, monetary and institutional segmentation has led to different macroeconomic developments in each of the constituent republics. Not only have the negative growth rates of production and real wages and the positive growth rates of unemployment and inflation been varied, but the differences have grown over time. As a result, during segmentation there has been an increasing divergence of key macroeconomic aggregates in the constituent republics (Table 8. 1).

Economic differences between Yugoslavia's constituent republics did not start with the transition. The disparities in the level of development between the regions have been well documented. Perhaps most importantly, the regions show divergent economic growth paths. In spite of major internal redistributions the gap between the developed and less developed regions grew during the whole post-war period (Ottolenghi and Steinherr 1993). These differences are such that they spawned three sets of explanations for Yugoslavia's break-up. The first and most widespread approach (e.g. Dubravcic 1993) interprets the differences in levels of economic development as the main cause of the break-up. The second (Mihailovic 1981) sees the lag of some regions as the result of redistributions which have become unsustainable. The third (Bicanic and Skreb 1994) connects these increasing differences to the economy's failure to generate sustained economic growth ever since its amalgamation in 1918 in spite of numerous growth-promoting policies.

Table 8.1 Economic divergence during segmentation (1989–91)

	1 Aggregate GDP change	2 1989 p/c income	3 1989 ppp* p/c income	4 Rate of unemploy- ment	5 Consumer price index
Bosnia- Hercegovina	—	1609	3590	17.0	—
Croatia	49.0	3182	7110	14.1	123.0
Macedonia	78.7	1581	3330	24.5	115.0
Slovenia	87.6	5675	12,520	10.1	115.0
Yugoslavia	80.4	2158	4630	21.4	188.0

* ppp = purchasing-power parity

Sources:
1. 1991 level with 1989 = 100, source: *Economic Bulletin for Europe*, no. 45 (1993), Geneva: UN, 1994; and for Croatia *Bulletin*, National Bank of Croatia, no. 10–12/1993.
2. Marsenic (1992).
3. *PlanEcon*, vol. 6, no. 52 (28 December 1991).
4. December 1991 level, source: *Economic Bulletin for Europe*, no. 45 (1993).
5. December 1991 level, source: *Economics of Transition, Statistical Tables*, vol. 1, no. 3 (1993); and for Yugoslavia Nikolic (1992).

Economic divergence during segmentation is not part of long-term growth or related to the level of development. It is a result of the economics of transition and the post-transitionary crises. In spite of these differences, until economic transition started all regions reacted uniformly to economic policies and they exhibited the same economic cycles. With economic transition the uniform reaction to policy breaks down, especially as regards readiness to implement it. These differences are transparent and backed by formal decisions of representative bodies. In this sense economic segmentation is different.

Re-contracting negotiations

Negotiations for recontracting the relationship among constituent republics began in January 1990. They started after the results of the multi-party elections of 1989 had changed the political climate in the constituent republics and after the federal presidency had changed its composition to reflect the results of the multi-party elections. The participants in these negotiations were the delegations of constituent republics and the federal presidency. Initially two proposals were made, one for a stronger federal system and the other for a loose confederation. They were joined by the third compromising attempt of a two-track, partially federative partially confederative solution. All the proposals are published in *Yugoslav Survey* (1991a, b).

Even though economic issues did not play a central role in the negotiations they had an important one. The negotiating positions concerned all aspects of passing, implementing and monitoring common economic policies and determining the policy scope for constituent republics. Given the range of negotiating positions (from various confederative and federative arrangements to increasingly centralized federations) predictable and expected differences emerged. Arguments for preventing republican and federal 'free riding', preventing regional redistributions of transition costs, strengthening central accountability to republics and concern for biased central brokerage of regional interests prevailed on one end of the spectrum. The opposite side pointed to the greater efficiency of centralized economic policies regarding their speed and decisiveness, to the negative-sum, overblown and particularist regional interests and to the greater existing expertise of the centre. Importantly, both sets of economic arguments were termed in the context of transition policies and the complexities they involve and in this sense were 'forward looking'. Another important 'forward looking' economic issue appeared in all the proposals. Regardless of negotiating positions great concern was shown for maintaining established economic links. In most cases provisions were found to protect them institutionally.

As the negotiations[6] led to an impasse and no solution was reached by a deadline, the constituent republics sought other means to pursue economic transition and stabilization. Two opted for independence and 'go-it-alone' policies (Slovenia and Croatia), another two followed the 'go-it-alone' path a little reluctantly (Macedonia and Bosnia-Hercegovina), while one (Serbia) and its somewhat reluctant ally (Montenegro) wanted to maintain as large a territory as possible under its dominance. The break-up and wars of the Yugoslav succession were the logical outcome. What makes the Yugoslav disintegration different from Czechoslovakia's dissolution and the Soviet Union's disintegration is that the latter two were based on a legal procedure and were not internally contested.

As a result of Yugoslavia's disintegration five states were created. With the international recognition of two (Slovenia and Croatia) in January 1992 the phase of segmentation ended four years after it had started. Subsequently, another two of the successor states have been recognized. Bosnia-Hercegovina was recognized in April 1992, while Macedonia's diplomatic isolation lasted into 1993. The remaining two former Yugoslav republics established a new federation in April 1992 and they remain internationally unrecognized, as do

Table 8.2 Basic macroeconomic indicators of Yugoslavia's successor states

	Area, million km²	Population 1991, million	GDP 1992 $ billion, ppp*	1992, ppp* income p/c
Bosnia-Hercegovina	51.2	4.4	(14)	(3930)
Croatia	56.6	4.7	26.3	5600
Macedonia	25.3	2.2	7.1	3110
Slovenia	20.3	2.0	21.0	10,700
Federal Republic of Yugoslavia	102.4	10.3	44.0	4200

* ppp = purchasing-power parity

Source: CIA Factorbook. Washington, DC: US Government Printing Office, 1993.

the two self-proclaimed republics declared by the Serb rebels in Croatia and Bosnia-Hercegovina and the one proclaimed by the Albanians in Serbia.

The economic divergence of Yugoslavia's successor states

With economic independence each of the five new economies embarked on its own path of economic development. The numerous differences which emerged after two and a half years of economic independence can be grouped under the following five headings: (1) the establishment of full national economic sovereignty; (2) defining transition paths; (3) macroeconomic stabilization policies; (4) changing patterns of international trade; and (5) macroeconomic changes. The first three reflect policies and their implementaion, the last two changes in the real economy. Two years after independence, regions which had for over seventy years been part of one economic space became dramatically different.

Completing economic sovereignty

Establishing full economic sovereignty in the new economies was surprisingly easy. Every one of the new national economies introduced its own currency, two of them more than once. Slovenia introduced the 'tolar' as a new permanent currency in October 1991 (Mencinger 1993), Croatia first introduced the 'Croatian dinar' as a temporary currency in December 1991 and the 'kuna' as a permanent currency in June 1994 (Skreb 1994), Macedonia introduced the 'denar' as a new permanent currency in April 1992 (Petkovski *et al.* 1993), the Federal Republic of Yugoslavia introduced a new 'dinar' in December 1991 and then a 'new dinar' in January 1992 and the 'super dinar' in January 1994 (Dyker 1993), while Bosnia-Hercegovina introduced its currency in 1991. In none of these cases, except in Bosnia-Hercegovina (whose economy collapsed and where multiple currencies were in use) and the Serb-rebel-controlled areas of Croatia, were any special difficulties registered. Inherited extensive fiscal federalism made new state budgeting easy to introduce since each successor state already had a sales tax collection system. Finally, the wars of the Yugoslav succession, by cutting mutual economic links, helped establish the new national economies. All the successor states not in conflict attempted to protect mutual trade by signing bilateral payment deals (where their trade would be trans-acted by means of special accounts) and by agreeing not to impose customs.

Divergent transition paths

The transition paths of the new economies largely continued along paths established during the period of segmentation. While they shared a common experience of grass-roots privatization, differences in the privatization of exist-ing assets and in marketization varied. Croatia (Bicanic 1993 and 1994b) remained the front-runner as regards privatization. By the deadline for enter-prise-initiated privatization almost all eligible enterprises submitted plans, and the privatization agency has dealt with most applications. Without the main features being changed, the privatization process was amended five times (to close inflationary accounting loopholes, attract foreign investors, protect small shareholders and simplify procedures). The expected revenue from privatiza-tion did not materialize and increasingly the state had to enter as buyer of last resort so that it emerged as the dominant shareholder, especially for the large firms. Most registered abuses (and their extent remains unclear) con-cerned managerial buy-outs and the attempts to purchase discount shares through 'ghost buyers' or to raise capital through managerial loans, insurance scams and bank loans. The major disappointment was the almost complete absence of foreign investors. Serbia's privatization (Bosnjak 1993) started offi-cially with the privatization legislation of August 1991, but was informally halted with the economic deterioration (hyperinflation, command economy, embargo and economic implosion). Montenegro's experience of privatization was similar (Bosnjak 1993). The law passed in 1992 has had very limited application. Slovenia (Cvikl *et al.* 1993), having frozen the federal privatiza-tion plan, could not agree on its own until late November 1992. Then it became one of the last acts of an outgoing government, while the one which replaced it started searching for a new privatization programme. As a result, Slovenia has not gone far down the privatization path, but with the announced acceleration of momentum it may catch up (Stiblar 1994). Macedonia (Petkovski et al. 1993) passed its privatization legislation in October 1992. It was part of a transitional package which included macroeconomic stabilization.

Divergent macroeconomic stabilization

An equal diversity of macroeconomic stabilization paths emerged in Yugoslavia's successor states. After independence Slovenia gave macroeconomic stability top priority and within six months reduced inflation from an October 1991 monthly rate of 20 per cent to an August 1992 monthly rate of 1.2 per cent. Inflation rate reduction was achieved (Cvikl et al. 1993) primarily by relying on monetary policy. A new currency was introduced, monetary reform (through which the National Bank achieved independence) implemented, and monetary austerity imposed. A floating exchange rate was introduced and all prices liberalized. Public expenditure was reduced and the 1991 budget deficit was 2.6 per cent of GNP (Cvikl et al. 1993). The macrostabilization policy did not include an incomes policy (this only emerged in 1994: Stiblar 1994). As a result of conservative monetary policies and decreasing public consumption while maintaining a balanced budget, Slovenian inflation rates remained low.

Croatia managed to reduce its inflation rate in its third attempt at macroeconomic stabilization (Bicanic 1994b). It failed in its first attempt in summer 1991 because it monetized the budget deficit with which it financed the war effort. When monthly inflation rates approached hyperinflationary levels (over 34 per cent monthly in October 1992) it embarked on its second attempt in December 1992. A heterodox policy of monetary austerity, incomes policy and public expenditure cuts was defined without specifying targets and with lukewarm political backing. It only briefly lowered monthly inflation rates (to 23 per cent in April 1993), but did not prevent a third inflationary cycle reaching hyperinflationary levels of 30 per cent a month by September 1993. The third attempt (Bicanic 1994a) was a 'heterodox' policy package with monetary policy targets implying severe monetary austerity, incomes controls with wage limits, foreign exchange targets and a balanced budget. Its implementation started in October 1993 when the monthly inflation rate was almost 40 per cent and within three months inflation rates were lowered. Indeed, since December 1993 the economy has experienced deflation (Bicanic 1994b).

Macedonia's first attempt at macroeconomic stabilization started in April 1992 when the monthly inflation rate was 86 per cent. Apart from introducing monetary independence the 'heterodox' policy of reliance on monetary austerity, a targeted reduction of public expenditure, a wage freeze (with exceptions) and a limited price freeze was followed (Petkovski *et al.* 1993). Three months after its introduction the monthly inflation rate was 17 per cent, and by August it was 6.6 per cent. Internal political disagreements, permitted wage increases, the Greek-imposed embargo on Macedonia and Macedonia's participation in the UN embargo on Serbia led to the beginning of a new inflationary cycle. The second macroeconomic stabilization package was introduced in October 1992. Based on an agreement with unions about wage restraint it decreased the extent of price control and devalued the currency, but attempted to maintain monetary austerity and public spending goals. With an unchanged economic environment and no external financial support Macedonia managed to maintain monthly inflation rates of around 10 per cent, thereby escaping the perils of high monthly rates.

The Federal Republic of Yugoslavia was established in March 1992. Its constituent republics are the former Yugoslav republics of Montenegro and Serbia. It showed least interest in consistent macroeconomic policies. In mid-1992 a stabilization programme with five anchors was planned for the time when UN sanctions would be lifted (Madzar 1993). All attempts at price control failed and the grey economy expanded to 30 per cent (Minic 1993). The country uprated its military effort and *ad hoc* controls were introduced. By August 1993 the Federal Republic of Yugoslavia's inflation rate reached record proportions: 1880 per cent monthly and 32,701,709 per cent annually. An attempt was made in August 1993 to recentralize the economy and to ration consumer goods (the latter failed by September owing to procurement problems: Dyker 1993). A more serious effort was made in January 1994 based on the introduction of a new currency with complete foreign currency backing. Even though it lowered inflation rates at the beginning of 1994 it was not followed up by any other measures and with the exhaustion of foreign currency reserves the government plans to introduce a new currency, this time backed by gold.

In assessing the different attempts at macroeconomic stability some similarities emerge. None of the four new economies in any of its attempts received any external financial support. The international financial community gave no loans (limiting itself to technical assistance) and no foreign private capital entered. Three (Slovenia, Croatia and Macedonia) started with no foreign currency reserves. There were initial devaluations, but during subsequent floating their currencies revalued. The same three successfully lowered their inflation rates from hyperinflationary levels within three months of the introduction of the policies (during which their currencies were revalued). The success was based on monetary austerity in all three cases, while the remaining elements of a heterodox policy varied. This was a result of lower inflation rates, which increased the demand for money through lowering the velocity of circulation

and remonetization, lowering inflationary expectations and monetary austerity. Two of them (Croatia and Macedonia) experienced more than one policy
attempt and even their current success may not be a lasting one if adequate
budgetary policies do not follow the initial success of monetary policy. Only
one (Slovenia) has managed to achieve lasting macroeconomic stabilization,
while two (Croatia and Macedonia) have to follow up monetary success with
additional policies. One (the Federal Republic of Yugoslavia) refrained from
adopting serious macrostabilizing efforts and ended up in hyperinflationary
chaos.

New patterns of international trade

The economic links between Yugoslavia's constituent republics were extensive.
With the changing of borders, every one of the new national economies found
its major trading partner was one of the successor states. During the recontracting negotiations this was clearly reflected in all the proposals tabled by
the special attention given to established links. Since the break-up was not
negotiated with independence, mutual trade got the same status as trade with
its pre-independence foreign trading partners. After decomposition the new
independent economies not in mutual conflict quickly signed special payments
regimes (mutual trade in a separate account, and refraining from customs on
traded goods).

Because of the violent way Yugoslavia disintegrated mutual (and often long-
standing) economic links changed dramatically. Macedonia became isolated
from the remaining successor states due to the wars of Yugoslav succession
(first the war in Croatia and then in Bosnia-Hercegovina), the UN embargo
on Serbia and, finally, the Greek economic blockade. As a result, Macedonia
lost its markets in former Yugoslavia. The Federal Republic of Yugoslavia faced
a UN embargo from 1992 onwards, but appropriated Yugoslav foreign reserves
of about $4 billion. It developed a foreign trade deficit.

Among the successor states the mutual trade of Croatia and Slovenia was
least affected by physical barriers and embargoes and somewhat more by war
(from the Croatian side). Changes in trade occurred under the influence of
the post-transition crises (which generally decreased exports and the demand
for imports) and new boundaries (which removed protection of mutual trade).
Both began their independence with their former Yugoslav neighbours emerging as their main trading partner. Both successfully redirected their trade on
to new Western markets. Thus by 1993, in the case of Croatia, Slovenia fell
from its rank as the main trading partner during the first year of independence to third place, behind Germany and Italy. The same is true of Slovenian
trade with Croatia.

Table 8.3 Economic divergence during independence (1992–93)

	1 Aggregate GDP change	2 1992 p/c income	3 1992 ppp* p/c income	4 Rate of unemploy- ment	5 Inflation rate
Bosnia- Hercegovina	—	—	(3930)	—	—
Croatia	90.9	2122	5600	17.2	1143.8
Macedonia	72.1	—	3110	28.6	1649.8
Slovenia	87.9	6186	10,700	15.0	42.9
Federal Republic of Yugoslavia	73.0	—	4200	25.0	hyper

* ppp = purchasing-power parity

1. 1993 level with 1992 = 100, source: *World Economic Outlook, May 1994*, Washington, DC: IMF, 1994; for Federal Republic of Yugoslavia data for 1992 only from Nikolic (1992).
2. For Croatia *Bulletin*, National Bank of Croatia, no. 10–12/1993; for Slovenia *Monthly Bulletin*, Bank of Slovenia, May 1994.
3. *CIA Factorbook*. Washington, DC: US Government Printing Office, 1993.
4. August 1993 level, source: *Economic Bulletin for Europe*, no. 45 (1993), Geneva: UN, 1994; for Slovenia *Monthly Bulletin*, Bank of Slovenia, May 1994.
5. Average 1992/93 value, source: for Croatia *Bulletin*, National Bank of Croatia, no. 10–12/1993, for Slovenia *Monthly Bulletin*, Bank of Slovenia, May 1994; for Macedonia *Bilten*, National Bank of Macedonia, no. 3/1994; for Federal Republic of Yugoslavia Nikolic (1992) and Dyker (1993).

Divergent macroeconomic aggregates

The macroeconomic divergence which started during segmentation continued once the constituent republics had achieved economic independence. The differences in economic aggregates increased even more dramatically. Two years after independence they resemble quite different economies. This is clear both from the macroeconomic data in Table 8.3 and from the institutional changes described.

The relevance of transition for Yugoslavia's disintegration

To explain Yugoslavia's disintegration, events during the segmentation phase require special scrutiny. The transition is a point of discontinuity in economic development. The economic legacy of socialism and 'socialized' ownership must be overcome and a new system developed for an institutionalized mixed ownership market economy. This requires not only short-term institutionalized changes, but medium- and long-term structural change as well. Both processes, however, have major short-term destabilizing, inequality-generating and asymmetric effects developing in an environment of falling production and consumption. The economic costs differ not only for social groups, but, at least as importantly, for regions as well. The resulting economic divergence is clearly visible from the data for economic segmentation (Table 8.1). Such developments provide strong incentives to break from the 'convoy effect' and introduce 'go-it-alone' policies.

The 'convoy effect' describes the interrelationships in defining federal transition policies during segmentation. Given the divergence, not all constituent republics are equally interested in pursuing transition and macroeconomic stabilization. Those least interested in change (and change requires building a new coalition; blocking is always easier) or those who could impose their choices on others (not all constituent republics had equal weight) can determine the speed and direction of transition in the whole federation. The 'convoy effect' thus prevents variations in transition paths and stabilization efforts and attempts to impose one solution on all the remaining constituent republics. Not surprisingly, the largest constituent republic determined actual transition paths and, equally importantly, the speed of their implementation. In Yugoslavia Serbia showed little interest in transition, especially in marketization and the hard budget constraint involved. It quite clearly attempted to slow it down and tried to avoid implementing the requirements of stabilization policies.

'Go-it-alone' policies resulted from the strong incentive to micromanage the transition in constituent republics. Both through their pro-active transition advancing policies (designed to define independent republican transition policies) and through reflexive and defensive policies (designed to prevent importing unwanted policy changes) they further increased divergence during segmentation. 'Go-it-alone' policies regularly first appear in the non-dominating constituent republic; thus they first appeared in Slovenia and then Croatia. They need not necessarily be pro-transition-motivated. Slovenia's case was pro-stabilization, that of Croatia and Macedonia was for protection from imported hyperinflation. An especially important aspect of 'go-it-alone' policies which wanted to slow down transition was their attempt to influence the economic costs, usually by monetizing budget deficits, retaining subsidies and issuing quasi-money. What both motives for 'go-it-alone' have in common is an attempt to break away from the convoy and the direction and speed it mandated. Even though the non-dominant constituent republics were the first to revert to 'go-it-alone' policies, in two cases the dominant partner embraced them.

There are three more economic reasons for divergence during segmentation and the final break-up. All three point to the greater efficiency of dealing with economic transition and macroeconomic stabilization in smaller new economies. The first concerns the need for a social consensus underlying transition and stabilization. The second relates to the fact that the break-ups decomposed the very complex policy requirements of economic transition and macroeconomic stabilization into smaller segments. The third points to the advantage of 'new beginnings'.

From the beginning (and at a time when the economic costs of transition were seriously underestimated) economists clearly saw that such a major point of discontinuity as the transition could be successfully tackled only if policies and their implementation were based on a wide-ranging social consensus. The subsequent extent of the post-transitionary crises only further underlined the importance of such a consensus. While recontracting negotiations could not (and did not) manufacture such a consensus, the new economies could. The new economies of the former Yugoslavia that succeeded in macroeconomic stabilization and transition clearly underline the importance of a social consensus. All of them managed to build such a consensus and reap the positive results.

The second issue concerns the complexity of the transition itself. Decomposing the transition into smaller and simpler policy tasks makes the transition and macroeconomic stabilization more manageable. Most importantly, it simplifies the inequality-generating and asymmetric effects of these policies. The successor states had different inherited economic structures which required different policy choices best addressed in separate economic environments. In addition, breaking up the policy into smaller and simpler goals prevented the negative spillovers which one set of policies implemented in a heterogeneous environment have.

Finally, there is the positive effect of a 'new beginning'. The need to define a new economic space with new laws and new institutions may have contributed to breaking down some barriers and entrenched opposition to transition and macroeconomic stabilization. It certainly brought about increased divergence among newly independent economies.

Notes

1. These two 'scenarios for the survival of socialism' have been named after the politician in charge of writing the report. The first was the 'Kreigher Commission Report' in 1983 and the second was the 'Vrhovec Commission Report' in 1986. While the first proposed pro-market reforms (increasing enterprise independence, introducing a hard budget constraint, limiting self-management etc.), the second was a return to basics (arguing for a return to the basic principles of self-management, limiting markets and affirming the leading role of the party). In spite of the first getting more extensive formal support, the second started the process of legislative reform which avalanched into the transition.
2. Three such 'crisis management' attempts were made. The first (and arguably most successful) attempted to introduce 'real prices and quotas' and was based on price reform (primarily for interest rates and the exchange rate), foreign trade quotas and restrictions (to deal with external imbalance) and wage controls. After initial success it was abandoned as the economic costs became apparent in the post-stabilization crises. The latter two followed in rapid succession in the late 1980s. The first of these was 'programmed inflation' and was based on pegging macroeconomic variables (interest rates, the exchange rate and some prices) to planned inflation rates (ones the government expected and hoped for). Instead of lowering inflation it led to rising inflation and macroeconomic imbalances. It was quickly followed by the 'four anchors policy', which concentrated policy on four key variables (interest rates, the exchange rate, wages and external balance). This policy was replaced before it could have any results.
3. The final policies of the transition path and the macroeconomic stabilization in fact coincided with proclamations about 'new socialism'.
4. It should be remembered that in Yugoslavia the transition was started by the League of Communists (as Yugoslavia's communist party called itself). Given the covert major differences within the party it is understandable that the laws would be hailed as a reform of socialism and not its undoing. Thus the sequencing is the opposite to the situation elsewhere, where political change preceded economic change.
5. The policies were introduced in December 1989. They are referred to as the 'Markovic Plan' after the name of the incumbent President of the Federal Executive Council.
6. One should add that negotiations about recontracting the other two post-Second World War federations, Czechoslovakia and the Soviet Union, could not find a modus for reintegration and led to the subsequent break-up of the federations involved.

References

Bicanic, I. (1992) 'Privatization in Yugoslavia's successor states', *RFE/RL Research Report*, vol. 1, no. 22, 29 May.
—— (1993) 'Privatization in Croatia', *East European Politics and Society*.
—— (1994a) 'Croatia's economic stabilization programme: a progress report', *RFE/RL*

Research Report, vol. 3, no. 22, 3 June.

—— (1994b) 'The Croatian economy: the economics of transition and stabilization in a small economy facing an adverse environment' in Kaufman (1994).

Bicanic, I. and Skreb, M. (1994) 'The Yugoslav economy from amalgamation to disintegration' in Good (1994).

Bosnjak, M. (1993) 'Privatization and entrepreneurship in the Federal Republic of Yugoslavia', *Yugoslav Survey*, no. 4.

Cvikl, M., Vodopivec, M. and Kraft, E. (1993) 'Costs and benefits of independence', *Communist Economies and Economic Transformation*, vol. 5, no. 3.

Dubravcic, D. (1993) 'Economic causes and political context of the dissolution of a multinational federal state: the case of Yugoslavia', *Communist Economies and Economic Transformation*, vol. 5, no. 3.

Dyker, D. (1993) 'Rump Yugoslavia's new economic policy package', *RFE/RL Research Report*, vol. 2, no. 41, 15 October.

Good, D. (ed.) (1994) *Economic Transformation in Central and Eastern Europe: Lessons and Legacies from the Past*. London: Routledge.

Kaufman, R. (ed.) (1994) *East-Central Europe in Transition*. Joint Economic Committee of the US Congress. Washington, DC: Government Printing Office.

Madzar, L. (1993) 'Rump Yugoslavia mired in economic problems', *RFE/RL Research Report*, vol. 2, no. 39, 1 October.

Marsenic, D. (1992) 'Some data about the Federal Republic of Yugoslavia', *Yugoslav Survey*, vol. 4.

Mencinger, J. (1993) 'How to create a currency? The experience of Slovenia', *Weltwirtschaftliches Archiv*, vol. 129, no. 2.

Mihailovic, K. (1981) *Ekonomska Stvarnost Jugoslavije*. Belgrade.

Minic, J. (1993) 'The black economy in Serbia: transition from socialism?', *RFE/RL Research Report*, vol. 2, no. 34, 27 August.

Nikolic, M. (1992) 'The economy of the Federal Republic of Yugoslavia in 1992', *Yugoslav Survey*, vol. 4.

Ottolenghi, D. and Steinherr, A. (1993) 'Yugoslavia: was it a winner's curse?', *Economics of Transition*, vol. 1, no. 2.

Petkovski, M., Petreski, G. and Slavenski, T. (1993) 'Stabilization efforts in the Republic of Macedonia', *RFE/RL Research Report*, vol. 2, no. 3, 15 January.

Skreb, M. (1994) 'Banking in Croatia', *The Vienna Institute Monthly Report*, no. 2.

Stiblar, F. (1994) 'Slovenia: a country study' in Kaufman (1994).

Stojanovic (1991) 'Yugoslavia and the IMF 1944-1990', *Yugoslav Survey*, vol. 3.

Uvalic, M. (1992) *Investment and Property Rights in Yugoslavia: the Long Transition to a Market Economy*. Cambridge: Cambridge University Press.

—— (1993) 'The disintegration of Yugoslavia: its costs and benefits', *Communist Economies and Economic Transformation*, vol. 5, no. 3.

Wyzan, M. (ed.) (1994) *First Steps towards Economic Independence*. Westport, CT: Praeger.

Yugoslav Survey (1991a), vol. 32, no. 1.

Yugoslav Survey (1991b), vol. 32, no. 3.

9 From Reform to Crisis: Economic Impacts of Secession, War and Sanctions in the Former Yugoslavia

Will Bartlett

This paper looks at recent economic performance and policy in the successor states of the former Yugoslavia in the early 1990s. The persistent economic crisis of the 1980s is outlined in the background. Some of the economic issues underlying the break-up of Yugoslavia are then briefly discussed. The main focus is on (1) the economic impacts of secession, war and sanctions and (2) policy responses in the microeconomic area of ownership reforms and restructuring and in the macroeconomic area of anti-inflationary stabilization programmes. Some conclusions are then drawn about the prospects for economic recovery and reconstruction in the region. Throughout the paper particular attention is paid to the new states of Slovenia, Croatia, Yugoslavia, and Macedonia, for which relevant information has been available. Access to information about economic performance and policy for Bosnia-Hercegovina has been much less readily available owing to the continuation of open warfare. However, references to Bosnia-Hercegovina have been made where appropriate and possible.

The background

The Yugoslav economy suffered a long crisis throughout the 1980s. The crisis was characterized by recurrent balance-of-payments problems, declining output and productivity, persistent inflationary pressures and a seemingly insoluble problem of foreign indebtedness. The Yugoslav debt had increased through-

out the 1970s, and by the early 1980s the country was unable to service it
(Stiblar 1992). The IMF encouraged the Planinc government to introduce an
austerity programme in 1982. The programme was moderately successful until
1984, but the Mikulic government relaxed the policy. In consequence, the
debt built up again until 1987 and a new crisis occurred (Bartlett 1987). A
new stabilization programme was begun in 1988, but there was fierce opposition to its harsh effects. The government lost credibility and had to resign
at the end of 1988.

Initially the new government under Ante Markovic had no stabilization
policy, but concentrated on structural reforms. The ownership structure of
the Yugoslav economy had been based upon a system of so-called 'social ownership' and workers' self-management and there was little room for private
business. The Enterprise Law which took effect in January 1989 was designed
to transform this situation. It opened the way for the development of a variety of forms of private ownership and provided equal treatment for privately-
owned and socially-owned firms. In addition, a privatization law permitted
firms to enter a process of voluntary self-privatization. Even though the structural ownership reforms stimulated an increase of entry of new private enterprises, they were too long-term to have much immediate impact on the
underlying tendency towards inflation. The economy ran into further problems, with hyperinflation at the end of 1989. In January 1990 a stabilization
package was introduced, designed to cut off inflationary pressures by a series
of short-term measures. The package involved a temporary wage freeze, a fixed
exchange rate, free market price setting and tight monetary and fiscal policies. By the middle of 1990 the package had achieved considerable success in
bringing down inflation, foreign debt was reduced, and Western financial institutions released new credits to support the economy (Bartlett 1991 and 1992).
However, as with previous stabilization packages of a similar nature throughout the 1980s, the success was only of short duration and as the wage freeze
came to an end the underlying inflationary pressures began to reassert themselves. By the end of 1990 Yugoslavia experienced the largest current account
deficit ever. In December 1990 convertible medium- and long-term debt
amounted to $16 billion. This was distributed between the republics and the
Federation itself, with the latter accounting for $3.6 billion. However, the
Federation as such had no original assets or sources of income to repay the
debt as it produced nothing except the armaments for the Yugoslav army.
Arguments about how repayments on the federal debt should be allocated
between republics provided a fertile ground for acrimonious disputes. A variety of criteria to divide the federal debt were proposed, ranging from a proportional division in relation to each republic's original debt obligations to
proportional division in relation to republican national product, exports or
imported equipment. Stiblar (1992) lists nine different criteria which had been

proposed at one time or another to divide the federal debt between the republics. Although the federal government was offered assistance by the international financial community to settle its debts the individual republics were not eligible for such support. Since most of the foreign exchange reserves were held by the federal central bank, the ability to repay foreign debts became an important issue in the debate about the viability of secessionary republics to pay their own way.

Table 9.1 Foreign debts of Yugoslav republics September 1990 (convertible area, $ million)

	Net debt	Debt ratio I	Debt ratio II
Bosnia	1144	25.4	32.6
Montenegro	589	62.3	80.1
Croatia	2237	22.0	28.3
Macedonia	741	26.6	34.2
Slovenia	1409	17.2	22.1
Serbia	2650	27.6	35.5
Kosovo	726	72.7	93.4
Voivodina	763	14.6	18.7
Federation	3609		
Total	13,868		30.1

Note: I: Original debt of republics; II: Including federal debt apportioned in proportion to original debt.
Source: Stiblar (1992).

The costs of the Markovic stabilization programme were high and unevenly distributed. Industrial production declined by 15 per cent in the year up to June 1990 and unemployment continued to increase. Various republics attempted to avoid the costs of the stabilization programme by taking measures which contradicted the federal government's intentions. Serbia, for example, introduced customs duties on imports from Slovenia and Croatia in an effort to protect the local industries, many of which were operating at a loss. In January 1991 the Serbian government funded pay increases and pensions in direct opposition to the Markovic policy, so increasing the money supply above the target levels. The dispute over the progress of the stabilization programme led the IMF to suspend a $1 billion stand-by arrangement and to the freezing of $32.8 billion of Western credits. By mid-1991 foreign currency reserves were at a dangerously low level and a debt crisis again occurred. The cycle of failed reforms and stabilization policies, IMF intervention and resurrection of familiar policy packages recurred. A fourth, but short-lived, 'shock therapy' programme was introduced in July 1991. But it was already too late to rescue the credibility of the federal government. The break-up of the country had begun.

The collapse and break-up of Yugoslavia: war, secession and sanctions

Could any of the reform packages tried repeatedly throughout the 1980s have had any success in preventing the economic collapse and gradual disintegration of Yugoslavia? Many commentators have focused on the system of self-management and social ownership as a fundamentally flawed system of industrial governance, which would eventually lead to persistent economic decline and consequent political instability. Ownership reforms were considered necessary to deal with the inherent inflationary pressures which appeared to characterize the self-managed economy. Insider employees were easily able to increase wages and prices in the knowledge that there would be no penalty in the form of reduced employment since their firms faced a soft budget constraint (Uvalic 1990) and many firms held a monopolistic position on their own republican markets. In addition, the banks, which were controlled by the enterprises, would provide credit to enterprises at negative real interest rates. This stimulated inflation (Madzar 1992).

Other commentators stressed the inadequacy of the political framework of a one-party state in a federal country with extensive decentralization of powers to regional and local levels. Under this political structure it would have been difficult for the federal government to introduce any consistent and credible macroeconomic policy under any system of property rights at the microeconomic level. The underlying inflationary trends were fundamentally linked to the secular increase in inequality between the republics of former Yugoslavia. Each republic had its own national bank and there was loose control over the money supply. By increasing the credits available to its own republican enterprises each republic attempted to lay claim to a greater share of resources, while having to bear only a partial cost of the resulting inflation. The more developed republics were more successful in this conflict and their economies pulled further and further away from those in the less developed south. The economic tensions between the republics eventually spilled over into uncontainable political conflict and eventually into secession and open warfare (initially between the breakaway republics of Slovenia and Croatia and the federal army).

Slovenia and Croatia declared their independence in June 1991. The ensuing war in Slovenia lasted only ten days (from 27 June 1991). In early July a three-month moratorium was agreed with the EU. When this ended in October a new currency (the tolar) was introduced. Slovenian independence was finally recognized on 23 December 1991. The war in Croatia lasted a year and was far more destructive. As soon as a truce had been signed in

Croatia, Bosnia-Hercegovina declared independence in February 1992. Full-scale war broke out in Bosnia in April 1992 following international recognition of the new state. Macedonia declared independence in 1991, but was only formally recognized by the UN in April 1993. Macedonia has so far been spared the trauma of being caught up in armed hostilities, but political tension in the new republic remains high, not least because of a serious diplomatic dispute with its most powerful neighbour, Greece. In April 1992 the remaining republics of Yugoslavia reconstituted themselves as the Federal Republic of Yugoslavia, consisting of the republics of Serbia (including the former autonomous provinces of Kosovo and Voivodina) and Montenegro. Serbia was by far the dominant partner in the new federation. In protest at the Yugoslav support for and involvement in the war in Bosnia, UN sanctions were promptly imposed on the Federal Republic of Yugoslavia (FR Yugoslavia) in May 1992.

The economic impact of secession, war and sanctions

ECONOMIC PERFORMANCE 1989–93

Yugoslav GDP already started to decline at the end of the 1980s. The continuing long economic crisis had been one of the causes of discontent that had led to the break-up of Yugoslavia and the subsequent wars of secession. However, these events themselves led to an even greater and more disastrous decline in economic activity. The decline in GDP plumbed new depths in Slovenia, with a fall of 9 per cent in 1991, before a slow recovery began to take place in 1993. Elsewhere the picture has been one of continuous decline. In Croatia GDP fell by 16 per cent in the war year of 1991, and although the decline since then has not been so precipitate, it has nevertheless continued. In both the FR Yugoslavia and Macedonia the decline has been worse and worse with each passing year. In Bosnia-Hercegovina no statistics on the scale of the disaster are available, although it is clear that the effects of war must have been even worse than elsewhere. Nevertheless, even there local agreements have sometimes been able to maintain levels of economic activity, as in the Bihac region where trade agreements between the opposing factions for a time insulated the local economy from some of the worst effects of the war. Indeed, probably the greatest losses have come from the disruption of trade between surplus and deficit areas rather than from the breakdown of the production system itself.

The reform programme of 1990 under the Markovic government had succeeded in bringing down inflation from seriously high levels in 1989 throughout Yugoslavia. But, as we have seen, the cost was incurred in falling levels

Table 9.2 GDP growth (% pa)

	Slovenia	Croatia	FR Yugoslavia	Macedonia
1989	−1.8	−1.6	−0.6	
1990	−4.7	−8.6	−8.4	−10.2
1991	−9.3	−15.5	−11.1	−12.1
1992	−6.0#	−12.9	−26.1	−13.4
1993	1 .0#	−3.2	−30.0	−15.0

Source: Slovenia: *EBRD Economic Review*, July 1993, and *Bank of Slovenia Monthly Bulletin*, May 1994 (#); Croatia: *EBRD Economic Review*, July 1993, and National Bank of Croatia; Macedonia: EBRD; FR Yugoslavia: CESMECON (1994).

of economic activity. After the onset of the war in 1991 the level of price inflation again began to increase, as the national banks in Croatia and Serbia struggled to finance the war budget by deficit financing. The imposition of UN sanctions on the FR Yugoslavia only exacerbated this tendency and monthly inflation reached 1,000,000 per cent in December 1993, the highest rate of hyperinflation ever recorded. The real incomes of pensioners, the unemployed and public sector workers in the FR Yugoslavia fell to less than $5 per month. In August 1993 the government introduced price controls and a black market emerged. By the end of December 1993, most articles were being purchased on the black market.

Table 9.3 Consumer price inflation (% pa)

	Slovenia	Croatia	FR Yugoslavia	Macedonia
1989	1306	1200	2644	1346
1990	550	610	124	708
1991	118	123	231	215
1992	201	664	19,830	1791
1993	32	1517	3.5×10^{13}	335~

Note: ~ Estimate.
Source: Slovenia: *Bank of Slovenia Bulletin*; Croatia: *EBRD Economic Review*, July 1993, and National Bank of Croatia; FR Yugoslavia: FRY Statistical Institute; Macedonia: *Macedonia Basic Economic Indicators*, Statistical Office of Macedonia, May 1993.

The reduction in the levels of economic activity was accompanied by rising levels of unemployment. However, owing to the practice of maintaining job stability, unemployment did not increase as much as one might have expected. It was only in Slovenia that a genuine shake-out of labour took place (Bartlett and Uvalic 1992). This contributed to an increase in the competitiveness of Slovenian industry and the eventual return to positive economic growth. In the FR Yugoslavia, by contrast, the state maintained high levels of overmanning, despite the precipitous collapse of industrial production. It is estimated that some 1,250,000 workers still in employment are actually redundant, but the government does not permit lay-offs while sanctions are in force. It is estimated that only 600,000 of these posts can be considered genuine temporary redundancies, that is, ones which could be rescued if sanctions were lifted (CESMECON 1994). Hence the official figure of 720,000 registered unemployed should be increased to 1,370,000. On this basis the real unemployment rate at the end of 1993 was 47 per cent of the labour force. In Macedonia registered unemployment increased from 150,000 in 1989 to 172,000 in 1992. In fact there are now more unemployed than there are employed in the entire industrial sector. By 1993 the registered unemployment rate had reached 28 per cent. However, in view of the sharp fall in economic activity there can be little doubt that, as in the FR Yugoslavia, there are also substantial numbers of 'hidden unemployed' among the labour force in the social sector of the economy, who keep their jobs more for political than for economic reasons.

Table 9.4 Unemployment rate (%)

	Slovenia	Croatia	FR Yugoslavia	Macedonia
1989	2.9	8.0	18.7	22.0
1990	4.7	9.3	21.3	22.9
1991	8.1	14.7	22.4	n.a.
1992	11.6	15.4	24.6	n.a.
1993	14.5	14.5	24.6	28.0

Notes: Data for FR Yugoslavia calculated from data for the former republics of Serbia including Kosovo and Voivodina, and Montenegro. Unemployment is measured as a percentage of the workforce employed in the social sector and registered unemployed.
Source: Slovenia: *EBRD Economic Review*, July 1993, and *Bank of Slovenia Bulletin*; Croatia, Macedonia: *Statisticki Godisnjak Jugoslavije*, 1990, 1991, National Bank of Croatia and EBRD; FR Yugoslavia: FRY Statistical Institute.

The secession of Slovenia was backed up by an already favourable performance in the area of foreign trade. Throughout the period of conflict Slovenia has been able to maintain a positive balance on the current account. In Croatia, however, there was a trade deficit in both 1990 and 1991. Remarkably, the current account was brought into surplus in 1992. More than 80 per cent of exports are now traded with Western economies and foreign exchange reserves were built up to $167 million by the end of 1992, to $340 million by May 1993 and to $1.1 billion by August 1994. Owing to sanctions the foreign trade of the FR Yugoslavia has collapsed. Apart from smuggled goods, exports are banned and imports consist only of humanitarian commodities such as food and clothing. (There are reports that Croatia and the FR Yugoslavia trade in substantial amounts of oil and electricity.) Macedonia has historically run a current account deficit and trade has been substantially reduced due to the double embargo.

Table 9.5 Current account balance ($USm)

	Slovenia	Croatia	FR Yugoslavia	Macedonia
1989	1100	4.8		−149
1990	600	−0.2		−496
1991	200	−10.1		−171
1992	929#	5.4~		−62
1993	196#	n.a.		n.a.

Note: ~ Estimate.
Sources: Slovenia: *EBRD Economic Review*, July 1993, and Bank of Slovenia, *Monthly Bulletin*, April 1994 (#); Croatia: *EBRD Economic Review*, July 1993; Macedonia: *Macedonia Basic Economic Indicators*, Statistical Office of Macedonia, May 1993.

THE EFFECTS OF SECESSION

Secession can be expected to have a number of economic effects on the economies of a former federation. These effects involve the disruption and redirection of trade patterns, the effects of restrictive macroeconomic policies which accompany the introduction of a new currency, and the fiscal changes associated with cessation of inter-regional equalization grants. The economic impact of these effects can be distinguished according to their short-run negative costs and their long-run positive gains. In the Yugoslav case these have been partly obscured by the effects of war and sanctions. However, the pure effects of secession can be seen most clearly in Slovenia. Although Slovenia was affected indirectly by the wars in Croatia and Bosnia-Hercegovina, the war on Slovene territory lasted only ten days and the economy was spared the scale of war damage which occurred elsewhere. And although war and sanctions deepened the losses associated with redirecting trade away from traditional markets, this effect would eventually have occurred in any case as a by-product of Slovenian independence and the long-run trend towards the fragmentation of the Yugoslav market. The short-run costs of secession in Slovenia were experienced as a rapid decline in production. Since 36 per cent of Slovenian trade went to the rest of the former Yugoslavia in 1987 it is not surprising that the short-term trade effects of secession would be severe. These were no doubt exacerbated by the effects of war and sanctions. In any case, the fall in GDP, which had already been taking place, speeded up after the secession, the balance of payments deteriorated and unemployment rose sharply. The initial focus of stabilization policy was in the area of restrictive monetary instruments (designed to support the introduction of the new currency) and the M1 money supply actually fell in the first month after secession (Cvikl, Vodopivec and Kraft 1993). Nevertheless, inflation was gradually brought under control and in the absence of further external shocks the economy began to regain lost ground. By 1993 the Slovenian economy was one of the few economies in eastern Europe to register a positive rate of GDP growth.

THE EFFECTS OF WAR

The direct effects of the fighting have been felt mainly in Croatia and Bosnia-Hercegovina. It is estimated that between 1991 and 1992 some 6000 people died in the war in Croatia and 21,500 were wounded. The effective size of the country was reduced by one-third as the Serb-held areas proclaimed their independence. Several cities were completely destroyed and over a quarter of a million people were displaced from their homes. Between a quarter and a third of industrial plant was destroyed or severely damaged, including eleven thermal and hydro-electric plants (Valentic 1993). Economic losses were especially severe in leather processing, textiles, metal manufacturing, machine-building and food processing. In addition, heavy losses were sustained in agriculture. More than 120,000 head of cattle, 65,000 sows, 14,000 horses and 230,000 sheep have been killed or taken away. At least 30,000 tractors and other farm implements were destroyed or lost. The losses in agriculture are estimated at around $4.5 billion. Infrastructure losses have also been extensive such as in telecommunications, oil and gas pipelines, airports (Dubrovnik, Zadar and Osijek), and ships on the Sava, Drava and Danube. The total direct losses are estimated at $20 billion, and equal the pre-war GDP for 1990 (Hromatko 1993). One of the most serious economic effects of the war has been the disruption of communications between the north of the country and the Dalmatian coast, which is virtually cut off by the continuing of hostilities on part of the main coastal road. This severance of the country and the continual threat of warfare has destroyed the tourist industry along most of the Dalmatian coast. Many tourist facilities are given over to refugees and their families. Overall, Croatia has the highest burden of refugees next to Bosnia, as measured by the proportion of refugees in the population (see Table 9.6).

The impact of the war can be seen in a comparative perspective from Figure 9.1, which shows the indices of industrial production in Croatia and the FR Yugoslavia from 1991 to 1993. Before the war began these two indices moved more or less synchronously. However, from the beginning of the war in June 1991, the index of industrial production for Croatia fell sharply below that for the FR Yugoslavia. The two indices did not reconnect until the end of the war and the start of sanctions against FR Yugoslavia.

Table 9.6 Refugees (1992)

	Number	Per cent of population
Slovenia	70,000	3.5
Croatia	725,100	15.8
Serbia	414,500	4.2
Bosnia	681,000	15.1
Montenegro	57,600	9.6
Macedonia	31,300	1.5

Source: Kukar (1993).

THE EFFECTS OF SANCTIONS

Sanctions against the FR Yugoslavia were imposed in May 1992 and strength-ened in August 1992 and again in April 1993. Following the collapse of the most recent negotiations on the war in Bosnia-Hercegovina they were to be strengthened again in August 1994. The embargo is not a total blockade. Medicines and certain foodstuffs are not affected, although their sale should be notified to the UN Sanctions Committee in New York. Other goods are authorized on humanitarian grounds including clothing, detergent, and other goods which contribute to personal survival. This means that luxury imported clothing can be found on sale in Belgrade shops. Despite some popular mis-conceptions, this is not a violation of the sanctions regime. Over 1000 lor-ries a week cross the border from Bulgaria and Hungary loaded with authorized and notifiable goods. Transit across the Macedonian border is a different case. Although only 800–900 lorries cross over this border, many contain goods which violate the sanctions regulations. However, the trade is controlled by the Macedonian government and even this border could not be described as an open door. The operational unit which monitors the embargo is known as the Sanctions Assistance Mission Communications Centre in Brussels (SANCOM). It co-ordinates seven international teams of customs officers on each of the borders of the FR Yugoslavia. According to officials of SANCOM, the embargo is one of the most effective there has ever been, and has led to extreme shortages of all types of manufactured goods. The shortage of oil is particularly severe and SANCOM officers report that it is a common prac-tice for individuals travelling across the border to carry petrol in soft drink cans and other dangerous forms of carriage. Other indications of the effec-tiveness of the embargo are not hard to find. As can be seen from Table 9.7, economic activity has fallen to less than half the level achieved in 1989 and the standard of living has experienced a similar decline. By July 1993 the real wages of university professors had fallen to the equivalent of $18 a month, to $15 for military officers and to $5 for army privates. Agriculture has been least affected and, although agricultural output fell by 15 per cent in 1992, it remained unchanged in 1993. Owing to the resilience of the agricultural economy, farmers are to some extent protected from the effects of the embargo and it is the urban population, especially those with least connection with farming, who have really lost out. This may well explain the loss of political support for the government in the cities and the resilience of that support in the countryside.

Table 9.7 Output decline in FR Yugoslavia

	GMP ($ billion)	Growth rate (%)	GMP per capita
1989	24.6	−0.64	2300
1990	22.7	−8.4	2200
1991	19.0	−11.1	1800
1992	14.0	−26.1	1300
1993	10.0	−30.0	900

Source: CESMECON (1994).

In addition, the effectiveness of the embargo can also be seen from the movements in monthly index of industrial production. Figure 9.1 compares these data for Croatia and the FR Yugoslavia.

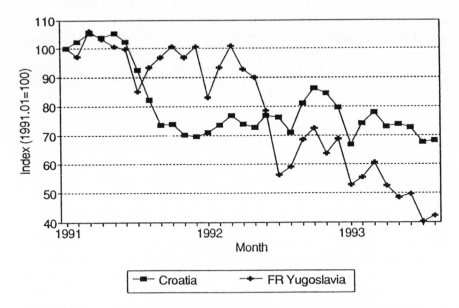

Figure 9.1 Index of industrial production, Croatia and FR Yugoslavia

The index for the FR Yugoslavia dropped below that for Croatia for the first time in June 1992, immediately following the imposition of the UN embargo. In 1993 alone industrial production declined by 37.7 per cent, largely owing to the effect of sanctions. Since the import content of most industries is relatively high (about 30–40 per cent), the lack of imports has been fatal for them and the most import-dependent industries suffered to the greatest extent. During 1993 the output of the pharmaceutical industry fell by 72 per cent, ferrous metallurgy by 71.4 per cent, shipbuilding by 68.3 per cent and motor vehicle production by 65.2 per cent, and a decline in excess of 50 per cent was recorded in oil derivatives, ferrous metals, metal processing machinery, electrical apparatus and textiles.

Although the effect of sanctions was serious in the FR Yugoslavia, they also affected the surrounding countries. One of the most seriously affected has been Macedonia which, as a republic of the former Yugoslavia, conducted up to 80 per cent of its trade across the Macedonian–Serbian border. In addition to the disruption of trade across this border, the Macedonians have also suffered from a separate embargo directed against them by Greece. This was first imposed in 1992, in protest against the title of the new state to which Greek nationalists objected. It has continued intermittently since then and has been imposed with particular tightness since February 1994. The disruption of trade routes through the former Yugoslavia has increased transport costs significantly. Re-routing trade flows through Bulgaria to the Black Sea, back through Romania, Hungary and to the West puts approximately an extra DM 1000 on transport costs per truck.

Economic policies

PRIVATIZATION
Croatia was the first republic to press ahead with its own privatization law, which was introduced in April 1991. Two agencies were set up, the Privatization Fund and the Privatization Agency (later to be merged into a single Privatization Fund in November 1992). The method of privatization was mainly through internal sale of enterprises to their employees, with substantial discounts related to length of service. The small privatization programme for enterprises with assets of less than DM 5 million was relatively straightforward. For other enterprises the deadline for autonomous privatization expired in July 1992. By then about two-thirds of the 3900 social sector enterprises in Croatia had submitted privatization proposals. However, relatively few of these proposals were approved, and these were mainly the small and medium-sized social enterprises covering only 27 per cent of the workforce. No large social sector enterprises have yet been privatized. The privatization programme has been criticized

as offering unfair advantages to insider management teams, who were often able to buy the enterprises on the basis of undervalued assets. In addition, there were frequent instances of political interference by the Privatization Agency, which in some cases replaced the existing management team with others more closely linked to the governing party, a procedure especially problematic in the case of media enterprises (Bicanic 1993). Enterprises which did not meet the July 1992 deadline were converted into state-owned enterprises. Over 100 new state enterprises were created in sectors such as utilities, railways and public services, employing altogether 15 per cent of the labour force. However, this did not solve the underlying soft budget problem as these firms could still pressure banks to cover their losses. In addition, even those enterprises which were privatized often had a high share of state participation through the ownership shares of the two state Pension Funds and the Croatian Fund for Development (Cuckovic 1993).

In Macedonia, a privatization law was passed in June 1993, and came into force in July 1993. The approach adopted by the government was based largely upon the direct sale of enterprises (Zografski 1993). The opposition parties proposed that more weight should be given to the free distribution of shares to employees and to workers in social services. The law was fiercely contested in the Assembly, with over 300 amendments being tabled. In the event only one was adopted. A new Privatization Agency will be established on the basis of the existing Agency, which was originally established in 1989 under the Markovic government. The part of the programme which is most likely to succeed is the 'small privatization', one through which relatively simple rules are to be drawn up for the privatization of up to 970 small and 350 medium-sized socially-owned firms. Anyone can buy these small enterprises, either outright or in instalments over five years. Alternatively the enterprises can be sold through an employee buy-out of at least 51 per cent of social capital (Zografski 1993).

In Slovenia, privatization legislation was passed in November 1992, but the first decrees were not issued until March 1993. A mixed approach to privatization was adopted, which permitted the direct sale of enterprises, employee purchase of shares, or share transfers (up to a maximum of 20 per cent to investment companies, 10 per cent to a Compensation Fund and 10 per cent to the state Pension Fund). Enterprises were given until the end of 1994 to register their preferred privatization plan. More recently a mass privatization programme has been introduced with the licensing of investment funds to collect ownership certificates from citizens for buying shares in the socially-owned enterprises.

SMALL BUSINESS DEVELOPMENT

Slovenia has been a path-breaker within the former Yugoslavia in terms of policies towards small business development and is one of the few countries in Eastern Europe to have established a Ministry of Small Business. It has a number of active programmes in place designed to promote the development of the small business sector. Small enterprises in Slovenia now produce 13 per cent of turnover (GDP), and account for 38 per cent of investment and 6.1 per cent of employment. In 1992 there were over 16,000 registered private companies. In addition there are 70,000 employed in craft firms. This represents 10 per cent of all employment and they produce 8 per cent of turnover. Taken together, small enterprises and craft firms employ 150,000 people in 38,000 small firms, out of a total workforce of around 700,000. According to Maks Tajnikar, the Minister for Small Businesses, 50 per cent of new starts survive for more than five years. This is a higher survival rate than in most Western countries and indicates both a lack of competition in the Slovene market and the relatively low-level risk faced by the small firms. The Ministry of Small Business (since incorporated into the Ministry of Industry) is trying to develop new measures to promote small firms. To begin with, they have lifted the restrictions on the number of employees which a firm can have. New laws are being prepared to regulate small firms and to bring both craft firms and small enterprises under the same legislative umbrella. A number of measures have been proposed by the ministry. In 1991 a fund to promote small business was established to provide loan guarantees and it also subsidizes some loans provided by the banks. The fund has the equivalent of DM 2 million available for such purposes and capital of DM 8 million overall. Around 200 firms received assistance from the fund by the end of 1992. In addition, the ministry's finance centre is organizing a consortium of Slovene banks to provide a venture capital fund for small firms. Aid for small business development from the EU's Phare programme was initiated in August 1992. The ministry has also been engaged in developing support networks for small firms, involving the Chamber of the Craft Sector, the Chamber of Commerce and local governments ('local communities') in the network. There are 54 local funds based in these local communities, with a total capital available of DM 10 million. In conjunction with the network partners they are trying to organize and manage a number of other activities, for example, innovation centres, training, entrepreneurship programmes, women in entrepreneurship and contacts with business fairs. In addition, the ministry has established a foreign relations department. It has a Ecu 2.1 million programme financed by Phare. This is designed to support small business and involves some technical assistance from the UK.

In Macedonia, the small business sector is also being built on an established base of small firms, although policy towards their further development is less advanced than in Slovenia. Estimates made by the Economics Department of Skopje University suggest that there are probably around 20,000 functioning private enterprises actively trading. Of these, 64 per cent are registered as private enterprises; 31.2 per cent are registered as limited liability companies; 1.3 per cent are registered as socially-owned enterprises. As a result of the rapid increase in the number of private firms, the great majority (92.8 per cent) of all enterprises are in private ownership; only 2.8 per cent are in social ownership and a further 2.5 per cent are in mixed ownership (i.e. with part of equity in social capital, part held as private capital). A mere 1.8 per cent of enterprises are organized as co-operatives. The predominant activity of enterprises is in commerce. A sectoral breakdown shows that 64.5 per cent of enterprises are in commerce, 9.4 per cent in industry, 7.3 per cent in financial and other services, 4.2 per cent in the craft sector, 3.5 per cent in agriculture and 3.4 per cent in construction. It is estimated at present that the small business sector accounts for only about 10 per cent of industrial output. It accounts for 22 per cent of revenues and 17 per cent of employment. In consequence of the difficulties of collecting taxes from small firms, it provides only 6 per cent of public revenue, and contributes only 1 per cent of the state pension fund and 1 per cent of the health care fund.

Table 9.8 Growth of the private sector (number and %)

	Slovenia⁻	Croatia	FR Yugoslavia (%)	Macedonia
1990	7935	17,350+	20.1	7234
1991	13,309	32,051+	21.3	15,280
1992	16,141	54,684+	26.6	37,232
1993		66,091#		44,589

Notes: ⁻ Excluding 'craft firms', + December, # April.
Sources: Croatia: The State Statistical Institute, Zagreb; Macedonia: Statistical Office of Macedonia; Slovenia: Prasnikar and Valencic (1992); FR Yugoslavia: CESMECON (1994).

The small private business sector is also developing rapidly in Croatia, where there is the largest number of registered small firms of any of the former republics, although it is estimated that only half of these are actively trading. At the end of 1992, just over one tenth of the labour force in Croatia was employed in private firms, mainly in trade and services (Cuckovic and Kalodjera 1993). Data are not available for the number of small firms in the FR Yugoslavia, but the slow growth in their number is indicated by the increase in the share of registered firms in the private sector from 20 per cent in 1990 to 27 per cent in 1992.

Overall, this form of 'bottom-up' transformation will probably provide the most important basis for the development of the private sector in view of the slow pace of formal 'top-down' privatization in most of the republics of the former Yugoslavia.

STABILIZATION AND ANTI-INFLATION POLICIES

The most successful post-secession stabilization policy is to be found in Slovenia. The introduction of the new currency in October 1991 helped to insulate Slovenia from the inflationary trends emerging elsewhere in the former Yugoslavia. A new central bank law was passed and a strict monetary policy introduced (Pleskovic and Sachs 1994). This involved the introduction of an extremely high real interest rate. In addition a tight fiscal stance resulted in budgetary surpluses of 2.7 per cent of GDP in 1991, 0.1 per cent in 1992 and 1.5 per cent in 1993. These measures helped to stabilize prices and the exchange rate, but led to a sharp short-run reduction in output and employment. It was not until 1993 that the real fruits of the policy began to emerge as output began to increase in Slovenia, in contrast to the steep declines in output which continued to plague the rest of the country.

Croatia was faced with equally difficult problems of macroeconomic stabilization when it became independent in 1991. Foreign exchange reserves were virtually zero and a strategic aim of economic policy was to build up these reserves. Bank deposits of foreign currency were frozen. The deposits were converted into long-term government debt which could be drawn on only to buy housing units from the state (Jones 1994). Inflation threatened to get out of hand in 1993 with prices rising at a monthly rate of 28 per cent, and an anti-inflationary policy was introduced in October. A three-phase approach was adopted beginning with disinflation. Only after this phase was successfully completed was it intended to move on to the second phase of structural reforms (including further privatization and demonopolization) and eventually to the third phase of reconstruction. The main elements of the first phase of the anti-inflation programme included a restrictive monetary policy, a restrictive fiscal policy, an incomes policy, removal of exchange controls and the introduction of internal currency convertibility (Jurkovic and Skreb 1994). The aim was to eliminate inflationary expectations through a sharp elimination of price increases. Monetary policy operated on the basis of a quantitative restriction of base money, combined with a low central bank base rate, which was reduced to 3 per cent per month. Limits to personal purchases of foreign exchange were removed. Monetary policy was so restrictive that commercial banks soon ran out of dinars to exchange for foreign currency on the newly liberalized foreign exchange market. Many businesses began to complain that they could not pay their employees. A dinar auction was introduced to ration the domestic money supply. Banks were free to set their own exchange rate and the National Bank built up sufficient reserves to be able to intervene in the market in order to stabilize the exchange rate. By November the dinar had actually appreciated by 10 per cent. An important element of the policy was wage restriction. The total wage bill was to rise by no more than 25 per cent in October and by 4 per cent in November and December, although there were no restrictions on wages paid in the private sector. In addition, the indexation of wages and pensions was abolished. The idea was that once inflation had been stabilized, the loss-making state enterprises could be restructured. The policy enjoyed a remarkable degree of success. Inflation fell from 38 per cent a month in October to 1.4 per cent in November and prices began to fall in December and January 1994, remaining stable thereafter. However, living standards also continued to fall and there is some doubt about the willingness of the labour force to accept the incomes policy. Nevertheless, by May 1994 the situation was stable enough to permit the introduction of a new currency, the Croatian kuna, a symbolically important break with the past.

In the FR Yugoslavia an anti-inflation programme was introduced at the beginning of 1994, following elections in December 1993 (which returned the Socialist Party of Serbia with a minority of seats and forced the governing party into a coalition with the tiny New Democracy party). The Program of Economic Recovery of Yugoslavia (January 1994) halted new base money production and introduced a new dinar (the 'super dinar'), which was pegged at 1:1 with the DM. New money creation was to be completely backed by foreign currency reserves and was freely convertible in domestic banks. The government was also committed to a fixed exchange rate. The old dinar remained in circulation, but was not convertible into the new dinar. The new currency was placed on a gold standard regime. By dipping into the country's gold reserves, more than 100,000 gold coins were produced, worth about 150 dinars each. They were used to pay the farmers and to avoid printing dinars to pay for the wheat crop, a key factor in stimulating the previous hyperinflation. The programme was extremely successful in eliminating inflation and prices have since remained stable. Industrial production began to recover and in June 1994 had increased by 2.3 per cent over the level recorded at the beginning of the year (CESMECON 1994), although this only compensated marginally for previous losses.

In Macedonia, an anti-inflation policy was adopted in April 1992 to arrest a tendency towards hyperinflation, which had earlier become apparent from February onwards. As elsewhere, the policy combined restrictive monetary and fiscal policy with a wage freeze which pegged wages to the level of March 1992; there was also a partial price freeze (Petkovski et al. 1993; Wyzan 1993). A new currency, the denar, was introduced, and the exchange rate was stabilized. Monthly inflation dropped from 86 per cent in April to 70 per cent in May and 17 per cent in June. However, the uncertain political situation undermined the programme and the parliament voted for an increase in wages for public sector workers. This happened just as Greece began its embargo against Macedonia. Industrial production fell sharply in 1992: estimates of the extent of the fall vary between 15 per cent (EBRD, 1994) and 50 per cent (Petkovski *et al.* 1993). The new government formed in September 1992 (with Branko Crvenkovski, leader of the Social Democratic Alliance, as prime minister) continued with the stabilization efforts. However, these programmes have been criticized for failing to establish an appropriate monetary policy. The policy failed to control the growth of money supply due to the practice of offering special 'selective' credit to the agricultural sector (Wyzan 1993). A new set of measures were introduced in December 1993 which for the first time had the support of the international financial agencies. Selective credits were phased out by the end of March 1994, and the core rate of inflation was reduced to 2 per cent per month. The programme has a greater chance of success than previous efforts owing to the availability of international assistance through the international financial community (including the World Bank and the IMF). However, the continuation of the Greek embargo and UN sanctions against the FR Yugoslavia will create major difficulties for the Macedonian economy and will probably undermine this latest stabilization policy.

Prospects

Prospects for future economic prosperity depend much more on the conditions for a political settlement than on the adoption of almost any conceivable economic policy. This is not to say that domestic economic policies have no effect in conditions of war, sanctions and secession. In those cases where the successor states have adopted restrictive monetary and fiscal policies they have been able to overcome tendencies towards hyperinflation which have emerged under these circumstances and, at least for a time, to stabilize output even in apparently intractable circumstances such as those prevailing in the FR Yugoslavia. However, long-term reconstruction can hardly follow from such policies alone and Slovenia is likely to be the only republic able to recover and develop in the absence of a generalized peace agreement.

Attempts at economic reconstruction were already being made in Croatia at the end of the war without any external assistance. There, the government has established a Ministry of Reconstruction, which was transformed into the Agency for Reconstruction in 1992 (with about 50 regional or local offices in different parts of the country). The Croatian Credit Bank for Reconstruction was established in mid-1992. The bank has financed 33,000 projects in housing and business premises repair (DM 40,000), twelve infrastructure projects in 1992 and 1993 (DM 27 million), fourteen economic projects worth DM

18 million, a small public service project worth DM 26,000, a livestock breeding project (DM 9.5 million) and grants to municipal authorities worth DM 5 million. Croatia was admitted to the IMF in December 1992, to the World Bank in February 1993 and to the EBRD in April 1993 (Hromatko 1993). Following the success of the stabilization policy Croatia negotiated a $192 million credit from the IMF in October 1994, designed to underpin further assistance from other multilateral institutions. But the division of the country and the loss of much of the tourism industry will be a long-term burden on the Croatian economy.

In the FR Yugoslavia, as in Macedonia, little can be done in the way of reconstruction under the present conditions of international sanctions and blockade, although since war damage has not been an issue, these economies could potentially enjoy a fairly rapid recovery once trade routes are again opened up.

It is in Bosnia-Hercegovina, where the worst effects of the war have been experienced and which has effectively ceased to exist as a unitary state, that prospects for the future look most bleak. Even if the war were to end, the country would be reliant on massive international aid for at least a decade to enable economic reconstruction to take place.

Slovenia has clearly come out of the process of break-up in the most favourable position and a process of economic recovery has already begun. The Slovenian experience suggests that secession carries short-run costs, but, because of the reorientation of macroeconomic policy it permits, also carries the possibility for long-term benefit. The ownership reforms have been slow to take place in Slovenia, although there has been substantial entry of new small private firms. This suggests further that rapid privatization is not a prerequisite for successful transformation of a self-managed market economy. The most important element required is monetary stability and the opening up of the economic system to a plurality of ownership forms.

Cvikl, Vodopivec and Kraft (1993) argue that in Slovenia the long-run gains of secession will offset the short-run costs, but it is hard to see how this conclusion can be extended to the former Yugoslavia as a whole. Many years of substantial economic growth will be required, even in Slovenia, to make good the losses that occurred in the early 1990s. Elsewhere in the former Yugoslavia it seems that it will be well into the next century before the region is likely to regain the levels of prosperity that, in 1989, made the country look like the best prospect for successful transition to Western-style capitalism in Eastern Europe.

Acknowledgements

I am grateful to Taki Fiti, Marko Skreb, Boris Begovic, Vesna Mukaetova, Nevenka Cuckovic, Janez Prasnikar, Simona Svetec and Max Watson for providing essential information in the preparation of this paper.

References

Bartlett, W. (1987) 'The problem of indebtedness in Yugoslavia: causes and consequences', *Rivista internazionale di scienze economiche e commerciali*, vol. 34, nos 11–12.

—— (1991) 'Economic change in Yugoslavia: from crisis to reform' in Sjöberg, Ö. and Wyzan, M. (eds) *Economic Change in the Balkan States: Albania, Bulgaria, Romania and Yugoslavia*. London: Pinter.

—— (1992) 'Foreign trade and stabilization policy in a self-managed economy: Yugoslavia in the 1980s' in Allcock, J., Horton, J. and Milivojevic, M. (eds) *Yugoslavia in Transition: Choices and Constraints*. Oxford: Berg.

Bartlett, W. and Uvalic, M. (1992) *Economic Transition, Unemployment and Public Policy in the Former Yugoslavia in the 1980s*. Bristol: Centre for Mediterranean Studies Occasional Paper no. 6.

Bicanic, I. (1993) 'Privatization in Croatia', *East European Politics and Societies*, vol. 7, no. 3.

CESMECON (1994) *Economic Developments in FR Yugoslavia*. Belgrade: CESMECON.

Cuckovic, N. (1993) 'Privatization in Croatia: what went wrong?', *History of European Ideas*, vol. 17, no. 6.

Cuckovic, N. and Kalodjera, D. (1993) *Regulatory Environment for the Growth of the New Private Enterprise in Croatia*. Reform Round Table Working Paper No. 4, Institute for Development and International Relations, Zagreb.

Cvikl, M., Vodopivec, M. and Kraft, E. (1993) 'Costs and benefits of independence', *Communist Economies and Economic Transformation*, vol. 5, no. 3.

EBRD (1994) *Transition Report*. London: European Bank for Reconstruction and Development.

Hromatko, I. (1993) 'Losses and reconstruction', *Razvoj / Development International*, vol. 8, no. 1.

Jones, C. (1994) 'The havoc of war', *The Banker*, January.

Jurkovic, P. and Skreb, M. (1994) *Financial Reforms in Croatia*. NBC Working Papers. Zagreb: National Bank of Croatia.

Kukar, S. (1993) 'Causes and consequences of the refugee problem in Slovenia', *Migration*, no. 19.

Madzar, L. (1992) 'The economy of Yugoslavia: structure, growth, record and institutional framework' in Allcock, J., Horton, J. and Milivojevic, M. (eds) *Yugoslavia in Transition: Choices and Constraint*. Oxford: Berg.

Petkovski, M., Petreski, G. and Slaveski, T. (1993) 'Stabilization efforts in the Republic of Macedonia', *RFE/RL Research Reports*, vol. 2, no. 3.

Pleskovic, B. and Sachs, J. (1994) 'Political independence and economic reform in Slovenia' in Blanchard, O., Froot, F. and Sachs, J. (eds) *The Transition in Eastern Europe: Country Studies*, vol. 1. Chicago: University of Chicago Press.

Stiblar, F. (1992) 'External indebtedness of Yugoslavia and its federal units' in Richter, S. (ed.) *The Transition from Command to Market Economies in East-Central Europe*. Boulder, CO: Westview Press.

Uvalic, M. (1992) *Investment and Property Rights in Yugoslavia: the Long Transition to a Market Economy*. Cambridge: Cambridge University Press.

—— (1993) 'The disintegration of Yugoslavia: its costs and benefits', *Communist Economies and Economic Transformation*, vol. 5, no. 3.

Valentic, N. (1993) 'On the reconstruction and development of Croatia', *Razvoj / Development International*, vol. 8, no. 1.

Wyzan, M. (1993) 'Monetary independence and macroeconomic stabilization in Macedonia: an initial assessment', *Communist Economies and Economic Transformation*, vol. 5, no. 1.

—— (1994) 'Macedonia' in Wyzan, M. (ed.) *First Steps towards Economic Independence: New States of the Postcommunist World*. Westport, CT: Praeger.

Zizmond, E. (1993) 'Slovenia – one year of independence', *Europe–Asia Studies*, vol. 45, no. 5.

Zografski, E. (1993) 'Privatization in the Republic of Macedonia'. Paper presented to the Round Table on Economic Transition in South East Europe, Skopje: Development Fund of the Republic of Macedonia, 27–28 April.

10 Nationalism and the Post-1989 Transition to Democracy and Market Economies in the Balkans: a Historical Perspective

Robert Bideleux and Ian Jeffries

Introduction

There are certain essential requirements for a fully consummated transition to stable, liberal, pluralistic democracies and healthy competitive market economies in the Balkans. These include the creation (or revival) of 'civil society'[1] and, above all, the firm establishment of impartial ('neutral') states and the rule of law, resting upon and underpinned by broad and inclusive 'civic' (rather than narrow and exclusive 'integral' or 'ethnic') conceptions of citizenship, statehood and nationhood. The latter is not just the most crucial requirement, but also the most difficult to accomplish. If it is not achieved, all attempts to attain inter-ethnic peace and reconciliation, political and economic stabilization, inward investment and closer links with the West (especially the European Union) are likely to be frustrated or to go awry. Conversely, if it is achieved, the difficult tasks of promoting inter-ethnic peace and reconciliation, political and economic stabilization, capital inflows, reconstruction and gaining fuller acceptance into the wider political and economic community (especially the European Union) will be made much easier. The Balkan states are not richly endowed with either natural resources or physical capital and this makes their people (human resources), even more than normal, their most precious asset. Hence the overriding importance of re-establishing their inter-ethnic, political and social relations on a more secure, fairer and more reassuring footing, in order to encourage their various social and ethnic groups to subscribe to a shared set of political and economic institutions, laws and 'rules of the game' and to pull together to attain economic and social reconstruction.

This paper, through the perspective of history, seeks to identify the kind of society which we believe to be most conducive to healthy democracy and market economies in the Balkan countries today. The key words are *tolerance* in society and *pragmatism* in the handling of the transition to market economies.

'Civil society' and the role of the state in the transition

Precocious pockets of 'civil society' did emerge in the interstices of Balkan society during the nineteenth and early twentieth centuries, notably among the predominantly commercial and professional German and Jewish minorities, as the development of capitalism and education stimulated the growth of autonomous professional and business activities and associations, especially among the monied, educated and independent-minded ethnic minorities. There was also a growth of autonomous mercantile activities among the larger ethnic groups in the Balkans during the eighteenth and nineteenth centuries. Balkan merchants sponsored the expansion of education, publishing, political activities and autonomous 'national' intelligentsias, who, in turn, saw themselves as the champions and apostles of the emerging Balkan nations in the ensuing struggles for 'national liberation' from 'alien' Ottoman, Habsburg and Tsarist imperial rule. Once the Balkan nations attained independent statehood, however, these nationalist merchants and intelligenti naturally tended to become servitors or clients or protégés of the new 'national' states, in which they automatically acquired a more exalted status as key constituents of the now dominant ethnic groups. Thus they tended to be less autonomous or independent of the state than the leading members of certain ethnic and religious minorities, including the Hungarian minorities in Transylvania and Vojvodina, the Italian minorities in Dalmatia and Slovenia and the Greek minorities in Albania, Bulgaria and Romania, as well as the Balkan Germans and Jews. Moreover, the Balkan Orthodox Churches had ancient traditions of collaboration with and subservience to the state, be it Byzantine, Ottoman or 'national'. In the Balkans (as in Russia), the Orthodox Churches were quintessentially statist churches. None of them nurtured or represented a civil society independent of the state, challenging it or providing an alternative source of authority, in the way Catholic and Protestant Churches did in western Europe or (to a lesser extent) Lutheran, Calvinist and Catholic Churches did in the northern Balkans. In the newly independent Balkan states, as in the previous imperial polities, there was in effect no major source of authority other than (or independent of) the state itself and the church that served it. These were the historical roots of the predominantly subservient or collaborationist orientations of the ascendant Balkan Orthodox Churches, 'national' bourgeoisies and 'national' intelligentsias, which lingered on in even more emasculated forms under communist rule and still impede the growth of (independent) civil society. This relative lack of (independent) civil society was a factor encouraging authoritarianism.

It was also unfortunate that the fledgeling would-be democracies and 'national' states of the inter-war Balkans were governed by a political class weaned on centuries of often indirect, venal, corrupt and nepotistic imperial rule (Byzantine as much as Ottoman). Their main institutions were generally controlled by 'national' leaderships who upheld increasingly narrow, exclusive and intolerant 'integral' or 'ethnic' conceptions of the state and the nation. They favoured 'native' capitalists, professionals and intelligentsias (who were increasingly dependent on state patronage and political nepotism) and gradually 'froze out' or discriminated against the more autonomous, cosmopolitan and independent-minded ethnic minorities (indeed, the word 'cosmopolitan' eventually became a term of abuse and an anti-semitic euphemism for 'Jew'). Thus there came to be no possibility of a 'neutral' state, one that fairly and uniformly upheld and applied the law without ethnic, racial or religious bias or favour. In practice there was one law for the ethnic minorities and other 'outsiders' and another (very bendable) law for the ruling clientele. Patronage, nepotism and clientelism prospered at the expense of (weak) civil institutions and marginalized ethnic and social groups, particularly as chronic political and economic instability, the rise of European fascism, mounting threats to national security and the 1930s Depression intensified the trends towards inward-looking 'ethnic' and 'economic' nationalism and etatism.

The post-1918 land reforms, which assisted the emergence of independent peasant smallholder agriculture and radical peasant parties and co-operative movements, initially appeared to offer the best hopes and prospects for the development of political and social pluralism, civil society, libertarian values and local autonomy in the inter-war Balkans, especially in Romania, Croatia and Slovenia. (Unfortunately, Bulgaria's important peasant party lapsed into brutality and authoritarianism under its charismatic leader Aleksandur Stamboliski between 1919 and 1923, and it never fully recovered from the subsequent right-wing backlash and repression and fears that it might revert to authoritarian rule again if it ever returned to power. It damaged the political prospects of peasant parties throughout the Balkans, but not irreparably so. The Croatian Peasant Party went on to become the major party in Croatia, while the liberal Romanian National Peasant Party won a massive electoral victory in 1928, only to be stymied by the onset of the 1930s Depression and the rise of fascism.) In the end, however, the relatively loose, diffuse and rudimentary organization of the peasant parties and co-operative movements were no match for the more concentrated power and wealth of the often corrupt industrial and banking interests who were much better placed to guard their privileged positions in the state and in the economy, to monopolize state patronage and gradually fragment and suppress the independent activity and representation of the peasantry, using a combination of repression and 'salami tactics'. This pattern was to be repeated in the aftermath of the Second World War and there is the danger that it could happen again today. After several decades of communist industrialization, the industrial lobbies today are now unquestionably much bigger and more powerfully organized and connected to the state than they were between 1918 and 1945 and even stronger *vis-à-vis* the re-emergent (but proportionately less important) private farmers.

The few remaining pockets of autonomous 'civil society' in the Balkans were largely destroyed during the Second World War, not least through genocide against Jews and other ethnic minorities. After the war most of the Jewish survivors (sooner or later) emigrated either to the West or Palestine/Israel, while most of the remaining Balkan Germans eventually left for Germany, if they had not already done so. The new host nations were enriched at the expense of the old. The post-war neo-Stalinist regimes in the Balkans soon completed the work done by illiberal nationalists and fascists, bringing all public activities and institutions under one-party control and destroying the last vestiges of 'civil society' and state 'neutrality'. Balkan politics during the 1940s was extraordinarily violent and bloody. Large-scale resistance to foreign occupation in Yugoslavia, Albania and Greece was accompanied and probably exceeded by internal 'civil' (i.e. extremely uncivil) warfare and settling of old scores between communists and anti-communist nationalists and between mutually antagonistic ethnic groups during the Second World War. In the later 1940s, in the wake of these wars, the newly established Balkan communist regimes executed many thousands of actual or alleged 'fascists' and 'collaborators', while Greece resumed its devastating civil war between communist and anti-communist nationalists with barely a break. The tattered remains of the old independent-minded professional and business groups and of the pre-war liberal intelligentsias were either liquidated by communist purges or swamped by raw, new, wholly subservient 'creative' and 'technical' intelligentsias, formed by (and dependent upon) state and party patronage. The latter were in large measure recruited from the ranks of the proletariat and the peasantry, thereby 'creaming off' and 'buying off' potential leaders and spokesmen of the proletarian and peasant opposition and discontent at the same time as creating new intelligentsias that consciously owed their positions and privileges to communist patronage. Thus the major political problem in the post-communist Balkan states is that 'neutral' political and civil institutions either have never existed or were destroyed by the combined effects of intolerant authoritarianism, fascism, the 1930s Depression, the Second World War and communist dictatorship, all of which to a large extent destroyed or drove abroad the social and ethnic groups which could most readily produce or recreate an autonomous, pluralistic and liberal-minded 'civil society'.

'Civil society' cannot, by definition, be created or recreated 'from above', that is, by state action. That would be a contradiction in terms or a form of 'incorporation' leading to a 'corporatist' monolith rather than autonomous pluralism. Creatures of the state tend to remain subservient to the state. In the Balkans, however, it is conceivable that the exhaustion, insolvency, retrenchment and atrophy or creeping sclerosis of the post-communist state will of itself cede or vacate many 'social spaces' which can (and should) be filled or taken over by autonomous social groups, associations and individuals outside state control and direction, creating or re-creating the vital social foundations for political and economic pluralism. Over and above their immediate private aims, ambitions and motives, professionals, legitimate entrepreneurs, writers, journalists, broadcasters, intellectuals, universities, trade unions and farmers' organizations now have a historic opportunity and a civic responsibility to maximize their autonomy and self-reliance and to minimize their dependence on the state, in order to secure the conditions in which vigorous, free and pluralistic democracies and market economies can flourish. Their performance in this regard will determine their countries' futures, at least as much as the volume of Western assistance and the more technical aspects of managing the transition to competitive market economies. In this sense the future is in their own hands. If they pass up this historic responsibility and opportunity, they will be the first to suffer and they will only have themselves to blame, for the construction or reconstruction of vigorous, autonomous and pluralistic 'civil society' is not something that can be done for them by the state or politicians or Western aid. Indeed, in the post-communist Balkans the state itself does not have the resources or capacity to control every activity, solve every problem and meet every economic and social need. Nor should it either attempt or be expected to do so, as that would be the fast track back to authoritarian 'corporatism' and paternalism.

Thus it is important to acknowledge the inherent limitations of the post-communist state (even with democratically elected and honest governments) and to recognize the dangers of expecting it to do more than it is capable of doing. *Both* the politicians who direct the state *and* their constituents need to see the state not as the universal controller, arbiter and provider, but as a relatively 'neutral' or impartial setter and upholder of free, fair and widely accepted political and economic frameworks and ground-rules within which (to avoid anarchy and the insidious rise of criminality) groups, associations and individuals should strive to conduct their affairs, resolve their problems and differences and meet their economic and social needs as autonomously as possible. The state which attempts to do, provide and resolve everything runs the risk of arousing excessively high expectations, overheating the economy, overloading the public services and over-stretching its fiscal resources. Nevertheless, we are not advocating a 'minimalist' role for the state. What we are doing is warning of the acute dangers posed by expecting too much of the state, especially when so much of the existing state apparatus has been inherited from a rather murky past and the rule of law is not firmly entrenched. But the state still has an important role to play in the transition, for example, labour retraining schemes, social welfare provision and control over the privatization process (in order to prevent abuse by state enterprise managers and other members of the former *nomenklatura*). We see a vital role here for large-scale Western technical aid in helping the transitional states develop an honest, politically neutral and efficient civil service, legal system and regulatory system (apart from helping retrain workers and managers and helping finance a social safety net to shield the many 'losers'). A generous attitude by the EU in opening up its markets to goods from the Balkan states is also necessary for an export-led recovery to be attainable.

It is interesting to see how the debate on handling the economic transition has changed over the past four years. We have always been sceptical of the wisdom and feasibility of attempting a 'big bang' solution, that is, a rapid and comprehensive change in the economic system. (Typically the term 'shock therapy' is used in a broad sense to include not only changes in the economic system but also the severe austerity measures necessary for macroeconomic stabilization. But we believe that 'shock therapy' is a term best reserved for the latter only; for example, the claim in 1993 that Russia had not undergone 'shock therapy' only makes sense if this narrower definition is used. Clearly, chronic inflation has to be tackled as a matter of urgency. But in general, any adverse effects on output and employment must be taken into account and care must be taken to ensure that 'the punishment fits the crime', that is, that the magnitude of stabilization measures is proportionate to the scale of the inflationary problem.) In the early 'heady' days, the proponents of the 'big bang' approach were generally too optimistic about the time needed to adjust (e.g. for the creation of the necessary institutional framework of a market economy) and the costs involved in the transition. But we are equally aware that doing next to nothing ('Ukrainianization', referring to the early years of Ukrainian independence) brings about economic catastrophe. Moreover, the rhetoric often conceals considerable agreement in a new area of economics in which clear definitions are hard to come by and theorists have, as usual, attempted to impose neat categories on a messy world. In this context it is worth noting that the free-marketeering but pragmatic Prime Minister of the Czech Republic, Václav Klaus, has engineered a remarkably successful and rapid transition while using subsidies to avoid sudden, large-scale bankruptcies and lay-offs. Obviously not 'everything' can be done 'at once' (nobody has ever suggested this) and there is no one solution to the many differing circumstances facing individual countries. But we see merit in the idea of (1) a 'critical mass' of co-ordinated measures on a sufficient scale to provide an irreversible and ongoing momentum to the reform process and (2) a credible programme for which a democratically elected government must seek and maintain popular approval (as rightly stressed by the United Nations Economic Commission for Europe: 1993: 9). Many of the alleged protagonists would probably agree that as much as possible should be done as quickly as possible, but this raises all sorts of questions. The debate, it seems to us, boils down to the question of what is politically and economically feasible. But choosing the appropriate blend and scale of measures best suited to individual countries is a political art, best exemplified by the pragmatism shown by Klaus.

Klaus has been a consistent advocate of pragmatism. In an article published in 1992 he stated the following:

> We know that just as an economy cannot be centrally planned, so an economic transition cannot be centrally planned and administered. The economic transition is a process with many forces, many constraints, many policies. We have to react, and react rationally ... So the sequencing issue very often discussed in economic literature is partly artificial, a rationalistic illusion of the intellectuals. (Cited in Jeffries 1993: 338)

It is worth quoting at length Klaus's more recent reflections on the first five years of transition:

> Communism was so evil, so oppressive and so inefficient a system of government that no country could ever hope to move on and create a normally functioning society and economy until it had undergone a comprehensive and painful transformation. Such a change takes years to complete; it cannot be accomplished merely with some sort of overnight shock therapy ... For the countries of Central and Eastern Europe, the important thing is to push ahead with the process of self-transformation, and to resist any temptation to settle for half-measures or to make useless political and social concessions. The reforming politician must guard against 'reform fatigue'.

Klaus then warns that such a politician

> must be able to formulate a clear and lucid vision of a future which is both attractive and achievable; he must explain this vision to his citizens and defend it against populists of all shades; he must implement a consistent reform strategy and introduce unpopular and painful measures as and when they are needed; and he must

not defer to rent-seekers and lobbyists who pursue their own short-term advantage to the detriment of society as a whole.

One must take into account the fact that the transformation of any society

is a complex and dynamic process, not merely an exercise in applied economics or political science ... A system of political parties has to be created as a means for achieving a basic political and economic consensus ... To privatize, deregulate and liberalize, and yet to retain an appropriate degree of macroeconomic stability: such is the essential aim. Most of Europe's post-communist countries have already introduced a first set of reform measures.

Unfortunately, Klaus believes,

some have done so hesitantly or inconsistently, falling short of the critical mass of reforms needed to change the basic system and so deliver some tangible results. Where that is so, initial euphoria has evaporated and with it the early mood of national unity; in some cases there is a high degree of political instability.

Finally, Klaus tackles the problem of the role of the state:

The totalitarian practices of communism and the irrationalities of state-owned and centrally planned economy were easy to criticise. That does not mean, however, that it is now easy to find an optimal equilibrium point in the real world between the freedom of individuals and the need for regulation by the state – not to mention by supranational institutions. (*The Economist*, 10 September 1994, pp. 45–6)

With de-industrialization proceeding rapidly and given the particular importance of agriculture in the Balkan states, we think it vital to stress the need to provide appropriate infrastructural support to private agriculture in such forms as clear property rights, credit institutions, efficient marketing structures and extension services. We feel there are important lessons to be learned from the past. Cochrane (1993) has written that 'To the extent that the land reforms of the 1920s failed to improve conditions for the rural population, it was because this necessary support was lacking' (p. 855).

Land reforms of the 1920s failed to alter significantly the structure of agriculture. One reason is that the reforms in many cases were not fully implemented; but another reason ... was the failure ... in most cases ... to follow up the land reforms with the institutions needed to support the new farmers ... extension services throughout the region were virtually unheard of.

Even in Bulgaria, where Stamboliski promoted a more extensive and effective system of co-operatives and credit institutions, 'overall government policies tended to favour industry' and 'state investment favoured non-agricultural sectors' (p. 851). While Bulgaria, Czechoslovakia and Croatia, for example, had well-developed networks of co-operatives, many of which provided credit to farmers, 'the effectiveness of these institutions was often greatly circumscribed by government policies that tended to tax agriculture ... Other countries, notably, did not even provide this limited support to farmers' (p. 853). We have an uncomfortable feeling that, in this as in some other respects, history is repeating itself. The growth of agricultural output in 1993 in Albania and Romania was very encouraging, but sustained progress still requires infrastructural support and growing internal and external markets.

The rule of law

Liberal parliamentary democracies and free market economies rest upon the rule of law, including such principles as equality before the law, the legal accountability of ministers, officials and firms, the legal enforceability of property rights and contracts, legal safeguards against arbitrary arrest and dismissal, and legally protected rights of expression, assembly and association. Moreover, parliamentary democracy rests on a form of social contract, ideally one that is freely and clearly articulated and accepted by all sections of the population and embodied in a constitution or constitutional law. Much of the Western economic advice given to the post-communist states seems to have taken for granted the very things that they (to varying degrees) lack most: 'civil society', politically and ethnically impartial states, and the rule of law (including an infrastructure of enforceable 'capitalist' commercial, company, financial, taxation, labour and trade union laws). The rule of law is a prerequisite for the proper functioning of democracies and market economies, not just internally but *a fortiori* in their international relations and transactions. There is an ongoing debate about the relationship between 'democratization' and 'marketization', but it is clear that, if they are to be fully consummated, both require the rule of law (or a *Rechtstaat*, a law-governed society) and a state that is politically and ethnically 'neutral' or impartial in its maintenance and enforcement of the rules, laws and contracts on which both democracy and the market system depend. A *Financial Times* editorial of 12 November 1993 (p. 17) rightly emphasizes the following:

> Markets need rules and they need an effective state to enforce them, but they are endangered by the arbitrary exercise of power ... A legal system subordinate to the executive, along with a corrupt judiciary, offers a poor environment for the development of market economies ... Contracts become impossible to enforce reliably. Credit becomes hard to get and expensive, because it is difficult for lenders to pursue claims for collateral. Without a proper institutional background, long-term

private investment ... will, in these days of free global movement of capital, find another home.

The crucial advantages which have placed Poland, Hungary and the Czech Republic well ahead of the Balkan states in the post-1989 transitions to democracy and market economies and at the front of the queues for eventual admission to the EU and NATO are not so much their significantly higher levels of education, skill, technology and economic development as the fact that they have become relatively law-governed societies in which the legal underpinnings of democracy and the market system are upheld and enforced in a politically and ethnically 'neutral' fashion. This is also what has made them the preferred locations for Western companies and investment in Central and Eastern Europe.

Democracy and a market economy can function after a fashion without the full application of the rule of law and civil society can exist without any rule of law, but then all three will fail to develop fully or to realize their full potential. In parts of Italy and Greece, for example, the rule of law is honoured more in the breach than in the observance and both states experience massive tax evasion. Yet northern Italy has a highly developed 'civil' society despite its weak rule of law. However, in so far as the state is unable (or unwilling) to enforce the rule of law, substitutes have to be found. Businessmen have to use other means of enforcement of property rights and contracts. These include (1) 'strong-arm' tactics, 'protection rackets' and other 'mafia'-type sanctions (not necessarily voluntarily employed by businessmen); (2) insistence on 'cash-on-delivery', avoiding the use of banks and credit; (3) reliance on private bonds of trust, such as family ties. The examples of Italy, Greece and many Latin American states provide useful reminders that such supposedly transitional phenomena may turn out to be more or less permanent features of society.

The rule of law has acquired an added significance in relation to the EU. As a voluntarily entered and law-governed association of liberal parliamentary democracies which have accepted and established a 'single market' and a number of 'common' institutions and policies, the EU rests upon a supranational rule of law, involving the uniform application and acceptance of a common set of laws, policies and legally binding treaty provisions. Therefore states which are not essentially law-governed, market-oriented liberal democracies cannot be accorded full membership of the EU. Indeed, only such states can reap all the benefits of participation in the international community in the widest sense.

The two Europes: 'civic' versus 'ethnic' nationalism

Western European politics is essentially in a post-nationalist phase (in this respect, as in several others, Greece remains more Balkan than western European). There is no denying that nationalism is still a potent, vibrant force in areas such as Wales, Scotland, Northern Ireland, the Basque country and Catalonia, but, even within Britain and (to a lesser extent) Spain, nationalism is largely confined to the fringes of western European politics. Moreover, except for a few violent extremists, the ethnic minorities in western European states for the most part accept (and operate within) the laws and the political 'rules of the game' of the larger polities in which they are embedded. In the main they champion their 'national rights' and 'national causes' through legal channels, including the ballot box, the media, the law courts and parliamentary debate. Conversely, those who legally and non-violently champion the rights and 'national causes' of ethnic minorities in western Europe are not denounced or assaulted or prosecuted as 'traitors' and 'fifth columnists', as they sometimes have been in Serbia, Croatia, Bulgaria and Greece in recent years. In contrast to the recurrent outbreaks of racist violence against Turkish and non-European immigrants in western European cities, however, the historic inter-ethnic disputes in western Europe have come to be conducted for the most part within the law and on the basis of considerable mutual tolerance and respect. One side can flatly disagree with what the other side says and yet defend the right to say it, so long as there is no recourse to violence or terrorism (as there is by ETA and the IRA).

The prejudice, discrimination and violence against Turkish and non-European immigrants in many western European cities in recent years represents an altogether different ball game, an expression of racism and xenophobia rather than nationalism in the state-building, nation-building, territorial mould. It poses serious dangers for western European democracy, but, as with European anti-semitism, no states, territories or borders are in dispute. The crucial point is that the great majority of western European 'nation-states' have long completed the processes of state-building and nation-building which are still the stock-in-trade of eastern European politics. Only in Belgium, northern Spain and possibly the UK does there appear to be a remote possibility that the existing polity could wholly unravel and the processes of state-building and nation-building begin anew. For the vast majority of western Europeans, politics has become largely concerned with prosaic 'bread and butter' issues such as unemployment, inflation, taxation, pensions, education and health care. It rarely concerns more inflammable, primordial matters such as ethnicity, the nature of the state and the nation, national security, territorial claims, border disputes, the plight of co-nationals in neighbouring states or (except in Italy) the levels of incompetence, corruption or criminality of the state apparatus.

These matters are generally regarded as 'settled'.

Likewise the EU is mainly concerned with mundane issues of 'low politics' (such as trade, farm price support, health and safety regulations, the environment and student exchanges) rather than with more emotionally charged issues of 'high politics'. Indeed, the EU was mainly created in order to defuse (and to a large extent lay to rest) the issues of 'high politics' which had repeatedly convulsed western Europe between 1870 and 1945. In western Europe since the 1950s it has been possible for the consolidation of relatively tolerant and inclusive 'civic' nations to proceed without fear, secure in the knowledge that neighbouring states are doing likewise and pose no threat. In south-eastern Europe, however, it may prove to be as difficult to build tolerant, liberal, inclusive 'civic' nations and 'civic' nationalism in states that are surrounded by strident, intolerant and exclusive 'ethnic' nationalism as it was to try to build 'socialism in one country' in a hostile capitalist world.

In the western European nations which have attained stable, comfortable and secure statehood since the 1950s, nationalism has lost much of its former emotive force and its power to mobilize opinion. It has largely become either a harmless and ineffectual form of nostalgia, a clinging to comforting illusions and to symbols and reminders of an idealized vanishing past, or a ritual, often jingoistic commemoration of wartime heroics (although even this is slowly dying away as the last generations of World War veterans 'pass out' for the last time). Most western Europeans adhere or subscribe to a hierarchy of identities, loyalties and emotional attachments revolving around their family, locality and local community, the region and the state in which they reside, their national and/or ethnic self-identification and a consciousness of being in various senses 'part of Europe' or 'European'. Family, locality, local community and region engender identities, loyalties and attachments which are just as 'real' or strong or fraught with practical implications as those generated by state, national and ethnic allegiances. Moreover, the things that western European nations hold in common, along with the high levels of cultural and biological inter-penetration and cross-fertilization of European nations, outweigh the differences that hold them apart (especially in the eyes of non-Europeans).

Nationalism and the primacy of national identities, loyalties and attachments may have performed 'functional' roles in the integration of 'national' markets, in the transference of sovereignty from monarchs to peoples and parliaments and in the era of warfare based upon huge conscript armies and obligatory 'national service', which began with the *levées en masse* to defend *la patrie en danger* during the French revolutionary wars of the 1790s. But in late twentieth-century Europe, market integration and the necessary scale of economic activity have far outgrown the narrow confines of national markets, while sovereignty is no longer vested in monarchs. In these respects nationalism has outlived its usefulness. Today, moreover, western European states neither base their military security on, nor fight wars with, huge conscript armies. Instead, professional soldiers and military engineers deploy capital-intensive high-technology weapons, with the result that most citizens are no longer expected to be ready to die for their nation and no longer receive any military training. In this respect, too, old-fashioned nationalism has become functionally and technologically redundant or obsolete. But in south-eastern Europe, unfortunately, communist regimes maintained large conscript armies and obligatory 'national service' long after they had been abandoned in most western European states. Furthermore, the resurgence of south-eastern European nationalism, combined with the reopening of long-suppressed territorial disputes and eruptions of armed conflict within and between post-communist states since 1989, has revived or reinstated actual or potential battlegrounds. As a result, nationalism and 'national' calls to arms have again been pressed into service to persuade growing numbers of people to fight and to be ready to die for their embattled nation ('right or wrong'). Moreover, the post-1989 economic disintegration and economic crises have precipitated scrambles to safeguard 'national' markets and 'national' economic resources, including land, industries and mineral rights. These forms of economic nationalism hardly encourage Western investment.

Unfortunately, Balkan politics is still very much in a state-building, nation-building nationalist phase and is likely to remain so for one or two decades to come. The seemingly solid, settled and secular (albeit repressive) polities created by communist rule have unravelled and, in the case of the former Yugoslav Republics, the projects of state-building and nation-building have virtually begun all over again. In matters of political language and discourse, the clock has been turned back fifty or more years. What is more, the nationalism which generally pervades Balkan politics is mainly a narrow, intolerant, exclusivist, quasi-religious 'integral' or 'ethnic' nationalism rather than a broad, tolerant, inclusive, secular 'civic' nationalism of the sort that prevails in western Europe. This contrast, over and above any legal, economic or technical impediments, is the fundamental obstacle to the Balkan states becoming credible candidates for membership of the EU in the foreseeable future. The nationalistic politics of the Balkans is wholly out of step with the post-nationalist politics of western Europe. We fully concur with William Pfaff's view that there still exists a fundamental cultural and 'moral' barrier to the unification of eastern with western Europe:

> The crucial distinction today is between those Europeans who believe in ethnic politics, ethnic exclusion and an intolerant ethnic nationalism and those who understand that the members of a common European civilization owe themselves and each other a commitment to national reconciliation – and to a liberal and secular

politics in which citizenship is a political quality and nationality is cultural, and the two are understood to be quite separate ... If the ... Balkan nations wish to be members of 'Europe', they must understand that the challenge is to reconcile their nations, as it was in Western Europe in the 1940s and early 1950s. If they are not prepared to change in that respect, they automatically exclude themselves from a changed Europe. (*International Herald Tribune*, 21 May 1994, p. 6)

It is an unfortunate fact that the projects and programmes which most effectively arouse and engage political passions and energies in the Balkans are not the 'worthy' high-minded projects of democratization and liberal economic reform, but the more primordial projects of nationalism and nation-building. The biggest and most crucial challenge confronting the Balkan states is how to lead or channel these more primordial passions and energies towards rational and constructive political and economic reform and away from destructive chauvinism, bigotry, xenophobia, vindictiveness and 'ethnic cleansing'. It is conceivable that the energies and passions aroused and engaged by nationalism and nation-building could play positive, constructive roles in the creation of new democratic power-structures and consensual sources of social cohesion and political legitimacy. Maurice Keens-Soper (1989: 694–5) has argued that

> liberal democracy has almost everywhere been parasitic on nationalism. Democracy possesses no theory or force of its own capable of either generating or explaining the very ties of attachment upon which its workings in practice depend ... Democracy may presuppose the loyalty of citizens to nations.

Nevertheless, he also warns that 'nationalism does not guarantee democracy'. Most democracies are national, yet 'few of the world's nationalisms sustain democracy'.[2] This pinpoints a crucial (possibly intractable) contradiction and dilemma facing the transitions to democracy in the post-1989 Balkans. It may well be that stable democracies have normally required an undergirding of nationalism and an implicit or explicit belief that they are co-terminous with relatively homogeneous national communities, national territories and nation-states. Yet almost any thoroughgoing attempt to make national identities and attachments the basis of state loyalties, public duties and citizens' rights and allegiances in the troubled ethnic patchwork of south-eastern Europe must be deemed to be dangerously divisive and a recipe for endemic instability and conflict. In the Balkans, moreover, states are still mainly being defined in terms of outmoded, divisive, exclusive, inward-looking ethnic and linguistic identities. This threatens to institutionalize and perpetuate ethnic division and potential for inter-ethnic conflict within and between the existing (multi-ethnic) state territories. The ensuing introversion, seclusion and intolerance could constantly endanger democratization. But, in the first flush of their hard-won and/or recently regained 'national' independence, most of the Balkan states are unwilling to accept any limitation or reduction of their 'national' sovereignty or any equitable legal protection or guarantee of minority rights for the sake of the greater harmony, stability, peace and prosperity of their region. Most of them cling, fearfully and jealously, to archaic self-images and Quixotic perceptions of national valour.

In western Europe, happily, the rise of modern nationalism was largely preceded by the formation of relatively discrete and tidy nation-states, thanks to the unifying state-building activities of the western European monarchies from the fourteenth century to the mid-nineteenth century (i.e. at a time when the linguistic and cultural consciousness of their subjects was still relatively fluid, inchoate and malleable). These activities were assisted by the precocious development of capitalism, unified 'national' markets and self-conscious 'national bourgeoisies'. Consequently, the boundaries of states and 'nations' increasingly coincided (although the correspondence was never complete: witness the anomalous status of the so-called 'Celtic fringes' within Great Britain and of the Basque country and Catalonia within Spain). This outcome was in the main achieved by bringing 'national' identities and allegiances into conformity wth pre-existing state boundaries through political and administrative centralization and 'imposed' or 'induced' educational and cultural (including religious) homogenization, rather than by 'surgically' bringing state frontiers into conformity with pre-existing (and haphazard) ethnic geographies by means of wars of conquest, population exchanges, expulsions, genocide and 'ethnic cleansing'. (Nevertheless, such barbarities were not wholly absent from the western European experience of nation-building: witness the mass expulsions of Jews and Moors from Spain between 1492 and 1610 or the mass extermination of Jews by Nazi Germany.) In north-western Europe, moreover, nationalism became part of the transference of sovereignty from monarchs to their former subjects, the people, 'now transformed into citizens, the members of the nation' (Sugar 1971: 8, 12). The doctrine of national/popular sovereignty developed in conjunction with a new emphasis on 'the Rights of Man', equality before the law, habeas corpus, public accountability and the political consolidation of liberal capitalism. In north-western Europe, consequently, equal rights and obligations of citizenship were gradually extended to (almost) everyone born and/or residing within particular 'national' territories (almost) irrespective of language, race or creed. This was the origin of the broad, inclusive 'civic' definition of the nation, citizenship and citizens' rights. Thus 'the French' for example, are not a particular 'race' or 'blood line', but simply the people of France, including many 'naturalized' Germans, Italians, Algerians and Jews.

In the Balkans there was no gradual historical evolution towards relatively homogeneous, 'civic' nation-states. This was not simply a consequence of ethnic and linguistic diversity. In all probability western European nations are descended from just as many different ethnic and linguistic 'strains' as eastern Europeans. The crucial difference between the ethnic tapestries of Balkan and western Europe lies not in the numbers of 'aboriginal' ethnic and linguistic 'strains', but in the contrast between the extensive fusion, coalescence or 'unification' of diverse ethnic and linguistic 'strains' into discrete 'national' political units in the West and the equally extensive perpetuation of a multiplicity of separate ethnic and 'national' identities in the Balkans (Stavrianos 1958: 13). In south-eastern Europe, for reasons which were closely connected with the long persistence of multi-cultural imperial polities, successive waves of inward migration and settlement helped to establish layer upon layer of ethnic groupings, many of whom have preserved their separate identities down to the present day. In western Europe, by contrast, similar waves of inward migration and settlement led to cultural assimilation and fusion, partly because the more fragmented states system that developed in western Europe encouraged rulers to foster and consolidate 'national' rather than imperial polities, loyalties, identities and territories.

In western Europe the prevalence of relatively innocuous and inclusive 'civic' forms of nationalism and nation-state was greatly facilitated by the fortuitous existence of some 'natural' national frontiers (in the shape of seas and mountain chains) and by the good fortune that they emerged *before* the popularization of racial ideas and doctrines in the second half of the nineteenth century. In south-eastern Europe, by contrast, the topography furnished fewer 'natural' national frontiers and nationalism developed later, under the baleful influence of racial ideas and doctrines and German idealist philosophy, with the result that nations and nationalisms came to be based on much more exclusive *ethnic* and *linguistic* criteria. In other words, national identities, allegiances and aspirations were determined not by birth and/or residence in a particular state, but by Germanic conceptions of the *Volk* (membership of a particular linguistic, consanguinary or even 'racial' group).

Germany itself has, in fact, remained an 'ethnic nation', despite its membership of the EU. Since there was no unified German state until 1867 (or, some would argue, until 1870 or even 1918) and since Germany has always lacked 'natural' frontiers, a German national state (in reality, 'Greater Prussia') was derived from the preconceived notion of an ethnic German *Volk* or 'nation'. In the eyes of most German nationalists (between 1848 and 1945 at least) this included the ethnic Germans of Bohemia, Austria, Alsace, Lorraine, the Balkans and even Russia and Ukraine, with ultimately devastating consequences for Europe. Fortunately, while Germany has not ceased to define itself as an 'ethnic' nation (rather than a more inclusive 'civic' one) in its nationality/citizenship laws inherited from the pre-1918 German Empire (posing acute problems for millions of immigrants), present-day Germany has renounced its earlier Bismarckian, Wilhelminian and Hitlerian methods of 'nation-building'. There are also no 'historic' ethnic minorities with claims to territorial autonomy within the Federal Republic of Germany. Notwithstanding the inherent contradictions, Germany has accepted the permanent 'loss' of Austria, Alsace, Lorraine, the Sudetenland and the German territories transferred to Poland in 1945 (despite continuing to define itself as an ethnic German nation-state), because its attempts to unite all ethnic Germans in one German state ended in disaster for both Germany and Europe. In fact, Germany has now become 'ultra-European' and an 'engine' of European integration. It has also adopted a relatively positive attitude toward Central and Eastern European countries in this regard. Europe has been spared any further *directly* destabilizing consequences of the German *Volk* concept since 1945. Indirectly, however, the 'ethnic' conception of the nation is still fomenting poisonous inter-ethnic conflicts in parts of eastern Europe (particularly in the Balkans). It is also dangerously exacerbating Germany's increasingly explosive immigrant problems and making them more difficult to defuse or resolve, with potentially pernicious consequences for the EU. Peoples who define themselves as consanguinary or 'racial' entities (the Teutonic 'race', the Slav 'race' or even the Jewish 'race') may be less easily transformed or assimilated than peoples who constitute inclusive 'civic' nations. They may also be more receptive to racist (and hence fascist) doctrines. Certainly racial and ethnic conceptions of nationhood are *inherently* more exclusive, more intolerant of 'ethnic minorities' and more dangerous to mankind than 'civic'/territorial conceptions of nationhood. Indeed, the problems of 'ethnic minorities' have loomed large in south-eastern Europe since 1878, partly because most of the new 'nation-states' were defined (or thought of themselves) in ethnic and almost racial, rather than 'civic', terms.

In south-eastern Europe, even after the dissolution of the great eastern empires in 1917–18, the frontiers of the existing states and those of the emerging nations rarely coincided; consequently, nationalism developed not in support of, but in protest against the existing state structures and territories (Kohn 1944: 329). Thus, whereas in western Europe nationalism and the idea of the nation were fostered as part of a process of democratization and as a means of identifying citizens with the already existing states, in south-eastern Europe nations were 'imagined' or 'postulated' as pre-existing ethnic or cultural entities from which *future* nation-states could be derived. In western Europe states have created nations, whereas in south-eastern Europe nations have eventually created states. Indeed, nationalists 'created, often out of myths of the past and dreams of the future, an ideal fatherland', which was not yet a political reality. Hence 'they were able to adorn it with traits for the realization of which they had no immediate responsibility, but which influenced the nascent nation's wishful image of itself and of its mission' (Kohn 1944: 330).

At first these dreams of past and future 'national' greatness took the forms of lofty idealism, poetic licence and harmless escapism and romanticism. Above all, the national vernacular or mother tongue became 'almost sacred, the mysterious vehicle of all the national endeavours'; and the reform, modernization and standardization of vernacular languages became 'a mighty movement ... which shook the awakened people ... with an almost religious enthusiasm' (Jászi 1929: 262–3). Alongside this quasi-religious literary and linguistic 'revivalism', national 'apostles' set out to reinvent history. 'We find everywhere a curious searching for historical ancestors. Every nation tried to reconstruct its past as the most glorious' (p. 259). At times this bordered on farce. Thus Vuk Karadzic, the father of the Serb linguistic–literary revival and of the concept of a 'Greater Serbia' (and a forebear of the present-day leader of the Bosnian Serbs, Radovan Karadzic), advanced pseudo-historical claims that 'the Serbs were "the greatest people of the planet", that their culture was 5000 years old, and that ... Jesus, too, with his apostles, was a Serb' (p. 264). (On 6 August 1994, after Milosevic imposed sanctions on the Bosnian Serbs for rejecting the Contact Group's peace plan, Radovan Karadzic said that 'Now we are totally alone; only God is with us'!)

Increasingly, moreover, 'eastern European nationalism became *messianic*', claiming rights for the nation rather than for individual citizens and demanding obedient service to the nation, which was seen as having an 'historic' or 'God-given' mission or destiny to fulfil (Sugar 1971: 11). To question or reject this 'mission' became tantamount to 'treason'; individuals who stood out against messianic nationalism were often regarded as 'traitors' to their nation. Messianic nationalism became increasingly intolerant, illiberal, exclusive and xenophobic. During the 1920s and 1930s this helped to make some East Europeans increasingly receptive to authoritarian forms of political and economic nationalism and hence to fascism. Indeed, the 'integral' or 'ethnic' conception of the nation postulated a collectivity whose claims and interests overrode and diminished the rights not only of ethnic minorities, but also of the individual members of the ethnic *majority*.

Conclusion

Nation-states not infrequently pursue policies which are inspired by a sense of their uniqueness, or by an urge to preserve, regain or reassert a sense of their own uniqueness. Such tendencies have been most marked among nations which have lacked long histories of independent statehood and whose specific identities have thus been all the more deeply rooted in and dependent upon the presumed existence of either real or imagined 'national' cultures. In such circumstances the promotion or preservation of a national language and culture becomes the major 'national' concern, especially as a means of self-defence against potential cultural, political, economic and demographic assimilation and colonization by bigger and more powerful neighbours (Jurgaitiene 1994: 170). For most of the Balkan nations, this cultural form of 'national asser-tion' supplied the main inspiration and impetus behind the struggles for national liberation. Patriotic sentiments were repeatedly mobilized at crucial junctures in their protracted national liberation struggles, demonstrating that nationalism remained a potent potential source of inspiration, unity, courage, heroism and self-sacrifice, capable of transcending sectional interests and class divisions. But it also encouraged uncritical idealization of (and faith in) inde-pendent statehood as a panacea, as the necessary and sufficient answer to 'national' problems and as an end in itself. In point of fact, however, the attainment of national independence is only a beginning, only a first step beyond which the 'national' coalition that headed the 'struggle' for indepen-dence is often riven by dissension over what to do next. In itself, national independence poses more problems than it resolves. Indeed, taken to its log-ical conclusion, the pursuit of national independence has led to extreme national self-reliance, autarky, national introversion, isolationism, fascism, xeno-phobia and counter-productive measures against foreign goods, capital, cul-ture and persons. Despite its powers to mobilize opposition and resistance to foreign ('alien') overlords and/or popular support for wars of conquest, nation-alism offers very little by way of *positive* or *constructive* policy guidance once national independence has been achieved. It then has to give way to prag-matism and the normal cut-and-thrust of competing functional interest groups and political ideologies, if healthy, pluralistic and tolerant political, economic, technological and cultural development is to be achieved.

Our plea for a tolerant, inclusive 'civic' conception of the nation is based on a belief not only that this is a worthy goal in itself, but also that it is a platform for successful economic development. Ethnic tolerance is conducive to a healthy democracy and economy. Full use can be made of people's abil-ities and resources and the haemorrhaging of scarce human capital avoided. Resources that would have been used to deal with ethnic (and religious) strife can be put to productive use, an ethnically impartial ('neutral') state can be built up and the danger of political parties developing along rigidly ethnic lines reduced. Foreign investment, firms and entrepreneurs are attracted, the support of the international community is gained and the chances of mem-bership of the EU enhanced. Above all, relations with those countries with a direct interest in the ethnic minorities are improved and the siren calls of the Zhirinovskys of this world are ignored. Armies rolling across borders to pro-tect their 'compatriots' would be truly catastrophic in every way. We profess to see a glimmer of hope in Bosnia. Even a truncated Bosnia, formed on the basis of a tolerant, harmonious and secular multi-ethnic view of society, could, we believe, look forward to eventual economic prosperity. By contrast, an ethnically cleansed, intolerant and introverted 'Greater Serbia', run by thugs and psychopaths, would face a bleak economic future.

Notes

1. 'Civil society': widespread activities by individuals who voluntarily associate together in various forms outside the control of the state; life outside the state; the self-organization of individuals in society.
2. There are, of course, more democracies now than when the article was written, not least in Latin America and the former communist bloc.

References

Cochrane, N. (1993) 'Central European agrarian reforms in a historical perspective', *American Journal of Agricultural Economics*, vol. 75, no. 3.

Jászi, O. (1929) *The Dissolution of the Habsburg Monarchy*. Chicago: University of Chicago Press.

Jeffries, I. (1993) *Socialist Economies and the Transition to the Market*. London: Routledge.

Jurgaitiene, K. (1994) 'Romantic nationalism and the challenge of Europeanization: the case of Lithuania' in Semanis, E. (ed.) *The Transition to Democracy*. Riga: University of Latvia.

Keens-Soper, M. (1989) 'The liberal state and nationalism in post-war Europe', *History of European Ideas*, vol. 10, no. 6.

Kohn, H. (1944) *The Idea of Nationalism*. New York: Macmillan.

Stavrianos, L. (1958) *The Balkans since 1453*. New York: Holt, Rinehart & Winston.

Sugar, P. (1971) 'External and domestic roots of East European nationalism' in Sugar, P. and Lederer, I. (eds) *Nationalism in Eastern Europe*. Seattle: University of Washington Press.

United Nations Economic Commission for Europe (1993) *Economic Survey of Europe in 1992–1993*. New York: United Nations.

Index